A Text Book Of

RDBMS
(RELATIONAL DATABASE MANAGEMENT SYSTEM)

For

BBA (Computer Applications)
Formerly known as BCA
Semester - III

As per New Revised Syllabus

MRS. SHEETAL GUJAR – TAKALE
M.E. (C.S.E.)
LECTURER, DEPARTMENT OF COMPUTER ENGINEERING,
VIDYAPRATISTAN'S COLLEGE OF ENGINEERING,
BARAMATI

ABHIJEET D. MANKAR
M.C.S.
LECTURER, DEPARTMENT OF COMPUTER SCIENCE,
TULJARAM CHATURCHAND COLLEGE,
BARAMATI

RDBMS (RELATIONAL DATABASE MANAGEMENT SYSTEM)

ISBN 978-93-5164-075-2

Third Edition : February 2016
© : Authors

The text of this publication, or any part thereof, should not be reproduced or transmitted in any form or stored in any computer storage system or device for distribution including photocopy, recording, taping or information retrieval system or reproduced on any disc, tape, perforated media or other information storage device etc., without the written permission of Authors with whom the rights are reserved. Breach of this condition is liable for legal action.

Every effort has been made to avoid errors or omissions in this publication. In spite of this, errors may have crept in. Any mistake, error or discrepancy so noted and shall be brought to our notice shall be taken care of in the next edition. It is notified that neither the publisher nor the authors or seller shall be responsible for any damage or loss of action to any one, of any kind, in any manner, therefrom.

Published By :
NIRALI PRAKASHAN
Abhyudaya Pragati, 1312, Shivaji Nagar,
Off J.M. Road, PUNE – 411005
Tel - (020) 25512336/37/39, Fax - (020) 25511379
Email : niralipune@pragationline.com

Printed By :
Repro Knowledgecast Limited,
Thane

☞ DISTRIBUTION CENTRES

PUNE
Nirali Prakashan : 119, Budhwar Peth, Jogeshwari Mandir Lane, Pune 411002, Maharashtra
Tel : (020) 2445 2044, 66022708, Fax : (020) 2445 1538
Email : bookorder@pragationline.com, niralilocal@pragationline.com

Nirali Prakashan : S. No. 28/27, Dhyari, Near Pari Company, Pune 411041
Tel : (020) 24690204 Fax : (020) 24690316
Email : dhyari@pragationline.com, bookorder@pragationline.com

MUMBAI
Nirali Prakashan : 385, S.V.P. Road, Rasdhara Co-op. Hsg. Society Ltd.,
Girgaum, Mumbai 400004, Maharashtra
Tel : (022) 2385 6339 / 2386 9976, Fax : (022) 2386 9976
Email : niralimumbai@pragationline.com

☞ DISTRIBUTION BRANCHES

JALGAON
Nirali Prakashan : 34, V. V. Golani Market, Navi Peth, Jalgaon 425001,
Maharashtra, Tel : (0257) 222 0395, Mob : 94234 91860

KOLHAPUR
Nirali Prakashan : New Mahadvar Road, Kedar Plaza, 1st Floor Opp. IDBI Bank
Kolhapur 416 012, Maharashtra. Mob : 9850046155

NAGPUR
Pratibha Book Distributors : Above Maratha Mandir, Shop No. 3, First Floor,
Rani Jhanshi Square, Sitabuldi, Nagpur 440012, Maharashtra
Tel : (0712) 254 7129

DELHI
Nirali Prakashan : 4593/21, Basement, Aggarwal Lane 15, Ansari Road, Daryaganj
Near Times of India Building, New Delhi 110002
Mob : 08505972553

BENGALURU
Pragati Book House : House No. 1, Sanjeevappa Lane, Avenue Road Cross,
Opp. Rice Church, Bengaluru – 560002.
Tel : (080) 64513344, 64513355,Mob : 9880582331, 9845021552
Email:bharatsavla@yahoo.com

CHENNAI
Pragati Books : 9/1, Montieth Road, Behind Taas Mahal, Egmore,
Chennai 600008 Tamil Nadu, Tel : (044) 6518 3535,
Mob : 94440 01782 / 98450 21552 / 98805 82331,
Email : bharatsavla@yahoo.com

niralipune@pragationline.com | www.pragationline.com
Also find us on www.facebook.com/niralibooks

Preface ...

This textbook **'RDBMS (Relational Database Management Systems)'** designed for the students of **B.B.A. (Computer Applications), Semester III**. RDBMS is one of the most rapidly growing areas of Computer and Information Technology. Basically, Relational Database Management systems is nothing more than a computer based record keeping system that is a system whose overall purpose is to record and maintain information.

The objective of Relational Database Management Systems is to provide a convenient and effective method of defining, sorting and retrieving the information stored in the database.

A special word of thanks to Shri. Dineshbhai Furia, Mr. Jignesh Furia and M.P. Munde for showing full faith in us to write this book. We also thank to Mahesh Swami, Mrs. Prachi Sawant and Vijay Shete of M/s Nirali Prakashan for their excellent co-operation.

Valuable suggestions communicated by the students and teachers are welcome.

AUTHORS

Syllabus ...

1. **Introduction to RDBMS** [2 Lectures]
    1.1 Introduction to popular RDBMS product and their features
    1.2 Difference Between DBMS and RDBMS
    1.3 Relationship among application programs and RDBMS

2. **PL/SQL** [20 Lectures]
    2.1 Overview of PL/SQL
    2.2 Data Types
    2.3 PL/SQL Block: 2.3.1 % type, % rowtype. 2.3.2 Operators, Functions, comparison, numeric, character, date, 2.3.3 Control Statement,
    2.4 Exception Handling: 2.4.1 Predefined, 2.4.2 User defined exceptions
    2.5 Functions, Procedures
    2.6 Cursor: 2.6.1 Definition, 2.6.2 Types of cursor- implicit, explicit (attributes), 2.6.3 Parameterized cursor
    2.7 Trigger
    2.8 Package

3. **Transaction Management** [10 Lectures]
    3.1 Transaction Concept
    3.2 Transaction Properties
    3.3 Transaction States
    3.4 Concurrent Execution
    3.5 Serializability: 3.5.1 Conflict Serializability, 3.5.2 View Serializability
    3.6 Recoverability: 3.6.1 Recoverable Schedule, 3.6.2 Cascadless Schedule

4. **Concurrency Control** [8 Lectures]
    4.1 Lock Based Protocol: 4.1.1 Locks, 4.1.2 Granting of Locks, 4.1.3 Two Phase Locking Protocol
    4.2 Timestamp Based Protocol: 4.2.1 Timestamp, 4.2.2 Timestamp ordering protocol, 4.2.3 Thomas's Write Rule
    4.3 Validation Based Protocol
    4.4 Deadlock Handling: 4.4.1 Deadlock Prevention, 4.4.2 Deadlock Detection, 4.4.3 Deadlock Recovery

5. **Recovery System** [8 Lectures]
    5.1 Failure Classification: 5.1.1 Transaction Failure, 5.1.2 System Crash, 5.1.3 Disk Failure
    5.2 Storage Structures: 5.2.1 Storage Types, 5.2.2 Data Access,
    5.3 Recovery and Atomicity: 5.3.1 Log based Recovery, 5.3.2 Deferred Database Modification, 5.3.3 Immediate Database Modification, 5.3.4 Checkpoints
    5.4 Recovery with Concurrent Transaction: 5.4.1 Transaction Rollback, 5.4.2 Restart Recovery
    5.5 Remote Backup System

Contents ...

1. **Introduction to RDBMS** — 1.1 – 1.34

2. **PL/SQL** — 2.1 – 2.108

3. **Transaction Management** — 3.1 – 3.28

4. **Concurrency Control** — 4.1 – 4.34

5. **Recovery System** — 5.1 – 5.30

* **University Question Papers** — P.1 – P.20

Chapter 1...
Introduction to RDBMS

Contents ...

This chapter introduces core concepts of RDBMS such as:

1.1 INTRODUCTION
    1.1.1 What is a Database ?
    1.1.2 Database Management System (DBMS)
    1.1.3 Relational Database Management System (RDBMS)
    1.1.4 Advantages of RDBMS
    1.1.5 Disadvantages of RDBMS
    1.1.6 Keys of RDBMS
1.2 DIFFERENCE BETWEEN RDBMS AND DBMS
1.3 RELATION AMONG DBMS AND APPLICATION PROGRAMS

1.1 INTRODUCTION

1.1.1 What is a Database ?

- A database is a collection of related data elements such as, Tables (entities), Columns (fields or attributes), and Rows (records). A database turns disparate pieces of data into information, based on needs, Collect essential information, Principle of parsimony.
- A database is a collection of data. A database could be as simple as a text file with a list of names. Or it could be as complex as a large, relational database management system, complete with in-built tools to help you maintain the data.
- A database is a collection of data organized in a particular way.
- Databases can be of many types such as Flat File Databases, Relational Databases, and Distributed Databases etc.

1.1.2 Database Management System (DBMS)   (April 11)

- A Database Management System (DBMS) is a computer program for managing a permanent, self-descriptive repository of data. This repository of data is called a database and is store in one or more files.
- A Database management System (DBMS) is a software program that enables the creation and management of databases.
- Most of today's database systems are referred to as a Relational Database Management System (RDBMS), because of their ability to store related data across multiple tables.

- There are many reasons why you could use a DBMS they are given below:
    1. **Sharing between applications:** Multiple application programs can read and write data to the same database.
    2. **Crash recovery:** The database is protected from hardware crashes, disk media failures, and some user errors.
    3. **Security:** Data can be protected against unauthorized read and write access.
    4. **Sharing between users:** Multiple users can access the database at the same time.
    5. **Data distribution:** The database may be partitioned across various sites, organizations, and hardware platforms.
    6. **Extensibility:** Data may be added to the database without disruption existing programs. Data can be reorganized for faster performance.
    7. **Integrity:** You can specify rules that data must satisfy. A DBMS can control the quality of its data over and above facilities that may be provided by application programs.

1.1.3 Relational Database Management System (RDBMS) (April 11)

- Edgar F. Codd at IBM invented the relational database in 1970. Referred to as RDBMS.
- RDBMS allows operations in a human logical environment. The main elements of RDBMS are based on Codd's 13 rules for a relational system.
- The relational database is perceived as a collection of tables. Each table consists of a series of row/column intersections. Tables (or relations) are related to each other by sharing a common entity characteristic.
- A Relational Database Management System (RDBMS) provides a comprehensive and integrated approach to information management.
- A relational model provides the basis for a relational database. A relational model has three aspects:
    1. Structures,
    2. Operations, and
    3. Integrity rules.
    1. **Structures:** It consists of a collection of objects or relations that store data. An example of relation is a table. You can store information in a table and use the table to retrieve and modify data.
    2. **Operations:** They are used to manipulate data and structures in a database. When using operations. You must adhere to a predefined set of integrity rules.
    3. **Integrity Rules:** The rules are laws that govern the operations allowed on data in a database. This ensures data accuracy and consistency.

1.1.3.1 Definition of RDBMS
- Relational Database Management System, RDBMS refers to a relational database plus supporting software for managing users and processing SQL queries, performing backups/restores and associated tasks.
- RDBMS usually include an API so that developers can write programs that use them.
- Typical RDBMS includes:
    - Microsoft Access
    - Microsoft SQL Server
    - IBM DB2
    - Oracle
    - MySQL

1.1.3.2 What is RDBMS? (Oct. 09, 13; April 13, 14)
- RDBMS stands for Relational Database Management System.
- RDBMS data is structured in database tables, fields and record. Each RDBMS table consists of database table rows. Each database table row consists of one or more database table fields.
- RDBMS stores data into collection of tables, which might be related by common fields.
- RDBMS also provide relational operators to manipulate the data stored into database tables. Most RDBMS use SQL as database query language.
- Edgar F. Codd introduced the relational database model. Many modern DBMS do not conform Codd's definition of a RDBMS, but nonetheless they are still considered to be RDBMS.

1.1.3.3 Characteristics of RDBMS (Oct. 10; April 14)
- RDBMS consist of following characteristics:
    1. **Data abstraction:** Relational abstraction enhances program-data independence.
    2. **Self-describing data:** Metadata describing structure of data stored together with data.
    3. **Concurrency:** Supporting shared concurrent access (transactions).
    4. **Support for multiple views:** External users can be provided with different views of the data.
    5. **Security:** Privacy/Confidentiality, Integrity, Availability, Accountability.

1.1.3.4 Features of RDBMS (Oct. 13)
- RDBMS consist of following features:
    1. Client server multi-tier support
    2. ANSI-SQL compatibility

3. Front-end support
4. Operating systems portability
5. Data Concurrency
6. Data Integrity features
7. Back-up and Recovery Facility
8. Data Import and Export facilities
9. Support for Web Enabled application
10. Support Data Warehousing
11. Support ERP
12. Network support for wide range Protocols
13. Support Distributed Database Processing.
14. Network support.

1.1.3.5 Components of RDBMS

- Relational database components includes:
    - Table
    - Row
    - Column
    - Field
    - Primary key
    - Foreign key
- Fig. 1.1 shows the components of RDBMS.

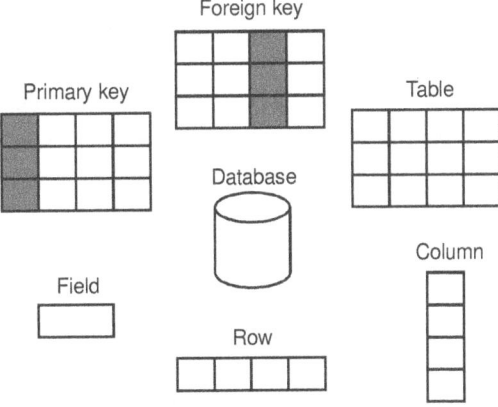

Fig. 1.1: Components of relational database

- A **Table** is a basic storage structure of an RDBMS and consists of columns and rows. A table represents an entity. For example, the E_DEPT table stores information about the departments of an organization.
- A **Row** is a combination of column values in a table and is identified by a primary key. Rows are also known as **records**. For example, a row in the table E_DEPT contains information about one department.
- A **Column** is a collection of one type of data in a table. Columns represent the attributes of an object. Each column has a column name and contains values that are bound by the same type and size. For example, a **'name'** column in the table E_DEPT specifies the names of the departments in the organization.
- A **Field** is an intersection of a row and a column. A field contains one data value. If there is no data in the field, the field is said to contain a NULL value.

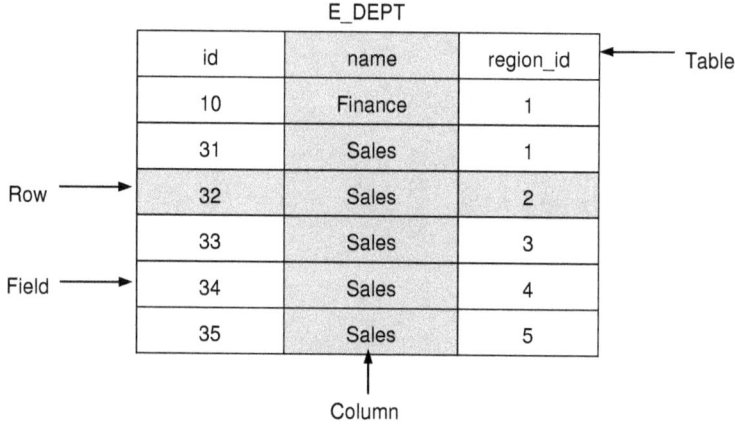

Fig. 1.2: Table, Row, Column and Field of RDBMS

- A **Primary key** is a column or a combination of columns that is used to uniquely identify each row in a table. For example, the column containing department numbers in the E_DEPT table is created as a **primary key** and therefore, every department number is different. A primary key must contain a value. It cannot contain a NULL value.
- A **Foreign key** is a column or set of columns that refers to a primary key in the same table or another table. You use foreign keys to establish principle connections between, or within, tables. A foreign key must either match a primary key or else be NULL. Rows are connected logically when required. The logical connections are based upon conditions that define a relationship between corresponding values, typically between a primary key and a matching foreign key. This relational method of linking provides great flexibility as it is independent of physical links between records.

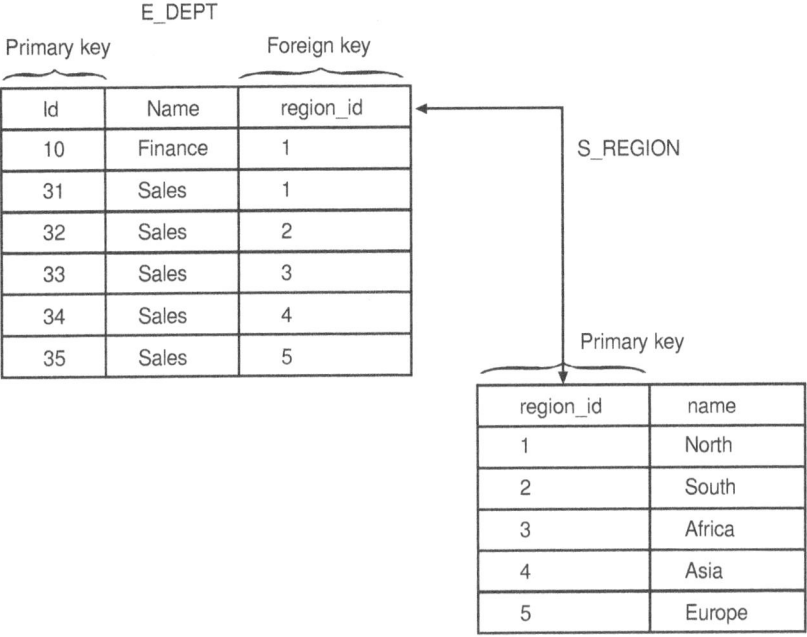

Fig. 1.3: Primary and Foreign key of RDBMS

1.1.3.6 RDBMS Properties

- An RDBMS is easily accessible. You execute commands in the Structured Query Language (SQL) to manipulate data. SQL is the International Standards Organization (ISO) standard language for interacting with a RDBMS.

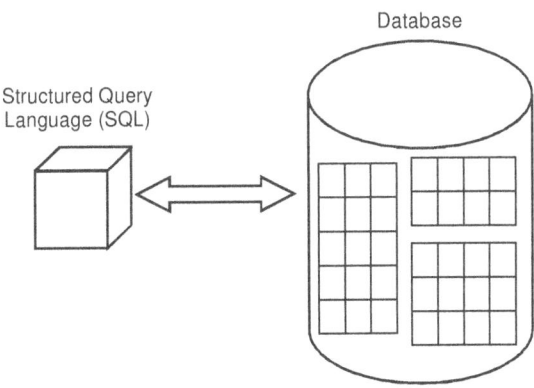

Fig. 1.4: SQL and Database

- An RDBMS provides full data independence. The organization of the data is independent of the applications that use it. You do not need to specify the access routes to tables or know how data is physically arranged in a database.
- A relational database is a collection of individual, named objects. The basic unit of data storage in a relational database is called **a table**. A table consists of rows and columns used to store values. For access purpose, the order of rows and columns is insignificant. You can control the access order as required.
- When querying the database, you use conditional operations such as joins and restrictions (conditions).
- A join combines data from separate database rows. A restriction limits the specific rows returned by a query.
- An RDBMS enables data sharing between users. At the same time, you can ensure consistency of data across multiple tables by using integrity constraints.

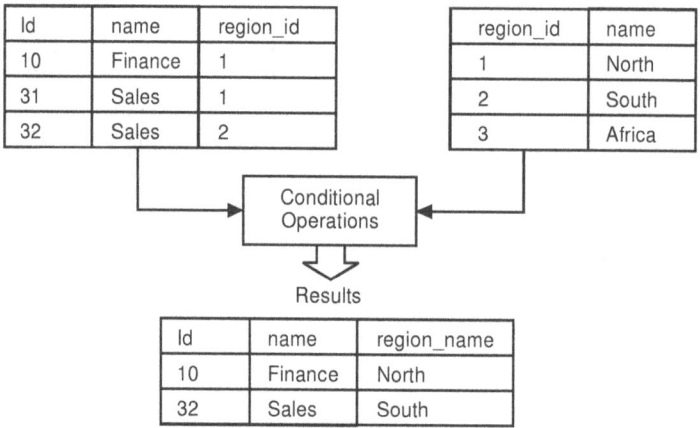

Fig. 1.5: Conditional operations

- An RDBMS uses various types of data integrity constraints. These types include entity, column, referential and user-defined constraints.
- The entity constraint, entity, ensures uniqueness of rows, and the column constraint ensures consistency of the type of data within a column.
- The other type, referential constraint, ensures validity of foreign keys, and user-defined constraints are used to enforce specific business rules.
- An RDBMS minimizes the redundancy of data. Redundancy means unnecessary duplication of data. This means that similar data is not repeated in multiple tables.

1.1.4 Advantages of RDBMS

- RDBMS consists of following advantages:
    1. Improved conceptual simplicity.
    2. Easier database design, implementation, management, and use.
    3. Ad hoc query capability (SQL).
    4. Powerful database management system.

1.1.5 Disadvantages of RDBMS

- RDBMS consists of following disadvantages:
    1. Possibility of poor design and implementation.
    2. Relational databases do not have enough storage area to handle data such as images, digital and audio/video.
    3. The requirement that information must be in tables where relationships between entities are defined by values.

1.1.6 Keys of RDBMS

- Every table must have some columns or combination of columns which uniquely identify each row in the table. For that we require a key. A key is simply a field used to identify a record. In other words, a key is subset of attributes with following properties:
    1. The value of key is unique for each tuple.
    2. No data redundancy.
- **Key can be classified as:**
    1. Primary key, 2. Candidate key, and 3. Foreign key.

1.1.6.1 Primary Key

- In a relation, there is one attribute or a group of attributes with values that are unique within that relation and thus can be used to uniquely identify the tuples of that relation.
- This key which uniquely identifies a row is known as primary key of that relation.
- For example, consider a relation customer, where social security number of the entity set customer is sufficient to distinguish one customer entity from another. So social security number is a primary key.

Social_Security No.	Cust_name	Address
100 - 205	John	Paris
103 - 102	Jimmy	New York
208 - 56	Juliee	Rye

1.1.6.2 Candidate Key

- The attribute which possess the unique identification property in a relation is called as **candidate key**. There can be more than one candidate keys in a relation.

- Candidate key should have following things:
  1. It must be unique
  2. A candidate key's value must exist. It cannot be null.
  3. The value of the candidate key must be stable. Its value cannot change outside the control of the system. In customer table, various employees were working and having unique identification number called as social security number (SSN).

Customer name	SSN	Basic
John	001-256	₹ 14,000
Martin	005-123	₹ 2,000
Paster	008-200	₹ 1,000
Mary	101-401	₹ 18,000
Johns	102-030	₹ 48,000

Candidate key

1.1.6.3 Foreign Key

- If any key in a given relation has reference to the value of a primary key of some other relation then it is called as foreign key.
- Foreign key can have duplicate values. It is used to search a record from two relations.

Relation = Dept

dept_no	Name
1	Production
2	Purchasing
3	Marketing

Relation = Emp.

Primary Key — Foreign Key

emp_id	Emp_name	Dept_no
10	Ramesh	2
25	Indranil	1

1.1.6.4 Super Key

- Super key is a set of one or more attributes which taken collectively allows us to identify uniquely an entity in the entity set.
- Consider the entity set account with attributes {acc_no. cust_name, bank_name, balance, address}.

- Here, acc_no is super key of account entity set. Similarly, (acc_no, cust_name) is a super key and (acc_no., bank_name) is a super key. But cust_name and bank_name independently are not the super keys.
- Super key may contain extra attributes i.e. if k is a super key, then any super set of k is also a Super key.

  Note: Candidate key is minimal superkey.

Popular RDBMS Products: (Oct. 09, 12; April 11, 13, 14)

I. SQL SERVER:
- SQL server is Database management software, uses own file structure, own logins and own security.
- SQL server uses Access through two main ways:
  1. Query Analyzer
  2. Enterprise Manager
- SQL server consists of three Services:
  1. **MS SQL Server:** For Data and Query processing.
  2. **SQL Server Agent:** For Schedulable jobs and alerts.
  3. **Microsoft Distributed Transaction Co-ordinator:** For Handling data from multiple sources.

History

Version	Year	Release Name
1.0 (OS/2)	1989	SQL Server 1.0 (16 bit)
1.1 (OS/2)	1991	SQL Server 1.1 (16 bit)
4.21 (WinNT)	1993	SQL Server 4.21
6.0	1995	SQL Server 6.0
6.5	1996	SQL Server 6.5
7.0	1998	SQL Server 7.0
-	1999	SQL Server 7.0 OLAP Tools
8.0	2000	SQL Server 2000
8.0	2003	SQL Server 2000 64-bit Edition
9.0	2005	SQL Server 2005

Contd...

10.0	2008	SQL Server 2008
10.25	2010	SQL Azure DB
10.5	2010	SQL Server 2008 R2
11.0	2012	SQL Server 2012
12.0	2014	SQL Server 2014

1. SQL Server 2005:

- SQL Server, released in October 2005, is the successor to SQL Server 2000 in addition to relational data. It included native support for managing XML data. It defined an XML data type that could be used either as a data type in database columns or as literals in queries.
- XML columns can be associated with XSD schemas and XML data being stored is verified against the schema. XML is converted to an internal binary data type prior to be stored in the database. Specialized indexing methods were made available for XML data. XML data is fetched using XQuery; SQL Server 2005 added some extensions to the T-SQL language to allow embedding XQuery queries in T-SQL. In addition, it also defined a new extension to XQuery, called XML DML allowing query-based modifications to XML data.
- SQL Server 2005 also allowed a database server to be exposed over web services using TDS packets encapsulated within SOAP requests. When the data is accessed over web services, results are returned as XML.
- SQL Server 2005 has been enhanced with new indexing algorithms and better error recovery systems. SQL CLR was introduced with SQL Server 2005 to let it combine with the .NET Framework.

2. SQL Server 2008:

- The current version of SQL Server, **SQL Server 2008**, was released on August, 2008. It aims to make data management self-tuning, self organizing, and self maintaining with the development of *SQL Server*.
- SQL Server 2008 also include support for structured and semi-structured data, including digital media formats for pictures, audio, video and other multimedia data.
- In latest versions, such multimedia data can be stored as BLOBs (Binary Large Objects), but they are generic bit streams. Intrinsic awareness of multimedia data will allow specialized functions to be performed on them.
- According to Paul Flessner, SQL Server 2008 acts as a data storage backend for *different varieties of data: XML, e_mail, time/calendar, file, document, spatial etc.* as well as perform *search, query, analysis, sharing and synchronization* across all data types.

- SQL Server 2008 also natively supports hierarchical data, and includes T-SQL constructs to directly deal with them (without using recursive queries).
- SQL Server 2008 supports the ADO.NET Entity Framework. The reporting tools, replication, and data definition is built around the Entity Data Model.
- SQL Server 2008 included the *Declarative Management Framework* which allowed configuring policies and constraints, on the entire database or certain tables, declaratively.
- The version of SQL Server Management Studio included with SQL Server 2008 supported IntelliSense for SQL queries against a SQL Server 2008 Database Engine.
- SQL Server 2008 also made the databases available via Windows PowerShell providers and management functionality available as Cmdlets, so that the server and all the running instances can be managed from Windows PowerShell.

3. **SQL Server 2008 R2**
- SQL Server 2008 R2 was announced at TechEd 2009, and was released to manufacturing on April 21, 2010.
- SQL Server 2008 R2 added certain features to SQL Server 2008 containing a master data management system branded as Master Data Services, central management of master data entities and hierarchies.
- SQL Server 2008 R2 included a number of new services, namely PowerPivot for Excel and SharePoint, Master Data Services, StreamInsight, Report Builder 3.0, Reporting Services Add-in for SharePoint, a Data-tier function in Visual Studio that enables packaging of tiered databases as part of application, and a SQL Server. Utility named UC (Utility Control Point), part of AMSM (Application and Multi-Server Management) that is used to manage multiple SQL, Servers.
- The first SQL Server 2008 R2 service pack (Service Pack 1) was released on July 11, 2011.

4. **SQL Server 2012**
- At the 2011 Professional Association for SQL Server (PASS) summit on October 11, Microsoft declared that the next major version of SQL Server would be SQL Server 2012. It was released to manufacturing on March 6, 2012.
- It was announced to be last version to natively support OLE D13 and instead to prefer ODBC for native connectivity.
- Some of SQL Server 2012's many new features and enhancements include AlwaysOn SQL Server Failover Cluster Instances and Availability Groups which provide a rich set of options that improve database availability, Contained Databases new and modified Dynamic Management Views and Functions, new Spatial features, Metadata discovery, Sequence objects and the THROW statement, performance improvements such as ColumnStore Indexes as well as improvements to OnLine and Partition level operations

and security improvements including Provisioning During Setup, new permissions, improved role management and default schema assignment for groups.

5. **SQL Server 2014:**
- SQL Server 2014 was launched on March 18, 2014, and released to the general public on April 1, 2014. Until November, 2013 there were two CTP revisions, CTP1 and CTP2.
- SQL Server 2014 provides a new in-memory capability for tables that can fit entirely in memory. Although small tables may entirely reside in memory in all versions of SQL Server, they also may reside on disk, so work is involved in reserving RAM, writing removed pages to disk, loading new pages from disk, locking the pages in RAM while they are being operated on, and many other tasks.
- By treating a table as guaranteed to be entirely resident in memory much of the 'plumbing' of disk-based databases can be avoided.
- For disk-based SQL Server applications, it also provides SSD bufferpool extension, which can improve application performance transparently by leveraging SSD as the intermediate memory hierarchy between DRAM and spinning media.
- SQL Server 2014 also enhances AlwaysOn (HADR) solution by increasing the readable secondaries count and sustaining read operations upon secondary-primary disconnections, and it provides new hybrid disaster recovery and backup solutions with Windows Azure, enabling customers to use their existing skills with the on-premises product offerings to take advantage of Microsoft's global datacenters.
- In addition, it takes advantage of new Windows Server 2012 and Windows Server 2012 R2 capabilities for database application scalability in a physical or virtual environment.

Services

- SQL Server also includes an assortment of add-on services. While these are not essential for the operation of the database system, these provide value added services on top of the core database management system.
- These services either run as a part of some SQL Server component or out-of-process as Windows Service and presents their own API to control and interact with them.

1. **Service Broker:** The Service Broker, being a part of the database engine, provides a reliable messaging and message queuing platform for SQL Server applications.
2. **Replication Services:** SQL Server Replication Services are used by SQL Server to replicate and synchronize database objects, either as a whole or a subset of the objects present, across replication agents, which can be other database servers across the network, or database caches on the client side.
3. **Analysis Services:** SQL Server Analysis Services adds OLAP and data mining capabilities. The OLAP engine supports MOLAP, ROLAP and HOLAP storage modes for data. Analysis Services supports the XML for Analysis standard as the underlying communication protocol.

4. **Reporting Services:** SQL Server Reporting Services is a report generation environment for SQL Server databases. It is administered through a web interface. Reporting services features a web services interface to support the development of custom reporting applications. Reports are created as RDL files.

5. **Notification Services:** Notification Services was provided as part of the Microsoft SQL Server platform for the first and only time with SQL Server 2005. With SQL Server 2005, SQL Server Notification Services is a mechanism for generating data-driven notifications, which are sent to Notification Services subscribers.

6. **Integration Services:** SQL Server Integration Services is used to integrate data from different data sources. It is used for the ETL capabilities for SQL Server for data warehousing needs.

Full Text Search Service :

- SQL Server Full Text Search service is a specialized indexing and querying service for unstructured text stored in SQL Server databases.
- The full text search index can be created on any column with text data. It allows for words to be searched.
- While it can be performed with the SQL pattern matching LIKE operator, using SQL Server Full Text Search service can be more efficient. Full allows for inexact matching of the source string, indicated by a Rank value which has range from 0 to 1000 - a higher rank means a more accurate match.
- It also provides linguistic matching ("inflectional search"), i.e., linguistic variants of a word (such as a verb in a different tense) will also be a match for a given word (but with a lower rank than an exact match).
- Proximity searches are also supported, i.e., if the words searched for do not occur in the sequence as mentioned in the query but are close to each other, they are also considered a match. T-SQL exposes special operators that can be used to access the FTS capabilities.
- The Full Text Search engine is divided into two processes - the Filter Daemon process and the Searchprocess.
- These processes interact with the SQL Server. The Search process includes the indexer (that creates the full text indexes) and the full text query processor.
- The indexer scans through text columns in the database. It can also index through binary columns, and use iFilters to obtain meaningful text from the binary blob (for example, when a Microsoft Word document is stored as an unstructured binary file in a database). The iFilters are hosted by the Filter Daemon process.
- Once the text is obtained, the Filter Daemon process breaks it up into a sequence of words and hands it over to the indexer. The indexer removes noise words, i.e., words like A, And etc., which occur frequently and are not useful for search. With the remaining words, an inverted index is created, associating each word with the columns they were found in. SQL Server itself includes a Gatherer component that constantly monitors changes to tables and runs the indexer in case of updates.

SQLCMD:
- It is a command line application that comes with Microsoft SQL Server, and shows the hidden management features of SQL Server. It allows SQL queries to be written and executed from the command prompt. It can also be used to create and run a set of SQL statements as a script.
- Such scripts are stored as a .sql file, and are used either for management of databases or to create the database schema during the deployment of a database.
- SQLCMD was introduced with SQL Server 2005 and continues with SQL Server 2012 and 2014. Its predecessor for earlier versions was OSQL and ISQL, which is functionally equivalent as it is connected to TSQL execution, and many of the command line parameters are identical, although SQLCMD adds extra versatility.

Features of SQL Server 2008

- In SQL Server 2008, improvements are made to core database engine, Analysis Services, Integration Services, Replication, Reporting Services and Service broker.

1. **Backup Compression:** SQL Server supports compressing backups, which can be restored to any edition of SQL server 2008.
2. **Configuration Servers:** This is a new method of managing multiple servers. An instance of SQL Server is chosen as a configuration server to maintain list of registered servers.
3. **Change Tracking:** SQL Server now allows applications to obtain incremental changes to user tables by tracking changes, which enables developing synchronization applications easier and faster.
4. **Query Processing on Partitioned Objects:** SQL Server 2008 improves query processing performance on partitioned tables for many parallel plans, changes the way parallel and serial plans are represented and improves the partitioning information provided in both compile-time and run-time execution plans.
5. **Partition Switching on Partitioned Tables and Indexes:** Partitioning data enables you to manage and access subsets of your data quickly and efficiently while keeping intact the integrity of the entire data collection. Now you can use partition switching to quickly and efficiently transfer subsets of your data by changing a partition from one table to another.
6. **Resource Governor:** Resource Governor is a feature that you can use to manage SQL Server workload and system resource consumption. Resource Governor enables you to restrict the amount of CPU and memory that incoming application requests can use.
7. **Extensible Key Management:** The Extensible Key Management (EKM) feature in the Enterprise, Developer, and Evaluation Editions of SQL Server 2008 allows third-party enterprise key management and hardware security module (HSM) vendors to register their devices in SQL Server.

8. **Transparent Data Encryption:** Transparent Data Encryption introduces a new database option that encrypts the database files automatically, without requiring to alter any applications.

9. **Server Administration:** SQL Server 2008 introduces Declarative Management, a new policy-based management framework for the SQL Server Database Engine.

10. **Spatial Data Storage, Methods and Indexing:** Spatial data describes information about the physical location and shape of geometric objects. These objects can be point locations or more complex objects such as countries, roads, or lakes.

11. **Transact-SQL Query Editor IntelliSense:** The Transact-SQL Editor now provides IntelliSense feature such as word completion and error underlining. IntelliSense is provided for frequently used Transact-SQL elements.

12. **Transact-SQL Error List Window:** SQL Server Management Studio has an Error List window that displays the syntax and semantic errors generated from the IntelliSense code in the Transact-SQL Query Editor.

13. **Data Collector:** SQL Server 2008 made available a data collector that you can use to obtain and save data that is gathered from several sources.

14. **Automatic Recovery from Corrupted Pages:** A database mirroring partner running on SQL Server 2008 or later versions automatically tries to resolve certain types of errors that prevent reading a data page.

15. **SQL Dependency Reporting Enhancements:** SQL Server 2008 made available a new catalog view and system functions to provide consistent and reliable SQL dependency reporting.

16. **SQL Server Extended Events:** SQL Server 2008 made available SQL Server Extended Events, an event infrastructure for server systems.

17. **Change Data Capture:** Change data capture is made to capture insert, update and delete activity applied to SQL Server tables and to make the details of the changes available in an easily consumed relational format.

18. **Optimized Bitmap Filtering:** The query optimizer can place bitmap filters run time in parallel query plans to improve the performance of queries against a star schema.

19. **Dynamic Management Views:** There are five new dynamic management views to show memory information.

20. **DDL Triggers and Event Notifications:** The class of events on which you can create DDL triggers and event notifications is expanded to contain numerous stored procedures that perform DDL-like operations.

II. ORACLE:

- The Oracle Database commonly known as Oracle RDBMS or Oracle, consists of a relational database management system (RDBMS) produced and marketed by Oracle Corporation.
- Larry Ellison and his friends Bob Miner and Ed Oates started the consultancy Software Development Laboratories (SDL) in 1977. SDL developed the original version of the Oracle software.
- The name *Oracle* comes from the code-name of a CIA-funded project Ellison had worked on while previously employed by Ampex.
- Users of Oracle databases refer to the server-side memory-structure as the SGA (System Global Area).
- The SGA typically contains cache information such as data-buffers, SQL commands and user information. Also, the database consists of online redo logs. Processes can in turn archive the online redo logs into archive logs which provide the basis for data recovery and for some forms of data replication.
- The Oracle RDBMS stores data logically in the form of tablespaces and physically in the form of data files. Tablespaces can contain various types of memory segments, such as Data Segments, Index Segments etc. Segments in turn comprise one or more extents. Extents comprise groups of contiguous data blocks.
- Data blocks form the basic units of data storage. At the physical level, datafiles comprise one or more data blocks, where the block size can vary between data files.
- Oracle database management handles its computer data storage with the help of information stored in the SYSTEM tablespace.
- The SYSTEM tablespace contains the data dictionary and often indexes and clusters.
- A data dictionary consists of a special collection of tables that stores information about all user-objects in the database.
- From version 8i, the Oracle RDBMS also supports "locally managed" tablespaces which can store space management information in bitmaps in their own headers rather than in the SYSTEM tablespace.
- The Oracle DBMS can store and execute stored procedures and functions within itself. PL/SQL (Oracle Corporation's proprietary procedural extension to SQL), or the object-oriented language Java can invoke such code objects and/or provide the programming structures for writing them.

Features of Oracle Database (Oct. 13)

1. **Scalability and Performance Features:**

   Oracle includes several software mechanisms to satisfy the following important requirements of an information management system:
   - Data concurrency of a multiuser system must be increased.

- Data must be read and modified in a consistent manner. The data a user is accessing or modifying is not modified until the user is finished with the data.
- High performance is required for maximum productivity from the many users of the database system.

This contains the following:

(i) Concurrency
(ii) Read Consistency
(iii) Locking Mechanisms
(iv) Quiesce Database
(v) Real Application Clusters
(vi) Portability

(i) **Concurrency:** A primary responsibility of a multiuser database management system is how to control **concurrency**, which is the access of the same data by many users at the same time. Without adequate concurrency controls, data could be updated or changed incorrectly, compromising data integrity. One way to manage data concurrency is to make each user wait for a turn. The aim of a database management system is to reduce that wait for each user so it is either nonexistent or negligible. All DML statements should precede with as little interference as possible and destructive interactions between concurrent transactions must be avoided. Neither performance nor data integrity can be sacrificed. Oracle handles such issues by using various types of locks and a multiversion consistency model. These features are based on the concept of a transaction. It is the application designer's responsibility to check that transactions fully use these concurrency and consistency features.

(ii) **Read Consistency:** Read consistency, as supported by Oracle, does the following:
- Guarantees that the set of data seen by a statement is agrees respect to a single point in time and does not change during statement execution (statement-level read consistency).
- Ensures that readers of data do not wait for writers or other readers of the same data.
- Ensures that writers of data do not wait for readers of the same data.
- Ensures that writers only wait for other writers if they attempt to update same rows in concurrent transactions.

The simplest way to think of Oracle's implementation of read consistency is to imagine each user operating its own copy of the database, hence the multiversion consistency model. To manage the multiversion consistency model, Oracle must create a read-consistent set of data when a table is read and simultaneously written. When an update occurs, the original data values modified by the update are recorded in the database undo records. As long as this update remains part of an uncommitted transaction, any user that later reads the modified data finds the original data values. Oracle uses current information in the system global area and information in the undo records to construct a **read-consistent view** of a table's data for a query.

Only when a transaction is committed the changes of the transaction are made permanent. Statements that start *after* the transaction is committed only see the changes made by the committed transaction.

The transaction is key to Oracle's strategy for providing read consistency. This unit of committed (or uncommitted) SQL statements:

- Dictates the start point for read-consistent views generated on behalf of readers.
- Controls when modified data can be seen by other transactions of the database for reading or updating.

The set of data returned by a single query is consistent with respect to a single point in time. However, in some situations, you might also require transaction-level read consistency. This is the ability to run set of queries within a single transaction, all of which are read-consistent with respect to the same point in time, so that queries in this transaction do not see the effects of intervening committed transactions.

You prefer a **read-only transaction**, if you don't need any modification.

(iii) **Locking Mechanisms:** Oracle uses **locks** to control concurrent access to data. When updating information, the data server holds that information with a lock until the update is committed. Until that happens, no one can make changes to the locked information. This guarantees the data integrity of the system.

Oracle provides unique non-escalating row-level locking. Oracle always locks only the row of information being updated. Because Oracle includes the locking information with the actual rows themselves, Oracle can lock an large number of rows so users can work concurrently without unnecessary delays.

1. **Automatic Locking:** Oracle locking is performed on its own basis and requires no user action. Implicit locking occurs for SQL statements as necessary, depending on the action requested. Oracle's lock manager on its own basis locks table data at the row level. By locking table data at the row level, contention for the same data is lowered. Oracle's lock manager maintains several different types of row locks, depending on what type of operation established the lock. The two general types of locks are **exclusive locks** and **share locks**. Only one exclusive lock can be placed on a resource (such as a row or a table); although, many share locks can be placed on a single resource. Both exclusive and share locks always allow queries on the locked resource but prohibit other activity on the resource (such as updates and deletes).

2. **Manual Locking:** Under some circumstances, a user might want to override default locking. Oracle allows manual changing of automatic locking features at both the row level and the table level.

(iv) **Quiesce Database:** Database administrators occasionally need separation from concurrent non-database administrator actions, that is, separation from concurrent non-database administrator transactions, queries, or PL/SQL statements. One way to provide such separation is to shut down the database and reopen it in restricted mode. You could also put the system into quiesced state without disrupting users. In quiesced state, the database administrator can safely perform certain actions whose executions require separation from concurrent non-DBA users.

(v) **Real Application Clusters:** Real Application Clusters (RAC) consists of several Oracle instances running on multiple clustered computers, which communicate with each other by means of a so-called interconnect. RAC uses cluster software to access a shared database that is stored on shared disk. RAC combines the processing power of these multiple interconnected computers to provide system redundancy, near linear scalability, and high availability. RAC also offers significant benefits for both OLTP and data warehouse systems and all systems and applications can efficiently take advantage of clustered environments.

You can scale applications in RAC environments to satisfy increasing data processing demands without changing the application code. As you add resources such as nodes or storage, RAC extends the processing powers of these resources beyond the limits of the individual components.

(vi) **Portability:** Oracle provides unique portability across all major platforms and makes sure that your applications run without modification after changing platforms. This is because the Oracle code base is similar across platforms, so you have similar feature functionality across all platforms, for complete application transparency. Because of this portability, you can easily upgrade to a more powerful server as your requirements changes.

2. **Manageability Features:** People who administer the operation of an Oracle database system, known as database administrators (DBAs), are responsible for creating Oracle databases, make sure their smooth operation, and monitoring their use. Oracle also offers the following features:

(i) **Self-Managing Database:** Oracle Database provides a high degree of self-management - automating routine DBA tasks and reducing complexity of space, memory, and resource administration. Oracle self-managing database features include the following:

1. Automatic undo management,
2. Dynamic memory management,
3. Oracle-managed files,
4. Mean time to recover,
5. Free space management,
6. Multiple block sizes, and
7. Recovery Manager (RMAN).

(ii) **Oracle Enterprise Manager:** Enterprise Manager is a system management tool that provides a combined solution for centrally controlling your heterogeneous environment. Combining a graphical console, Oracle Management Servers, Oracle

Intelligent Agents, common services, and administrative tools: Enterprise Manager provides a comprehensive systems management platform for controlling Oracle products.

(iii) Automatic Storage Management: Automatic Storage Management automates and simplifies the layout of datafiles, control files and log files. Database files are automatically distributed across all available disks and database storage is rebalanced whenever the storage configuration is modified.

(iv) Scheduler: The Scheduler allows database administrators and application developers control when and where various tasks take place in the database environment. For example, database administrators can arrange and monitor database maintenance jobs such as backups or data warehousing loads and extracts.

(v) Database Resource Manager: The Database Resource Manager controls the distribution of resources among various sessions by controlling the execution schedule inside the database.

3. **Database Backup and Recovery Features:** In every database system, the possibility of a system or hardware failure always exists. If a failure occurs and affects the database, then the database must be recovered. The goals after a failure are to make sure that the effects of all committed transactions are reflected in the recovered database and to return to normal operation as quickly as possible while protecting users from problems caused by the failure.

   Oracle provides various mechanisms for the following:
   - Database recovery required by different types of failures.
   - Flexible recovery operations to match any situation.
   - Availability of data during backup and recovery operations so users of the system can continue to work.

4. **High Availability Features:** Oracle has a number of products and features that provide high availability in cases of unplanned or planned downtime. These include Fast-Start Fault Recovery, Real Application Clusters, **Recovery Manager (RMAN)**, backup and recovery solutions, Oracle Flashback, partitioning, Oracle Data Guard, LogMiner, multiplexed redo log files, online reorganization. These can be used in various combinations to satisfy specific high availability needs.

5. **Business Intelligence Features:** This feature describes several business intelligence features.

   (i) Data Warehousing: A data warehouse is a relational database designed for query and analysis rather than for transaction processing. It usually contains historical data derived from transaction data, but it can contain data from other sources. It clearly separates analysis workload from transaction workload and make possible for an organization to join data from several sources.

(ii) Extraction, Transformation and Loading (ETL): You must load your data warehouse regularly so that it can serve its purpose of making business analysis easier. To do this, data from one or more operational systems must be extracted and copied into the warehouse. The process of extracting data from source systems and bringing it into the data warehouse is commonly called **ETL**, which stands for extraction, transformation, and loading.

(iii) Data Mining: With Oracle Data Mining, data never leaves the database — the data, data preparation, model building, and model scoring results all remain in the database. This enables Oracle to provide an infrastructure for application developers to combine data mining seamlessly with database applications. Some typical examples of the applications that data mining are used in are call centers, ATMs, ERM, and business planning applications. Data mining functions like model building, testing, and scoring are provided through a Java API.

6. Content Management Features: Oracle includes datatypes to handle different types of rich Internet content such as relational data, object-relational data, XML, text, audio, video, image, and spatial. These datatypes seem as native types in the database. They can all be queried using SQL. A single SQL statement can contain data belonging to any or all of these datatypes.

(i) XML in Oracle: XML, (eXtensible Markup Language) is the standard way to recognise and describe data on the Web. Oracle XML DB treats XML as a native datatype in the database. Oracle XML DB gives a number of easy ways to create XML documents from relational tables. The result of any SQL query can be automatically changed into an XML document. Oracle also includes a set of utilities, available in Java and C++, to simplify the task of creating XML documents.

Oracle includes five XML developer's kits, or XDKs. Each consists of a standards-based set of components, tools, and utilities. The XDKs are available for Java, C, C++, PL/SQL, and Java Beans.

(ii) LOBs: The LOB datatypes BLOB, CLOB, NCLOB, and BFILE make possible for you to store and manipulate large blocks of unstructured data in binary or character format. They provide efficient, random, piece-wise access to the data.

(iii) Oracle Text: Oracle Text indexes any document or textual content to give fast, accurate retrieval of information. Oracle Text allows text searches to be combined with regular database searches in a single SQL statement. The Oracle Text SQL API makes it simple and intuitive for application developers and DBAs to create and preserve Text indexes and run Text searches.

(iv) Oracle Spatial: Oracle includes built-in spatial features that allow you store, index, and manage location content and query location relationships using the power of the database. The Oracle Spatial Option gives advanced spatial features such as linear reference support and coordinate systems.

7. **Security Features:** Oracle contains security features that control how a database is accessed and used. For example, security mechanisms:
   - Prevent unauthorized database access
   - Prevent unauthorized access to schema objects
   - Audit user actions

   Associated with each database user is a schema by the same name. By default, each database user creates and has access to all objects in the corresponding schema.

   Database security can be classified into two categories: **system security** and **data security**.

   System security contains the mechanisms that control the access and use of the database at the system level. For example, system security includes:
   - Valid user name/password combinations
   - The amount of disk space available to a user's schema objects
   - The resource limits for a user

   System security mechanisms check whether a user is authorized to connect to the database, whether database auditing is active, and which system operations a user can perform.

   Data security contains the mechanisms that control the access and use of the database at the schema object level. For example, data security contains:
   - Which users have access to a specific schema object and the specific types of actions allowed for each user on the schema object.
   - The actions, if any, that are audited for each schema object.
   - Data encryption to stop unauthorized users from bypassing Oracle and accessing data.

III. MYSQL

- MySQL is a relational database management system (RDBMS). The program runs as a server providing multi-user access to a number of databases.
- MySQL is owned and sponsored by Swedish company MySQL AB, Sun Microsystems.

History

- Development of MySQL by Michael Widenius and David Axmark starting in 1994.
- First internal release on 23 May 1995.
- Windows version was released on 8 January 1998 for Windows 95 and NT.
- Version 3.19: 1996.
- Version 3.20: January 1997.
- Version 3.21: production release 1998.

- Version 3.22: alpha, beta from 1998.
- Version 3.23: beta from June 2000, production release 22 January 2001.
- Version 4.0: beta from August 2002, production release March 2003 (unions)
- Version 4.01: beta from August 2003.
- Version 4.1: beta from June 2004, production release October 2004 (R-trees, 13-trees, subqueries, prepared statements).
- Version 5.0: beta from March 2005, production release October 2005 (cursors, stored procedures, triggers, views, XA transactions).
- Sun Microsystems acquired MySQL AB on 26 February 2008.
- Version 5.1: production release 27 November 2008 (event scheduler, partitioning, plugin API, row-based replication, server log tables)
- MySQL 5.1 and 6.0 proved poor performance when used for data warehousing partly because of its inability to utilize multiple CPU cores for processing a single query.
- Oracle acquired Sun Microsystems on 27 January 2010.
- MySQL Server 5.5 is currently generally available (as of December 2010). Enhancements and features include:
    - The default storage engine is InnoDB, supporting transactions and referential integrity constraints.
    - Improved InnoDB I/O subsystem
    - Semisynchronous replication.
    - Improved SMP support
    - SIGNAL and RESIGNAL statement agrees with the SQL standard.
    - Support for supplementary Unicode character sets utf16, utf32, and utf8mb4.
    - New options for user-defined partitioning.
- MySQL Server 6.0.11-alpha was announced on 22 May 2009 as the last release of the 6.0. Future MySQL Server development uses a New Release Model. Features developed for 6.0 are being included into future releases.
- MySQL 5.6 was announced in February 2013. New features include performance improvements to the query optimizer, higher transactional throughput in InnoDB, new NoSQL-style memcached APIs, improvements to partitioning for querying and organize very large tables, TIMESTAMP column type that correctly stores milliseconds, improvements to replication, and better performance checking by expanding the data available through the PERFORMANCE_SCHEMA. The InnoDB storage engine now also supports full text search and improved group commit performance.
- MySQL 5.7 Development Milestone 3 was released in December 2013.

Features

- MySQL 5.1 is available in two different variants: the MySQL Community Server and Enterprise Server.
- They have a common code base and include the following features:
    1. A broad subset of ANSI SQL 99, as well as extensions.
    2. Stored procedures.
    3. Cross-platform support.
    4. Cursors.
    5. Triggers.
    6. Updatable Views.
    7. True VARCHAR support.
    8. INFORMATION_SCHEMA.
    9. Strict mode.
    10. X/Open XA Distributed Transaction Processing (DTP) support; two phase commit (2PC) as part of this, using Oracle's InnoDB engine.
    11. Independent storage engines such as, MyISAM for read speed, InnoDB for transactions and referential integrity, MySQL Archive for storing historical data in little space etc.
    12. Query caching.
    13. SSL support.
    14. Sub-SELECTs.
    15. Replication with one master per slave, many slaves per master, no automatic support for multiple masters per slave.
    16. Full-text indexing and searching using MyISAM engine
    17. Embedded database library.
    18. Partial Unicode support.
    19. ACID compliance using the InnoDB, BDB and Cluster engines.
    20. Shared-nothing clustering through MySQL Cluster.

Limitations:

- Like other SQL databases, MySQL does not currently agree with the full SQL standard for some of the implemented functionality, including foreign key references when using some storage engines other than the 'standard' InnoDB (or third-party engines which supports foreign keys).
- Until MySQL 5.7, triggers are restricted to one per action / timing, meaning that at most one trigger can be defined to be executed after an INSERT operation, and one before INSERT on the same table. No triggers can be defined on views.

Deployment:
- MySQL can be built and installed manually from source code, but this can be boring so it is more commonly installed from a binary package unless special customizations are required.
- On most Linux distributions the package management system can download and install MySQL with less effort, though further configuration is often needed to adjust security and optimization settings.
- Though MySQL began as a low-end alternative to more powerful proprietary databases, it has slowly evolved to support higher-scale needs as well.
- It is still most commonly used in small to medium scale single-server deployments, either as a component in a LAMP-based web application or as a standalone database server.
- Much of MySQL's attraction originates in its relative simplicity and ease of use, which is enabled by an ecosystem of open source tools such as phpMyAdmin.
- In the medium range, MySQL can be scaled by deploying it on more powerful hardware, such as a multi-processor server with gigabytes of memory.

High availability:
- Ensuring it requires a certain amount of redundancy in the system. For database systems, the redundancy traditionally takes the form of having a primary server acting as a master, and using replication to keep secondaries available to replace in case the primary fails.
- This means that the "server" that the application connects to is in reality a collection of servers, not a single server. In a similar manner, if the application is using pieces of database, it is in reality working with a collection of servers, not a single server.
- In this case, a collection of servers is usually referred to as a farm.

Cloud deployment:
- MySQL can also be run on cloud computing platforms such as Amazon EC2. Following are some common deployment models for MySQL on the cloud:
- **Virtual Machine Image** – cloud users can upload a machine image of their own with MySQL installed, or use a ready-made machine image with an optimized installation of MySQL on it, such as the one provided by Amazon EC2.[54]
- **MySQL as a Service** – some cloud platforms offer MySQL "as a service". In this configuration, application owners do not have to install and maintain the MySQL database on their own. Instead, the database service provider takes responsibility for installing and preserving the database, and application owners pay according to their usage. Notable cloud-based MySQL services are the Amazon Relational Database Service, Rackspace, HP Converged Cloud;Heroku and Jelastic.
- **Managed MySQL cloud hosting** – the database is not offered as a service, but the cloud provider hosts the database and organizes it as representative of application owner. As of 2011, of the major cloud providers, only Terremark and Rackspace offer managed hosting for MySQL databases.

Backup:

- **MySQL Enterprise Backup** – a hot backup utility added as part of the MySQL Enterprise subscription from Oracle. It provides native InnoDB hot backup, as well as backup for other storage engines.
- **mysqldump** – a logical backup tool included with both community and enterprise editions of MySQL. Supports backup from all storage engines.
- **Filesystem snapshot or volume manager snapshot** – backups are performed by using an external tool provided by the operating system (such as LVM) or storage device, with additional support from MySQL for ensuring consistency of such snapshots.
- **XtraBackup** – open source MySQL hot backup software. Some notable features include hot, non-locking backups for InnoDB storage, incremental backups, streaming, parallel-compressed backups, throttling based on the number of I/O operations per second, etc.

IV IBM DB2:

- DB2 is one of IBM's families of Relational Database Management System (RDBMS) software products within IBM's broader Information Management Software line.
- Although there are different "editions" and "versions" of DB2 which run on devices ranging from handhelds to mainframes, most often DB2 refers to DB2 Enterprise Server Edition, which runs on Unix (AIX), Windows or Linux servers; or DB2 for z/OS.
- DB2 powers the different IBM InfoSphere Warehouse editions. Alongside DB2 is another RDBMS: Informix, which was acquired by IBM in 2001.
- DB2 can be administered from either the command-line or a GUI. The command-line interface requires more knowledge of the product but can be more easily scripted and automated.
- The GUI is a multi-platform Java client that contains a variety of wizards suitable for beginners. DB2 supports both SQL and XQuery. DB2 has native implementation of XML data storage, where XML data is stored as XML (not as relational data or CLOB data) for faster access using XQuery.
- DB2 has APIs for .NET CLI, Java, Python, Perl, PHP, Ruby, C++, C, REXX, PL/I, COBOL, RPG, FORTRAN, and many other programming languages. DB2 also supports combining into the Eclipse and Visual Studio .NET integrated development environments
- An important feature of DB2 computer programs is error handling. The SQL Communications Area (SQLCA) structure was once used only within a DB2 program to return error information to the application program after every SQL statement was executed. The primary, but not singularly useful, error diagnostic is held in the field SQLCODE within the SQLCA block.
- The SQL return code values are:
    - 0 (zero) means successful execution.

- A positive number means successful execution with one or more warnings. An example is +100 which means no rows found.
- A negative number means unsuccessful with an error. An example is -911 which means a lock timeout (or deadlock) has occurred, triggering a rollback.

V MS-ACCESS: [Oct. 11]

- Microsoft Access is a Relational Database Management System (RDBMS), designed mainly for home or small business usage.
- Access is known as a desktop database system because it's functions are intended to be run from a stand alone computer. This is in contrast to a server database application (such as SQL Server), where it is intended to be installed on a server, then accessed remotely from multiple client machines.
- Microsoft (or MS) Access is a software package that you install just like any other software package, and is bundled as part of the Microsoft Office suite.
    1. **Tables:** The tables are the backbone and the storage container of the data entered into the database.
    2. **Relationships:** Relationships are the links you build between the tables. They join tables that have associated elements.
    3. **Queries:** Are the means of manipulating the data to display in a form or a report. Queries can sort, calculate, group, filter, join tables, update data, delete data, etc. Their power is great. The Microsoft Access database query language is SQL (Structured Query Language).
    4. **Forms:** Forms are the primary interface through which the users of the database enter data.
    5. **Reports:** Reports are the results of the manipulation of the data you have entered into the database.
    6. **Macros:** Macros are spontaneous way for Access to carry out a series of actions for the database. Access gives you a selection of actions that are carried out in the order you enter.
    7. **Modules:** Modules are the basis of the programming language that supports Microsoft Access, The module window is where you can write and store Visual Basic for Applications (VBA). Advanced users of Microsoft Access tend to use VBA instead of Macros.

Features

1. Users can create tables, queries, forms and reports, and link them together with macros. Advanced users can use VBA to write valuable solutions with advanced data manipulation and user control.
2. Access also has report creation features that can work with any data source that Access can "access".

3. Other features include: the import and export of data to various formats like Excel, Outlook, ASCII, dBase, Paradox, FoxPro, SQL Server, Oracle, ODBC, etc.
4. It also has the ability to link to data in its existing location and use it for viewing, querying, editing, and reporting. This allows the existing data to change while makes sure that Access uses the latest data. It can perform heterogeneous joins between data sets stored across different platforms.
5. There is also the Jet Database format (MDB or ACCDB in Access 2007) which can contain the application and data in one file. This makes it very convenient to distribute the entire application to another user, who can run it in disconnected environments.
6. Queries can be viewed graphically or edited as SQL statements, and SQL statements can be used directly in Macros and VBA Modules to manipulate Access tables. Users can mix and use both VBA and "Macros" for programming **forms** and logic and presents object-oriented possibilities. VBA can also be included in queries.
7. Microsoft Access present parameterized queries. These queries and Access tables can be referenced from other programs like VB6 and .NET through DAO or ADO.
8. The desktop editions of Microsoft SQL Server can be used with Access as an alternative to the Jet Database Engine. This support began with MSDE (Microsoft SQL Server Desktop Engine), a scaled down version of Microsoft SQL Server 2000, and continues with the SQL Server Express versions of SQL Server 2005 and 2008.
9. Microsoft Access is a file server-based database. Unlike client–server relational database management systems (RDBMS), Microsoft Access does not support database triggers, stored procedures, or transaction logging.
10. Access 2010 includes table-level triggers and stored procedures built into the ACE data engine. Thus a Client-server database system is not a need for using stored procedures or table triggers with Access 2010. Tables, queries, Forms, reports and Macros can now be developed specifically for web base application in Access 2010. Integration with Microsoft SharePoint 2010 is highly improved.

1.2 DIFFERENCE BETWEEN RDBMS AND DBMS (April 10; Oct. 11, 12)

RDBMS	DBMS
• RDBMS is a relational database management system	• DBMS is a database management system.
• RDBMS follows normalization concept.	• DBMS does not follow the normalization.
• In RDBMS relation is made between two tables.	• In DBMS relation is between two files.

Contd...

• RDBMS has the major difference of solving the queries easily as they are stored in table format and use many functional keys in solving the queries.	• DBMS is mainly a storage area and it does not employ any tables for storing the data or does not use any special function keys or foreign keys for the retrieval of the data.
• RDBMS supports client/server Architecture.	• DBMS does not support client/server Architecture.
• RDBMS allows simultaneous access of users to the database.	• Only one user can access the database at a time in DBMS.
• RDMBS stand for Relational Database Management System. This is the most common form of DBMS. Invented by E.F. Codd, the only way to view the data is as a set of tables. Because there can be relationships between the tables.	• DBMS stands for Database Management System which is a general term for a set of software dedicated to controlling the storage of data.
• It is used to establish the relationship concept between two database objects, i.e., tables.	• In DBMS no relationship concept.
• It treats data as tables internally.	• It treats data as files internally.
• It supports minimum 6 rules of E.F.Codd.	• It supports 3 rules of E.F.Codd out of 12 rules.
• It requires High software and hardware requirements.	• It requires low Software and hardware requirements.

• Example: (i) SQL-Server,
          (ii) Oracle
	• Example: (i) FoxPro,
	          (ii) IMS

1.3 RELATION AMONG DBMS AND APPLICATION PROGRAMS

- A database is information that is stored in a disk. The database management system (DBMS) is a set of programs, middleware if you will, which allow read and write access to the database.
- A database application is a set of programs that utilize the DBMS in order to store, retrieve, manipulate and report the data in the database. Enhanced DBMS's, such as D3, offer much more than just read/write capabilities.
- D3 provide a full featured operating environment for the applications to run in.
- A programmer is an application developer who creates the applications for the benefit of the end users. The end user is one who sits in front of a keyboard and exercises the application.

- A user runs software, which is a database application, to manipulate data contained in a database. One or more databases are stored in a DBMS and they are subject to the rules enforced and features provided by that DBMS.
- Outside of the technical definitions, users should not have any knowledge of the underlying mechanics of the database applications.
- That is, they should not have to know how to navigate the application or how the data in the application relates - a good application will simply perform the functions required and expected by the user so that they can focus on what they do and not the software that does it.

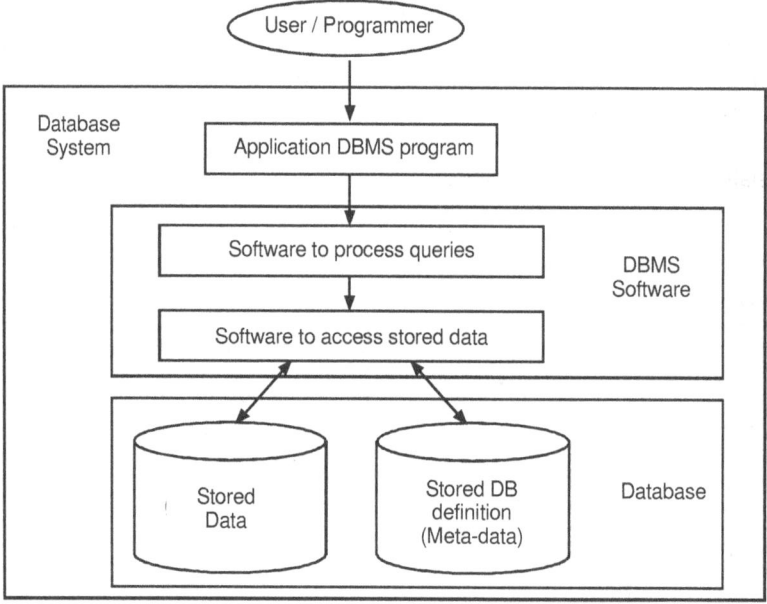

Fig. 1.6: Structure of database application

- Too many business applications expect the user to think a certain way in order to get things done - the software should "think" like the user. A DBMS is a wrapper around one or more databases.
- Each DBMS type claims to be better at maintaining data better than others. Examples, of DBMSs are Oracle, SQL Server, MySQL, D3, jBASE, dBASE, DB2, Universe, Interbase, etc.
- Again, the user should not have to worry about what DBMS they are using, only that their data is safe and being processed as they expect.
- The question is "who is the user?" If the user is Manisha, the data entry person, then she should not care. If the user is Manisha, the company owner, or Manisha, the IT director, then she should care if her DBMS is Oracle or MS Access.

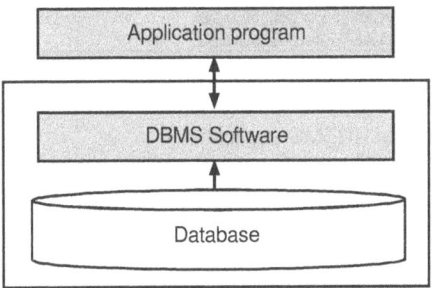 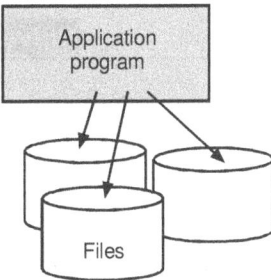

Fig. 1.7: Relation between DBMS and application program

- The difference is both technical and a matter of perception - would you buy stock in a large company if you knew they did all of their financials in MS Access?
- "Database application "also known as" application software which could be business software like accounts receivable or inventory management.
- It could also be a game which tracks player positions and scores, or a program to track your favorite restaurants. Good application software should be as independent as possible of the underlying DBMS, but in the real world many developers tie their software heavily into the DBMS to utilize the benefits the DBMS provides.
- By making software DBMS independent, you can more easily move your application and database to another DBMS. This portability can be of great value to the end-user.

Practice Questions

1. What do you mean by database?
2. What is RDBMS?
3. Define RDBMS.
4. Enlist various characteristics of RDBMS.
5. State advantages of RDBMS.
6. List out various features of RDBMS.
7. Describe the following RDBMS keys.
   (i) Primary key
   (ii) Foreign key
   (iii) Candidates key
8. Compare DBMS and RDBMS.
9. Enlist various properties of RDBMS.
10. With neat diagram explain components of RDBMS.
11. State disadvantages of RDBMS.
12. Enlist various RDBMS products. Describe two of them in detail.
13. Write short notes on:
    (i) IBM DB2.
    (ii) MySQLs

University Question & Answers

October 2009

1. What is RDBMS? State popular commercial RDBMS application. [2 M]
Ans. Please refer to Sections 1.1.3.2. & 1.2.
2. Write a note on any two products of RDBMS. [4 M]
Ans. Please refer to Page 1.17

April 2010

1. Give any two differences between DBMS and RDBMS. [2 M]
Ans. Please refer to Section 1.3.
2. Explain any four objects of oracle. [4 M]
Ans. Please refer to Section 1.2.2.

October 2010

1. Explain any two distinguishing characteristic of RDBMS. [2 M]
Ans. Please refer to Section 1.1.3.3.
2. What are the features of oracle? [4 M]
Ans. Please refer to Page 1.16.

April 2011

1. List four products of RDBMS. [2 M]
Ans. Please refer to Section 1.2.
2. Differentiate between DBMS and RDBMS. [4 M]
Ans. Please refer to Section 1.3.

October 2011

1. What are the main objects in MS-Access? [2 M]
Ans. Please refer to Page 1.28.
2. Differentiate between DBMS and RDBMS with example. [4 M]
Ans. Please refer to Section 1.3.

April 2012

1. What is RDBMS? List any two features of RDBMS. [2 M]
Ans. Please refer to Section 1.1.3.2 and 1.1.3.4.
2. Write short note on: System concepts. [4 M]
Ans. Please refer to Section 1.5.

October 2012

1. Give any two differences between DBMS and RDBMS. [2 M]
Ans. Please refer to Section 1.3
2. Explain any two popular products of RDBMS. [4 M]
Ans. Please refer to Page 1.10.

April 2013

1. What is RDBMS? List any four popular RDBMS products. [2 M]
Ans. Please refer to Section 1.1.3.2 Page 1.16.
2. Explain difference between DBMS and RDBMS. [4 M]
Ans. Please refer to Section 1.3.

October 2013

1. What is RDBMS? List any two features of RDBMS. [2 M]
Ans. Please refer to Section 1.1.3.2 and 1.1.3.4.
2. What are the features of oracle. [4 M]
Ans. Please refer to Page 1.16.

April 2014

1. What is RDBMS. [2 M]
Ans. Please refer to Section 1.1.3.2.
2. What are the characteristics of RDBMS? [2 M]
Ans. Please refer to Section 1.1.3.3.
3. Explain any two popular RDBMS products. [4 M]
Ans. Please refer to Page 1.10.

❖❖❖

Chapter 2...

PL/SQL

Contents ...

This chapter gives basic concepts of PL/SQL such as:

2.1 OVERVIEW OF PL/SQL
    2.1.1 What is PL/SQL
    2.1.2 PLSQL Engine
    2.1.3 Features of PL/SQL
    2.1.4 Adventages of PL/SQL
2.2 DATA TYPES
2.3 PLSQL BLOCK
    2.3.1 % type, % rowtype
    2.3.2 Operators, Functions, comparison, numeric, character, date
    2.3.3 Control Statement
2.4 EXCEPTION HANDLING
    2.4.1 Concept of Exception
    2.4.2 What is Exception Handling?
    2.4.3 Predefined
    2.4.4 User defined exceptions
2.5 FUNCTIONS
    2.5.1 What is a Function ?
    2.5.2 Creating a Function
    2.5.3 How to Execute a Function?
    2.5.4 Deleting a Function
2.6 PROCEDURES
    2.6.1 Creating a Procedure
    2.6.2 Executing a Procedure
    2.6.3 Deleting a Procedure
2.7 CURSOR
    2.7.1 Definition
    2.7.2 Types of cursor- implicit, explicit (attributes)
    2.7.3 Parameterized cursor
2.8 TRIGGER
    2.8.1 What is Trigger?
    2.8.2 Creating a Trigger
    2.8.3 Modifying a Trigger
    2.8.4 Enabling/Disabling a Trigger
    2.8.5 Deleting a Trigger

2.9 PACKAGE
    2.9.1 Package Strucutre
    2.9.2 Package Initialization

2.1 OVERVIEW OF PL/SQL (April 10, Oct. 10)

- PL/SQL stands for Procedural Language/SQL.
- PL/SQL extends SQL by adding constructs found in procedural languages, resulting in a structural language that is more powerful than SQL.
- With PL/SQL, you can define and execute PL/SQL program units such as procedures, functions, triggers, cursors and packages. PL/SQL program units generally are categorized as anonymous blocks and stored procedures.
- PL/SQL supports variables, conditions, arrays and exceptions. Implementations from version 8 of Oracle Database onwards have included features associated with object-orientation and some constructs such as loops.
- PL/SQL, however, as a complete procedural language that fills in these gaps, allows Oracle database developers to interface with the underlying relational database in an imperative manner.
- SQL statements can make explicit in-line calls to PL/SQL functions, or can cause PL/SQL triggers to fire upon pre-defined Data Manipulation Language (DML) events.

2.1.1 What is PL/SQL? (Oct. 10, 11, 13; April 12)

- PL/SQL is Oracle's procedural language extension to SQL.
- PL/SQL allows you to mix SQL statements with procedural statements like IF statement, Looping structures etc.
- PL/SQL is the superset of SQL. It uses SQL for data retrieval and manipulation and uses its own statements for data processing.
- PL/SQL program units are generally categorized as follows:
  1. Anonymous blocks and
  2. Stored procedures
1. **Anonymous block:** This is a PL/SQL block that appears within your application. In many applications PL/SQL blocks can appear where SQL statements can appear. Such blocks are called as Anonymous blocks.
2. **Stored Procedure:** This is a PL/SQL block that is stored in the database with a name. Application programs can execute these procedures using the name. Oracle also allows you to create functions, which are same as procedures but return a value and packages, which are a collection of procedures and functions.
- PL/SQL is a combination of SQL along with the procedural features of programming languages. It was developed by Oracle Corporation in the early 90's to enhance the capabilities of SQL.

2.1.2 PL/SQL Engine

- Oracle uses a PL/SQL engine to process the PL/SQL statements. A PL/SQL code can be stroed in the client sytem (client-side) or in the database (server-side).
- Every PL/SQL block is first executed by PL/SQL engine.
- This is the engine that compiles and executes PL/SQL blocks.
- PL/SQL engine is available in Oracle Server and certain Oracle tools such as Oracle Forms and Oracle Reports etc.
- PL/SQL engine executes all procedural statements of a PL/SQL of the block, but sends SQL command to SQL statements executor in the Oracle RDBMS.
- That means PL/SQL separates SQL commands from PL/SQL commands and executes PL/SQL commands using Procedural statement executor, which is a part of PL/SQL engine, (Refer Fig. 2.1).

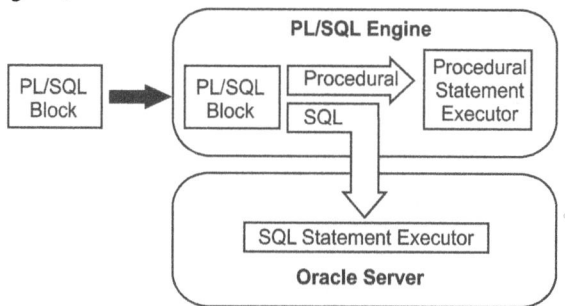

Fig. 2.1: PL/SQL Engine

2.1.3 Features of PL/SQL   (Oct. 10)

- The important features of PL/SQL are listed below:

   1. **Block structure:**

      PL/SQL is a block-structured language. Each program written in PL/SQL is written as a block. Blocks can also be nested. Each block is meant for a particular task.

   2. **Variables and Constants:**

      PL/SQL allows you to declare variables and constants. Variables are used to store values temporarily. Variables and constants can be used in SQL and PL/SQL procedural statements just like an expression.

   3. **Control structures:**

      PL/SQL allows control structures like IF statement, FOR loop, WHILE loop to be used in the block. Control structures are most important extension to SQL in PL/SQL. Control structures allow any data process possible in PL/SQL.

   4. **Exception handling:**

      PL/SQL allows errors, called as exceptions, to be detected and handled. Whenever there is a predefined error PL/SQL raises an exception automatically. These exceptions can be handled to recover from errors.

5. **Modularity:**
PL/SQL allows process to be divided into different modules. Subprograms called as procedures and functions can be defined and executed using the name. These subprograms can also take parameters.

6. **Cursors:**
A cursor is a private SQL area used to execute SQL statements and store processing information. PL/SQL implicitly uses cursors for all DML commands and SELECT command that returns only one row. It also allows you to define explicit cursor to deal with multiple row queries.

7. **Built-in functions:**
Most of the SQL functions that we have seen so far in SQL are available in PL/SQL. These functions can be used to manipulate variables of PL/SQL.

2.1.4 Advantages of PL/SQL   (Oct. 09)

- PL/SQL is completely portable, high perormance transaction processing language that gives the following advantages.
    1. **Block Structures:** PL/SQL consists of blocks of code, which can be nested within each other. Each block forms a unit of a task or a logical module. PL/SQL Blocks can be stored in the database and reused.
    2. **Procedural Language Capability:** PL/SQL consists of procedural language constructs such as conditional statements, (if else statements) and loops (FOR, WHILE loops etc.).
    3. **Better Performance:** PL/SQL engine processes multiple SQL statements simultaneously as a single block, thereby reducing network traffic.
    4. **Error Handling:** PL/SQL handles errors or exceptions effectively during the execution of a PL/SQL program. Once an exception is caught, specific actions can be taken depending upon the type of the exception or it can be displayed to the user with a message.
    5. PL/SQL supports both languages i.e. procedural language and object oriented language.
    6. PL/SQL is portable language that means the programs of PL/SQL are platform independent.
    7. PL/SQL is high transaction processing language; it does not require and particular operating system to run.
    8. PL/SQL having built-in libraries of packages.
    9. PL/SQL is highly productive language, i.e. it works with the front-end to develop the application.
    10. Performance of PL/SQL is high as in single line query entire block of statement can be processed.
    11. PL/SQL also permits dealing with errors and facilitates displaying user-friendly messages when errors are found.
    12. Fully portable.

2.2 DATA TYPES (April 10, 12, 13, 14; Oct. 13)

- Every constant, variable, and parameter has a *datatype* (or *type*), which specifies a storage format, constraints and valid range of values.
- PL/SQL provides a variety of predefined datatypes. For instance, you can choose from integer, floating point, character, Boolean, date, and collection, reference and LOB types.
- In addition, PL/SQL lets you define your own subtypes. This section covers the basic types used frequently in PL/SQL programs.

1. **Character Datatypes:**

Data Type Syntax	Explanation (if applicable)
char(size)	Where size is the number of characters to store. Fixed-length strings. Space padded.
nchar(size)	Where size is the number of characters to store. Fixed-length NLS string Space padded.
nvarchar2(size)	Where size is the number of characters to store. Variable' length NLS string.
varchar2(size)	Where size is the number of characters to store. Variable-length string.
long	Variable-length strings. (backward compatible)
raw	Variable-length binary strings
long raw	Variable-length binary strings. (backward compatible)

2. **Numeric Datatypes:**

Data Type Syntax	Explanation (if applicable)
number(p,s)	Where p is the precision and s is the scale. For example, number(7,2) is a number that has 5 digits before the decimal and 2 digits after the decimal.
numeric(p,s)	Where p is the precision and s is the scale. For example, numeric(7,2) is a number that has 5 digits before the decimal and 2 digits after the decimal.
float	
dec(p,s)	Where p is the precision and s is the scale. For example, dec(3,1) is a number that has 2 digits before the decimal and 1 digit after the decimal.
decimal(p,s)	Where p is the precision and s is the scale. For example, decimal(3,1) is a number that has 2 digits before the decimal and 1 digit after the decimal.

Contd...

integer	
int	
smallint	
real	
double precision	

3. Data/Time Datatypes:

Data Type Syntax	Explanation (if applicable)
Date	
Timestamp (fractional seconds precision)	Includes year, month, day, hour, minute, and seconds. For example: timestamp(6)
timestamp (fractional seconds precision) with time zone	Includes year, month, day, hour, minute, and seconds; with a time zone displacement value. For example: timestamp(5) with time zone
timestamp *(fractional seconds precision)* with local time zone	Includes year, month, day, hour, minute, and seconds; with a time zone expressed as the session time zone. For example: timestamp(4) with local time zone
interval year *(year precision)* to month	Time period stored in years and months. For example: interval year(4) to month
interval day *(day precision)* to second *(fractional seconds precision)*	Time period stored in days, hours, minutes, and seconds. For example: interval day(2) to second(6)

4. Large Object (LOB) Datatypes:

Data Type Syntax	Explanation (if applicable)
bfile	File locators that point to a binary file on the server file system (outside the database).
bob	Stores unstructured binary large objects.
clob	Stores single-byte and multi-byte character data.
nclob	Stores Unicode data.

5. Rowid Datatypes:

Data Type Syntax	Explanation (if applicable)
rowid	Fixed-length binary data. Every record in the database has a physical address or **rowid**.
urowid(size)	Universal rowid. Where size is optional.

1. Predefined Datatypes:
- A *scalar* type has no internal components.
- A *composite* type has internal components that can be manipulated individually.
- A *reference* type holds values, called *pointers*, that designate other program items.
- A LOB type holds values, called lob locators that specify the location of large objects (For example graphic images) stored out-of-line.

2. User-Defined Subtypes:
- Each PL/SQL base type specifies a set of values and a set of operations applicable to items of that type. Subtypes specify the same set of operations as their base type but only a subset of its values. Thus, a subtype does *not* introduce a new type; it merely places an optional constraint on its base type.
- Subtypes can increase reliability, provide compatibility with ANSI/ISO types, and improve readability by indicating the intended use of constants and variables.
- PL/SQL predefines several subtypes in package STANDARD. For example, PL/SQL predefines the subtypes CHARACTER and INTEGER as follows:

```
SUBTYPE CHARACTER IS CHAR;
SUBTYPE INTEGER IS NUMBER(38,0);   -- allows only whole numbers
```

- The subtype CHARACTER specifies the same set of values as its base type CHAR, so CHARACTER is an *unconstrained subtype*. But, the subtype INTEGER specifies only a subset of the values of its base type NUMBER, so INTEGER is a *constrained subtype*.

(a) Defining Subtypes:
- You can define your own subtypes in the declarative part of any PL/SQL block, subprogram, or package using the syntax:

```
SUBTYPE subtype_name IS base_type[(constraint)] [NOT NULL];
```

where subtype_name is a type specifier used in subsequent declarations, base_type is any scalar or user-defined PL/SQL datatype and constraint applies only to base types that can specify precision and scale or a maximum size.

Some examples follow:

```
DECLARE
    SUBTYPE BirthDate IS DATE NOT NULL;   -- based on DATE type
    SUBTYPE Counter IS NATURAL;           -- based on NATURAL subtype
    TYPE NameList IS TABLE OF VARCHAR2(10);
    SUBTYPE DutyRoster IS NameList;       -- based on TABLE type
    TYPE TimeRec IS RECORD (minutes INTEGER, hours INTEGER);
    SUBTYPE FinishTime IS TimeRec;        -- based on RECORD type
    SUBTYPE ID_Num IS emp.empno%TYPE;     -- based on column type
```

- You can use %TYPE or %ROWTYPE to specify the base type. When %TYPE provides the datatype of a database column, the subtype inherits the size constraint (if any) of the column. However, the subtype does *not* inherit other kinds of constraints such as NOT NULL.

- **Type Compatibility:** An unconstrained subtype is interchangeable with its base type. For example, given the following declarations, the value of amount can be assigned to total without conversion:

```
DECLARE
    SUBTYPE Accumulator IS NUMBER;
    amount NUMBER(7,2);
total   Accumulator;
BEGIN
    ...
    total:= amount;
    ...
END;
```

- Different subtypes are interchangeable if they have the same base type. For instance, given the following declarations, the value of finished can be assigned to debugging:

```
DECLARE
    SUBTYPE Sentinel IS BOOLEAN;
    SUBTYPE Switch IS BOOLEAN;
    finished  Sentinel;
    debugging Switch;
BEGIN
    ...
    debugging:= finished;
    ...
END;
```

- Different subtypes are also interchangeable if their base types are in the same datatype family. For example, given the following declarations, the value of verb can be assigned to sentence:

```
DECLARE
  SUBTYPE Word IS CHAR(15);
  SUBTYPE Text IS VARCHAR2(1500);
  verb     Word;
  sentence Text(150);
BEGIN
    ...
    sentence:= verb;
    ...
END;
```

Datatype Conversion

- Sometimes, it is necessary to convert a value from one datatype to another. For example, if you want to examine a rowid, you must convert it to a character string.
- PL/SQL supports both explicit and implicit (automatic) datatype conversion.

1. **Explicit Conversion:** To convert values from one datatype to another, you use built-in functions. For example, to convert a CHAR value to a DATE or NUMBER value, you use the function TO_DATE or TO_NUMBER, respectively. Conversely, to convert a DATE or NUMBER value to a CHAR value, you use the function TO_CHAR.

2. **Implicit Conversion:** When it makes sense, PL/SQL can convert the datatype of a value implicitly. This lets you use literals, variables and parameters of one type where another type is expected. In the example below, the CHAR variables start_time and finish_time hold string values representing the number of seconds past midnight. The difference between those values must be assigned to the NUMBER variable elapsed_time. So, PL/SQL converts the CHAR values to NUMBER values automatically.

```
DECLARE
    start_time    CHAR(5);
    finish_time   CHAR(5);
    elapsed_time NUMBER(5);
BEGIN
    /* Get system time as seconds past midnight. */
    SELECT TO_CHAR(SYSDATE,'SSSSS') INTO start_time FROM sys.dual;
    -- do something
    /* Get system time again. */
    SELECT TO_CHAR(SYSDATE,'SSSSS') INTO finish_time FROM sys.dual;
    /* Compute elapsed time in seconds. */
    elapsed_time:= finish_time - start_time;
    INSERT INTO results VALUES (elapsed_time, ...);
END;
```

- Before assigning a selected column value to a variable, PL/SQL will, if necessary, convert the value from the datatype of the source column to the datatype of the variable. This happens, for example, when you select a DATE column value into a VARCHAR2 variable.
- Likewise, before assigning the value of a variable to a database column, PL/SQL will, if necessary, convert the value from the datatype of the variable to the datatype of the target column. If PL/SQL cannot determine which implicit conversion is needed, you get a compilation error. In such cases, you must use a datatype conversion function.

2.3 PL/SQL BLOCKS (Oct. 10, 11; April 12)

- The basic unit in PL/SQL is a block. All PL/SQL programs are made up of blocks, which can be nested within each other.
- Typically, each block performs a logical action in the program. A typical PL/SQL block shown in Fig. 2.2.
- Each program consists of SQL and statements which is from a PL/SQL block.
- A PL/SQL Block consists of three sections:
  1. The Declaration section (optional).
  2. The Execution section (mandatory).
  3. The Exception (or Error) Handling section (optional).

1. Declaration Section:

The Declaration section of a PL/SQL Block starts with the reserved keyword DECLARE. This section is optional and is used to declare any placeholders like variables, constants, records and cursors, which are used to manipulate data in the execution section. Placeholders may be any of Variables, Constants and Records, which stores data temporarily. Cursors are also declared in this section.

2. Execution Section:

The Execution section of a PL/SQL Block starts with the reserved keyword BEGIN and ends with END. This is a mandatory section and is the section where the program logic is written to perform any task. The programmatic constructs like loops, conditional statement and SQL statements form the part of execution section.

3. Exception Section:

The Exception section of a PL/SQL Block starts with the reserved keyword EXCEPTION. This section is optional. Any errors in the program can be handled in this section, so that the PL/SQL Blocks terminates gracefully. If the PL/SQL Block contains exceptions that cannot be handled, the Block terminates suddenly with errors.

Every statement in the above three sections must end with a semicolon;. PL/SQL blocks can be nested within other PL/SQL blocks. Comments can be used to document code.

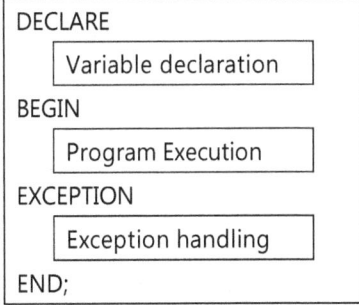

Fig. 2.2: PL/SQL Block

- For example:
  ```
  declare
      v_rollno students.rollno%type;
  begin
      -- get roll number of the students who joined most recently
      select max(rollno) into v_rollno;
      -- insert a new row into payments table
      insert into payments values (v_rollno, sysdate,1000);
      -- commit transaction
      commit;
  end;
  /
  ```
- Follow the procedure given below to create and run the above block.
  1. Type the above program in a text editor such as Notepad and save it in a text file. Assume the file is saved under the name INSPAY.SQL. And be sure to know the directory where the file is saved.
  2. Get into SQL*PLUS. Start it and logon if you have not already logged on.
  3. Use START command to execute the program that is in the file INSPAY.SQL.
     ```
     SQL> start c:\orabook\inspay.sql
     ```
     PL/SQL procedure successfully completed.
- If the block is successfully executed then PL/SQL displays the above message. If there are any errors during the execution then you have to correct the program, save the program and rerun it until you succeed.

Variables in PL/SQL

- Information transfer between PL/SQL program and data base through variable.
- Every variable stores certain type of values. Every variable has a specific type associated with it. That type are:
  1. One of the types used by SQL for database columns.
  2. A generic type used in PL/SQL such as NUMBER.
  3. Declared to be the same as the type of some database column.
- **Values for declaring a variable:**
  1. Variables must be declared first before the usage.
  2. Only TRUE or FALSE can be assigned to BOOLEAN type of variable.
  3. Attribute TYPE can be used to define a variable which is of type same as a database column's type definition.
  4. For customization the variable type user can use TYPE ....IS statement.

Scope of Variables

- PL/SQL allows the nesting of Blocks within Blocks i.e, the Execution section of an outer block can contain inner blocks. Therefore, a variable which is accessible to an outer Block is also accessible to all nested inner Blocks.

- The variables declared in the inner blocks are not accessible to outer blocks. Based on their declaration we can classify variables into two types.
    1. **Local variables:** These are declared in a inner block and cannot be referenced by outside Blocks.
    2. **Global variables:** These are declared in a outer block and can be referenced by its itself and by its inner blocks.
- For Example: In the below example we are creating two variables in the outer block and assigning thier product to the third variable created in the inner block. The variable 'var_mult' is declared in the inner block, so cannot be accessed in the outer block i.e. it cannot be accessed after line 11. The variables 'var_num1' and 'var_num2' can be accessed anywhere in the block.

```
DECLARE
    var_num1 number;
    var_num2 number;
BEGIN
    var_num1:= 100;
    var_num2:= 200;
    DECLARE
      var_mult number;
      BEGIN
        var_mult:= var_num1 *var_num2;
      END;
END;
/
```

Compiling and Executing a Simple block

- After typing code, type slash (/), SQL *plus sends your code to oracle for execution. After execution, your output displays line.
- PL/SQL procedure successfully completed.
- PL/SQL is always used with some other program or tool that handles input, output and other user interaction.
- Oracle now includes the DBMS_OUTPUT package with PL/SQL.

```
Declare
    a Number;
Begin
    a: = 5294;
    dbms_output.put_line('value of variable is =');
    dbms_output.put_line(a);
End;
/
```

- The dbms_out.put_line( ) procedure takes exactly one argument and output a line of text from the database server.
- To see this line of text as output use command.
    ```
    SQL > SET SERVEROUTPUT ON
    ```

Output:
```
Value of variable is =
   5294
```

Character set in PL/SQL

- The basic character set includes the following:
    1. Uppercase alphabets {A – Z}
    2. Lowercase alphatets {a – z}
    3. Numerals {0 – 9}
    4. Symbols ( ) + – */< > =! ;: . ' (a) %, "# $ ^ & – \ { }? [ ]
- Words used in a PL/SQL block are called **Lexical Units** Blank spaces can be freely inserted between lexical units in a PL/SQL block.

    Literals: A literal is a numeric value or a character string used to represent itself.

1. **Numeric Literal:** These can be either integers or floats.

    For example:
    ```
    25, 6.33, +702, -6.
    ```

2. **String Literal:** They are represented by one or more legal characters enclosed within single quotes.

    For example:
    ```
    'Hello', 'Isn"t it'
    ```

3. **Character Literal:**

    Character literals consisting of single characters.

    For example:
    ```
    '*', 'B'
    ```

4. **Logical Literal (Boolean Literal):**

    These are predetermined constants. The values that can be assigned to this data type are:
    ```
    TRUE, FALSE, NULL.
    ```

PL/SQL Constants

- As the name implies a constant is a value used in a PL/SQL Block that remains unchanged throughout the program.
- A constant is a user-defined literal value. You can declare a constant and use it instead of actual value.

- For example: If you want to write a program which will increase the salary of the employees by 25%, you can declare a constant and use it throughout the program, Next time when you want to increase the salary again you can change the value of the constant which will be easier than changing the actual value throughout the program.
- The General Syntax to declare a constant is:

  constant-name CONSTANT datatype:= VALUE;
    - Constant name is the name of the constant i.e. similar to a variable name.
    - The word CONSTANT is a reserved word and ensures that the value does not change.
    - VALUE - It is a value which must be assigned to a constant when it is declared. You cannot assign a value later.
- For example, to declare salary_increase, you can write code as follows:

  DECLARE
  salary_increase CONSTANT number (3) := 10;
- You must assign a value to a constant at the time you declare it. If you do not assign a value to a constant while declaring it and try to assign a value in the execution section, you will get a error. If you execute the below Pl/SQL block you will get error.

  DECLARE
      Salary_increase CONSTANT number (3);
  BEGIN
      salary_increase:= 100;
      dbms_output.put_line (salary-increase);
  END;

2.3.1 %type, %rowtype (Oct. 10, 13)

- Assign the same type to variable as that of the relation column declared in database. If there is any type mismatch, variable assignments and comparisons may not work the way you expect, so instead of hard coding the type of a variable, you should use the %TYPE operator.

  For example:
  DECLARE
      My_name emp.ename%TYPE;

  gives PL/SQL variable my_name whatever type was declared for the ename column in emp table.

- The %TYPE attribute provides the datatype of a variable or database column. This is particularly useful when declaring variables that will hold database values. For example, assume there is a column named title in a table named books. To declare a variable named `my_title` that has the same datatype as column `title`, use dot notation and the `%TYPE` attribute, as follows:

`my_title books.title%TYPE;`

- Declaring `my_title` with `%TYPE` has two advantages. First, you need not know the exact datatype of `title`. Second, if you change the database definition of `title` (make it a longer character string for example), the datatype of `my_title` changes accordingly at run time.

%rowtype: (Oct. 10, 13)

- A variable can be declared with %rowtype that is equivalent to a row of a table i.e. record with several fields. The result is a record type in which the fields have the same names and types as the attributes of the relation.

  For example:
  ```
  DECLARE
       Emp_rec   emp1%ROWTYPE;
  ```

- This makes variable emp_rec be a record with fields name and salary, assuming that the relation has the schema emp1(name, salary).
- The initial value of any variable, regardless of its type, is NULL.
- In PL/SQL, records are used to group data. A record consists of a number of related fields in which data values can be stored. The `%ROWTYPE` attribute provides a record type that represents a row in a table. The record can store an entire row of data selected from the table or fetched from a cursor or cursor variable.
- Columns in a row and corresponding fields in a record have the same names and datatypes. In the example below, you declare a record named `dept_rec`. Its fields have the same names and datatypes as the columns in the `dept` table.

  ```
  DECLARE
     dept_rec dept%ROWTYPE;   -- declare record variable
  ```
  You use dot notation to reference fields, as the following example shows:

  `my_deptno:= dept_rec.deptno;`

- If you declare a cursor that retrieves the last name, salary, hire date, and job title of an employee, you can use `%ROWTYPE` to declare a record that stores the same information, as follows:
  ```
  DECLARE
      CURSOR c1 IS
          SELECT ename, sal, hiredate, job FROM emp;
  emp_rec c1%ROWTYPE;  -- declare record variable that represents
                       -- a row fetched from the emp table
  ```

- When you execute the statement,

    FETCH c1 INTO emp_rec;

the value in the ename column of the emp table is assigned to the ename field of emp_rec, the value in the sal column is assigned to the sal field, and so on.

	emp_rec
emp_rec.ename	JAMES
emp_rec.sal	950.00
emp_rec.hiredate	03-DEC-95
emp_rec.job	CLERK

Program 2.1: Accept the deptno and print the no. of employees working in that department.

```
Declare
    v_deptno emp.deptno%type;
    v_count number;
Begin
    v_deptno:=&v_deptno;
    select count(*) into v_count
    from emp
    where deptno=v_deptno;
    dbms_output.put_line('No. of emp working in '|| v_deptno ||
                                              'are' || v_count);
End;
/
```

Output:
```
SQL> /
Enter value for v_deptno: 20
old 5: v_deptno:=&v_deptno;
new 5: v_deptno:=20;
No. of emp working in 20 are 2
```

Program 2.2: Accept the deptno and print the department name and location.

```
Declare
    v_deptno dept.deptno%type;
    v_dname dept.dname%type;
    v_loc dept.loc%type;
Begin
    v_deptno:=&v_deptno;
    select dname,loc into v_dname,v_loc
    from dept
```

```
        where deptno=v_deptno;
        dbms_output.put_line('Department name is '|| v_dname ||' and
                                        location is '|| v_loc);
    End;
    /
```

Output:
```
SQL> /
Enter value for v_deptno: 10
old 6: v_deptno:=&v_deptno;
new (6: v_deptno:= 10;
Department name is ACCOUNTING and location is NEW YORK
```

Program 2.3: Print name of employee having maximum salary. Also print salary.

```
Declare
    v_name emp.ename%type;
    v_Sal emp.sal%type;
Begin
    select ename,sal into v_name,v_sal
    from emp
    where sal = (select max(sal)
            from emp);
    dbms_output.put_line(v_name ||' is having maximum salary =
                                    '|| v_sal);
End;
/
```

Output:
```
SQL>/
KING is having maximum salary = 5000
```

Program 2.4: Accept employee name and print date of joined.

```
Declare
    v_name emp.ename%type;
    v_date date;
Begin
    v_name:='&v_name';
    select hiredate into v_date
    from emp
    where ename=v_name;
    dbms_output.put_line('Date of joined of '|| v_name || 'is'
                                    || v_date);
End;
/
```

Output:
```
SQL> /
Enter value for v_name: KING
old 5: v_name:='&v_name';
new 5: v_name:='KING';
Date of joined of KING is 17-NOV-81
```

Program 2.5: Accept salary and print no. of employees having salary less than or equal to accepted salary

```
Declare
   v_sal emp.sal%type;
   v_count number;
Begin
   v_sal:=&v_sal;
   select count(*) into v_count
   from emp
   where sal<=v_sal;
   dbms_output.put_line(' No.of  employees  having  salary  less
      than or equal to '|| v_sal || ' are ' || v_count);
End;
/
```

Output:
```
SQL> /
Enter value for v_sal: 3000
old 5: v_sal:=&v_sal;
new 5: v_sal:=3000;
No. of employees having salary less than or equal to 3000 are 8.
```

2.3.2 Operators, Function, Comparison, Numeric, Character, Date

Operators :

- PL/SQL operators are either unary or binary. Binary operators act on two values. An example of binary operators is the addition operator, which adds two numbers together. Unary operators only operate on one value.
- The negation operator is unary. PL/SQL operators can be divided into the following categories:
  1. Arithmetic operators
  2. Comparison operators
  3. Logical operators
  4. String operators

1. Arithmetic Operators:

Arithmetic operators are used for mathematical computations.

**	10**5	The exponentiation operator. 10**5 = 100,000.
*	2*3	The multiplication operator. 2 * 3 = 6.
/	6/2	The division operator. 6/2 = 3.
+	2+2	The addition operator. 2+2 = 4.
-	4-2	The subtraction operator. 4 -2 = 2.
-	-5	The negation operator.
+	+5	It complements the negation operator.

For example:

```
SQL>
SQL> SET SERVEROUTPUT ON
SQL> BEGIN
        DBMS_OUTPUT.PUT_LINE(4 * 2);   --multiplication
        DBMS_OUTPUT.PUT_LINE(24 / 3);  --division
        DBMS_OUTPUT.PUT_LINE(4 + 4);   --addition
        DBMS_OUTPUT.PUT_LINE(16 - 8);  --subtraction
     END;
     /
```

Exponentiation:

```
SQL>
SQL> SET SERVEROUTPUT ON
SQL> BEGIN
        DBMS_OUTPUT.PUT_LINE(4 ** 2);
     END;
     /
```

2. Comparison Operators:

Comparison operators are used to compare one value or expression to another.

All comparison operators return a boolean result.

Operator	Example	Usage
=	IF A = B THEN	The equality operator.
<>	IF A <> B THEN	The inequality operator.
!=	IF A != B THEN	Another inequality operator, synonymous with <>.

Contd....

~=	IF A ~= B THEN	Another inequality operator, synonymous with <>.
<	IF A < B THEN	The less than operator.
>	IF A > B THEN	The greater than operator.
<=	IF A <= B THEN	The less than or equal to operator.
>=	IF A >= B THEN	The greater than or equal to operator.
LIKE	IF A LIKE B THEN	The pattern-matching operator.
BETWEEN	IF A BETWEEN B AND C THEN	Checks to see if a value lies within a specified range of values.
IN	IF A IN (B,C,D) THEN	Checks to see if a value lies within a specified list of values.
IS NULL	IF A IS NULL THEN	Checks to see if a value is null.

3. **Relational Operators:**

=, <>, !=, ~=, <, >, <=, >=

String comparisons are case-sensitive.

String comparisons are dependent on the character set being used.

String comparisons are affected by the underlying datatype.

Comparing two values as CHAR strings might yield different results than the same values compared as VARCHAR2 strings.

It's important to remember that Oracle dates contain a time component.

Example:

True Expressions	False Expressions
5 = 5	5 = 3
'AAAA' = 'AAAA'	'AAAA ' = 'AAAA'
5 != 3	5 <> 5
'AAAA ' ~= 'AAAA'	'AAAA' ~= 'AAAA'
10 < 200	10.1 < 10.05
'Jeff' < 'Jenny'	'jeff' < 'Jeff'
TO_DATE('15-Nov-61' < '15-Nov-97')	TO_DATE('1-Jan-97' < '1-Jan-96')
10.1 <= 10.1	10 <= 20
'A' <= 'B'	'B' <= 'A'
TO_DATE('1-Jan-97') <= TO_DATE('1-Jan-97')	TO_DATE('15-Nov-61') <= TO_DATE('15-Nov-60')

4. Logical Operators:

- PL/SQL has three logical operators: AND, OR and NOT.
- The NOT operator is typically used to negate the result of a comparison expression. The AND and OR operators are typically used to link together multiple comparisons.
- The Syntax for the NOT Operator:

   `NOT boolean_expression`

   boolean_expression can be any expression resulting in a boolean, or true/false value.

- The Syntax for the AND Operator:

   `boolean_expression AND boolean_expression`

   boolean_expression can be any expression resulting in a boolean or true/false value. The AND operator returns a value of true if both expressions evaluate to true; otherwise, a value of false is returned.

Expression	Result
(5 = 5) AND (4 < 10) AND (2 >= 2)	true
(5 = 7) AND (5 = 5)	false
'Mon' IN ('Sun','Sat') AND (2 = 2)	false

- The Syntax for the OR Operator:

   `boolean_expression OR boolean_expression`

   boolean_expression can be any expression resulting in a boolean, or true/false, value. The OR operator returns a value of true if any one of the expressions evaluates to true.

- A value of false is returned only if both the expressions evaluate to false.

Expression	Result
(5 <> 5) OR (4 >= 100) OR (2 < 2)	false
(7 = 4) OR (5 = 5)	true
'Mon' IN ('Sun','Sat') OR (2 = 2)	true

Logical Operators in PL/SQL:

x	y	x AND y	x OR y	NOT x
True	True	True	True	False
True	False	False	True	False
False	True	False	True	True
False	False	False	False	True

5. String Operators:

- PL/SQL has two operators specifically designed to operate only on character string data.
- These are the LIKE operator and the concatenation (||) operator.
- The Syntax for the Concatenation Operator:
  ```
  string_1 || string_2
  ```

string_1 and string_2 are both character strings and can be string constants, string variables, or string expressions.

For example:
```
SQL>
SQL> SET SERVEROUTPUT ON
SQL>
SQL> DECLARE
        a     VARCHAR2(30);
        b     VARCHAR2(30);
        c     VARCHAR2(30);
     BEGIN
        c:= 'A' || ' AND ' || 'B';
        DBMS_OUTPUT.PUT_LINE(c);
        a:= ' C ';
        b:= ' D ';
        DBMS_OUTPUT.PUT_LINE(a || ' ' || b || ',');
        a:= ' E ';
        b:= ' F';
        c:= a || b;
        DBMS_OUTPUT.PUT_LINE(c);
     END;
     /
A AND B
 C   D ,
 E  F
```

6. Numeric Functions

All number functions return a numeric values unless otherwise specified. The number functions are given below

Function	Purpose
ABS	Gives absolute value of n
CEIL	Gives smallest integer >=n
COS	Gives cosine of angle.
COSH	Gives hyperbolic cosine of n
EXP	Gives value of e^n

Contd...

FLOOR	Gives largest integer <=n
LN	Gives natural logarithm of n where n>0
LOG	Gives base-m log of n where m>1 and n>0
MOD	Gives remainder of m/n
POWER	Gives value of m^n
ROUND	Gives m rounded to n places
SIGN	Gives -1 for n<0, 0 for n=0 and 1 for n>0
SIN	Gives sine of angle
SINH	Gives hyperbolic sine of n
SQRT	Gives square root of n
TAN	Gives tangent of angle
TANH	Gives hyperbolic tangent of n
TRUNC	Gives m truncated to n places

7. **Character Functions**

Function	Purpose
ASCII	Gives ASCII value of a character
CHR	Gives character for ASCII value
CONCAT	Gives string2 appended to string1
INITCAP	Gives string1 with the first letter of each word in capitals and rest in small
INSTR	Gives starting position of string2 in string1. Search starts at *pos* for the *nth* occurrence. If *pos* is negative, the search is performed in backward direction. Both *pos* and *n* default to 1. The function gives 0 if string2 not found.
INSTRB	Same like INSTR except *pos* is a byte position.
LENGTH	Gives character count in *str* and for data type CHAR, length contains trailing blanks.
LENGTHB	Same like LENGTH, gives byte count of *str* containing trailing blanks for CHAR
LOWER	Gives *str* with all letters in lowercase.

Contd...

LPAD	Left pads string to specified length with the character mentioned
LTRIM	Gives string with leading spaces(or characters mentioned in set) removed
NLS_INITCAP	Same like INITCAP except a sort sequence is specified
NLS_LOWER	Same like LOWER except a sort sequence is specified
NLS_UPPER	Same like UPPER except a sort sequence is specified
NLSSORT	Gives string in sort sequence specified
REPLACE	Gives string1 with all occurrences of string2 replaced by string3. If string3 is not given, then all occurrences of string2 are removed.
RPAD	Right pads string to specified length with the character mentioned
RTRIM	Gives string with trailing spaces(or characters mentioned in set) removed
SOUNDEX	Gives phonetic representation of string
SUBSTR	Gives substring of string starting at specified position for the length mentioned or to the end of string is length is not given.
SUBSTRB	Same like SUBSTR except works on bytes
TRANSLATE	It replaces all occurrences of set1 with set2 characters in string.
UPPER	Gives all letters of the string in uppercase

8. Date Functions

All date functions except MONTHS_BETWEEN return a DATE value.

Function	Purpose
ADD_MONTHS	Adds or subtract the specified number of months from date.
LAST_DAY	Gives last day of the month for given date.
MONTHS_BETWEEN	Gives month count between date1 and date2.
NEW_TIME	Gives date and time in other zone based on date and time in one time zone
NEXT_DAY	Gives first day of the week for day that is later than specified date
ROUND	Gives date rounded to specified unit in format. If no format is specified, date is rounded to the nearest day.
SYSDATE	Gives current system date and time.
TRUNC	Gives date with the time of day truncated as specified by format.

9. Conversion and Other Miscellaneous Functions

Function	Purpose
TO_CHAR (Dates)	Changes date to varchar2 based on format.
TO_CHAR (Numbers)	Changes number to varchar2 based on format.
TO_DATE	Changes string or number to date value based on format.
TO_NUMBER	Changes string to number value as per the given format.

Here are few examples based on above functions.

```
1.   SELECT ABS(-15) "Absolute" FROM DUAL;
     Absolute
     ----------
     15


2.   SELECT MOD(15,4) "Modulo" FROM DUAL;
     Modulo
     ----------
      3
3.   SELECT SQRT(121) FROM DUAL;
     SQRT(121)
     ----------
         11
4.   SELECT ASCII('A') FROM DUAL;
     ASCII('A')
     ----------
         65
5.   SELECT INITCAP('how are you') "init" FROM DUAL;
        init
     ----------
     How Are You
6.   SELECT INSTR('WHERE ARE YOU GOING','RE') "FIRST" FROM DUAL;
     FIRST
     ---------
         4
7.   SELECT INSTR('WHERE ARE YOU GOING','RE',1,2) "SECOND" FROM DUAL;
        SECOND
     ---------
         8
8.   SELECT LTRIM('****WHAT IS GOING','*') "LTRIM" FROM DUAL;
     LTRIM
     -------------
     WHAT IS GOING
```

```
9.    SELECT RTRIM('WHAT IS GOING--*#','*#') "RTRIM" FROM DUAL;
      RTRIM
      ---------------
      WHAT IS GOING--
10.   (If sysdate is 17-MAY-14)
      SELECT ADD_MONTHS(SYSDATE,1) "NEXT" FROM DUAL;
      NEXT
      ---------
      17-JUN-14
11.   (If sysdate is 17-MAY-14)
      SELECT LAST_DAY(SYSDATE) "LAST" FROM DUAL;
      LAST
      ---------
      31-MAY-14
```

2.3.3 Control Statements

- Control structures are the most important PL/SQL extension to SQL. Not only does PL/SQL let you manipulate Oracle data, it lets you process the data using conditional, iterative and sequential flow-of-control statements such as IF-THEN-ELSE, FOR-LOOP, WHILE-LOOP, EXIT-WHEN and GOTO. Collectively, these statements can handle any situation.

2.3.3.1 Conditional Statement in PL/SQL

- Often, it is necessary to take alternative actions depending on circumstances. The IF-THEN-ELSE statement lets you execute a sequence of statements conditionally. The IF clause checks a condition; the THEN clause defines what to do if the condition is true; the ELSE clause defines what to do if the condition is false or null.

1. IF-THEN Statement:

- The simplest form of IF statement associates a condition with a sequence of statements enclosed by the keywords THEN and END IF (not ENDIF), as follows:

```
IF condition THEN
   sequence_of_statements
END IF;
```

- The sequence of statements is executed only if the condition is true. If the condition is false or null, the IF statement does nothing. In either case, control passes to the next statement. An example follows:

```
IF sales > quota THEN
   compute_bonus(empid);
   UPDATE payroll SET pay = pay + bonus WHERE empno = emp_id;
END IF;
```

- You might want to place brief IF statements on a single line, as in
  ```
  IF x > y THEN high:= x; END IF;
  ```

2. IF-THEN-ELSE Statement:

- The second form of IF statement adds the keyword ELSE followed by an alternative sequence of statements, as follows:
  ```
  IF condition THEN
      sequence_of_statements1
  ELSE
      sequence_of_statements2
  END IF;
  ```
- The sequence of statements in the ELSE clause is executed only if the condition is false or null. Thus, the ELSE clause ensures that a sequence of statements is executed. In the following example, the first UPDATE statement is executed when the condition is true, but the second UPDATE statement is executed when the condition is false or null:
  ```
  IF trans_type = 'CR' THEN
      UPDATE accounts SET balance = balance + credit WHERE ...
  ELSE
      UPDATE accounts SET balance = balance - debit WHERE ...
  END IF;
  ```
- The THEN and ELSE clauses can include IF statements. That is, IF statements can be nested, as the following example shows:
  ```
  IF trans_type = 'CR' THEN
      UPDATE accounts SET balance = balance + credit WHERE ...
  ELSE
      IF new_balance >= minimum_balance THEN
          UPDATE accounts SET balance = balance - debit WHERE ...
      ELSE
          RAISE insufficient_funds;
      END IF;
  END IF;
  ```

3. IF-THEN-ELSIF Statement:

- Sometimes you want to select an action from several mutually exclusive alternatives.
- The third form of IF statement uses the keyword ELSIF (not ELSEIF) to introduce additional conditions, as follows:
  ```
  IF condition1 THEN
      sequence_of_statements1
  ELSIF condition2 THEN
  ```

```
      sequence_of_statements2
ELSE
      sequence_of_statements3
END IF;
```

- If the first condition is false or null, the ELSIF clause tests another condition. An IF statement can have any number of ELSIF clauses; the final ELSE clause is optional.
- Conditions are evaluated one by one from top to bottom. If any condition is true, its associated sequence of statements is executed and control passes to the next statement.
- If all conditions are false or null, the sequence in the ELSE clause is executed. Consider the following example:

```
BEGIN
   ...
   IF sales > 50000 THEN
      bonus:= 1500;
   ELSIF sales > 35000 THEN
      bonus:= 500;
   ELSE
      bonus:= 100;
   END IF;
   INSERT INTO payroll VALUES (emp_id, bonus, ...);
END;
```

- If the value of sales is larger than 50000, the first and second conditions are true. Nevertheless, bonus is assigned the proper value of 1500 because the second condition is never tested. When the first condition is true, its associated statement is executed and control passes to the INSERT statement.

Program 2.6: Program to find largest of two numbers.

```
DECLARE
A NUMBER;
B NUMBER;
BEGIN
A:=&a;
B:=&b;
If (A>B) THEN
Dbms_output.put_line ('A IS LARGEST');
ELSE
Dbms_output.put_line ('B IS LARGEST');
END IF;
END;
/
SQL>/
```

```
Enter value for A:6
Old 5: A:=&a;
New 5: A:=6
Enter value for B:7
Old 6: B:=&b
New 5: B:=7
B IS LARGEST
PL/SQL procedure successfully completed.
```

Program 2.7: Display whether the salary of Johnson is 50000 or not.

```
DECLARE
Jsal EMP.Sal%type;
BEGIN
SELECT Sal INTO Jsal
 From EMP
Where LastName='Johnson';
IF(Jsal==50000) Then
Dbms_output.put_line ('Salary of Johnson is 50000');
ELSE
Dbms_output.put_line ('Salary of Johnson is not 50000');
END IF;
END;
/
SQL>/
Salary of Johnson is 50000
PL/SQL procedure successfully completed.
```

Program 2.8: Program for calculation of net salary.

```
DECLARE
ename varchar2(15); /*size of ename is 15*/
basic number;
da number;
hra number;
pf number;
netsalary number;
BEGIN
ename:=&ename;
basic:=&basic;
da:=basic * (41/100);
hra:=basic * (15/100);
IF (basic < 3000) THEN
pf:=basic * (5/100);
```

```
ELSIF (basic >= 3000 and basic <= 5000) THEN
pf:=basic * (7/100);
ELSIF (basic >= 5000 and basic <= 8000) THEN
pf:=basic * (8/100);
ELSE
pf:=basic * (10/100);
END IF;
netsalary:=basic + da + hra -pf;
dbms_output.put_line('Employee name: ' || ename);
dbms_output.put_line('Providend Fund: ' || pf);
dbms_output.put_line('Net salary: ' || netsalary);
end;
```

Program 2.9: Program to find maximum of three numbers.

```
DECLARE
a number;
b number;
c number;
BEGIN
dbms_output.put_line('Enter a:');
a:=&a;
dbms_output.put_line('Enter b:');
b:=&b;
dbms_output.put_line('Enter c:');
c:=&c;
IF (a>b) and (a>c) THEN
dbms_output.putline('A is Maximum');
ELSIF (b>a) and (b>c) THEN
dbms_output.putline('B is Maximum');
ELSE
dbms_output.putline('C is Maximum');
END IF;
END;
```

2.3.3.2 Iterative Statement in PL/SQL (Oct. 11)

- An iterative control Statements are used when we want to repeat the execution of one or more statements for specified number of times
- There are following types of loops in PL/SQL:
    1. Simple Loop
    2. For Loop
    3. Exit When
    4. While Loop

1. Simple Loop:
- A simple loop is used when a set of statements is to be executed at least once before the
- loop terminates.
- An EXIT condition must be specified in the loop, otherwise the loop will get into an infinite number of iterations.
- When the EXIT condition is satisfied the process terminates from the loop.
- The General Syntax to write a Simple Loop is:
  ```
  LOOP
      statements;
      EXIT;
      or EXIT WHEN condition;
  END LOOP;
  ```
- These are the important steps to be followed while using Simple Loop.
  1. Initialise a variable before the loop body.
  2. Increment the variable in the loop.
  3. Use a EXIT WHEN statement to exit from the Loop. If you use a EXIT statement without WHEN condition the statements in the loop is executed only once.

Program 2.10: Insert each of the pairs (1, 1) upto (100, 100) into table T1.
```
DECLARE
i NUMBER:= 1;
BEGIN
LOOP
INSERT INTO T1 VALUES(i,i);
i:= i+1;
EXIT WHEN i>100;
END LOOP;
END;
```

Program 2.11: Print the numbers 1 to 5.
```
DECLARE
  i NUMBER:=0;
BEGIN
LOOP
 i:=i+1;
Dbms_output.put_line(i);
IF(i>=5) THEN
EXIT;
END IF;
END LOOP;
```

```
END;
/
SQL>/
1
2
3
4
5
```

Program 2.12: Print numbers 1 to 5 using EXIT WHEN <condition>.
```
DECLARE
  i NUMBER:=0;
BEGIN
LOOP
  i:=i+1;
Dbms_output.put_line(i);
EXIT WHEN i>=5;
END LOOP;
END;
/
SQL>/
1
2
3
4
5
```

2. While Loop:

- A WHILE LOOP is used when a set of statements has to re executed as long as a condition is true.
- The condition is evaluated at the beginning of each iteration. The iteration continues until the condition becomes false.
- The General Syntax to write a WHILE LOOP is:
  ```
  WHILE <condition>
      LOOP statements;
  END LOOP;
  ```
- Important steps to follow when executing a while loop:
  1. Initialise a variable before the loop body.
  2. Increment the variable in the loop.
  3. EXIT WHEN statement and EXIT statements can be used in while loops but it's not done oftenly.

Program 2.13: Print numbers 1 to 5.
```
DECLARE
    i number:=0;
BEGIN
WHILE i<=5 LOOP
 i:=i+1;
dbms_output.put_line(i);
END LOOP;
END;
/
SQL>/
1
2
3
4
5
```

Program 2.14: Program to find sum of odd numbers from 1 to 100. (Hint: value = 100)
```
DECLARE
n NUMBER;
value NUMBER;
sum NUMBER default 0;
BEGIN
value:=&value;
n:=1;
WHILE (n < value)
LOOP
sum:=sum+n;
n:=n+2;
END LOOP;
dbms_output.put_line('Sum of odd numbers between 1 and ' ||
                                    endvalue || ' is ' || sum);
END;
/
```

3. For Loop (April 10)

- A FOR Loop is used to execute a set of statements for a predetermined number of times. Iteration occurs between the start and end integer values given
- The counter is always started by 1. The loop exits when the counter reaches the value of the end integer. The General Syntax to write a FOR LOOP is:

    FOR counter IN val1..val2
        LOOP statements;
    END LOOP;

- o Val1 - Start integer value.
- o val2 - End integer value.
- Important steps to follow when executing a while loop:
  1. The counter variable is implicitly declared in the declaration section, so it's not necessary to declare explicity.
  2. The counter variable is incremented by 1 and does not need to be incremented explicitly.
  3. EXIT WHEN statement and EXIT statements can be used in FOR loops but it's not done oftenly.

Program 2.15: Print numbers 1 to 5.
```
DECLARE
N NUMBER:=5;
FOR I in 1..5 LOOP
Dbms_output.put_line(i);
END LOOP;
END;
/
SQL>/
1
2
3
4
5
```

Program 2.16: Program to find sum of odd numbers.
```
DECLARE
n NUMBER;
sum number default 0;
value Number;
begin
value:=&value;
n:=1;
for n in 1.. value LOOP
IF mod(n,2)=1 THEN
sum:=sum+n;
END IF;
END LOOP;
dbms_output.put_line('sum = ' || sum);
END;
/
```

PROGRAMS

Program 1: Accept two numbers and print the largest number.

```
Declare
    n1 number;
    n2 number;
Begin
    n1:=&n1;
    n2:=&n2;
    if(n1>n2) then
        dbms_output.put_line(n1 ||' is largest');
    else if (n1<n2) then
        dbms_output.put_line(n2 ||' is largest');
    else
        dbms_output.put_line('Both are equal');
    end if;
    end if;
End;
```

Output:

```
SQL> /
Enter value for n1:23
old 5: n1:=&n 1;
new 5: n1:=23;
Enter value for n2: 12
old 6: n2:=&n2;
new 6: n2:= 12;
23 is largest
SQL>/
Enter value for n1: 11
old 5: n1:=&n 1;
new 5: n1:=11;
Enter value for n2: 11
old 6: n2:=&n2;
new 6: n2:=11;
Both are equal
```

Program 2: Accept a number and check whether it is odd or even. If it is even no. print square of it otherwise cube of it.

```
Declare
   n1 number;
Begin n1:=&n1;
   if(mod(n1,2)=0) then
      dbms_output.put_line(n1 ||' is even no .');
      dbms_output.put_line('Square of '|| n1 ||' is '|| n1*n1);
   else
      dbms_output.put_line(n1 at ||' is odd no.');
      dbms_output.put_line('Cube of '|| n1 ||' is '|| n1 *n1*n1);
   end if;
End;
```

Output:

```
SQL> /
Enter value for n1: 2
old 4: n1:=&n1;
new 4: n1:=2;
2 is even no.
Square of 2 is 4
SQL> /
Enter value for n1: 3
old 4: n1:=&n1;
new 4: n1:=3;
3 is odd no.
Cube of 3 is 27
```

Program 3: Accept a number and print factorial of it.

```
Declare
   n number;
   i number;
   fact number:= 1;
Begin
   n:=&n;
   for i in 1..n
   loop
      fact:=fact*i;
   end loop;
   dbms_output.put_line(n ||'!='||fact);
End;
/
```

Output:
```
SQL>/
Enter value for n: 3
old 6: n:=&n;
new 6: n:=3;
3! = 6
```

Program 4: Accept a number and print it in reverse order.
```
Declare
    n number;
    r number;
Begin
    n:=&n;
    r:=0;
    while n>0
    loop
       r:=mod(n,10);
       dbms_output.put_line (r);
       n:=floor(n/10);
    end loop;
End;
/
```

Output:
```
SQL> /
Enter value for n: 234
old 5: n:=&n;
new 5: n:=234;
4
3
2
```

Program 5: Accept a string and print it in reverse order.
```
Declare
    s varchar2(30);
    c varchar2(1);
    l number;
Begin
    s:='&s';
    l:=length(s);
    while l>0
    loop
       c:=substr(s,1,l);
```

```
        dbms_output.put_line(c);
        l=l - 1;
    end loop;
End;
/
```

Output:
```
SQL> /
Enter value for s: smita
old 6: s:='&s';
new 6: s:='smita';
a
t
i
m
s
```

GOTO Statement

- This statement changes flow of control within block. Entry point is marked using tags << userdefined name >>.
- The GOTO statement can make use of this name to jump into that block for execution.

Syntax:
```
GOTO <codeblock name>;
```

For example:
```
Declare
    _____
    _____
    _____
Begin
   If a > 0 Then
      GOTO POS;
   Else
      GOTO NEG;
   END IF;
   <<POS>>
        dbms_output.put_line ('Positive Number');
   <<NEG>
        bms_output.put_line ('Negative Number');
END;
```

2.4 EXCEPTION HANDLING (April 13)

2.4.1 Concept of Exception

- The Exception section in PL/SQL block is used to handle an error that occurs during the execution of PL/SQL program.
- If an error occurs within a block, PL/SQL passes control to the EXCEPTION section of the block. If no EXCEPTION section exists within the block or the EXCEPTION section does not handle the error that's occurred then the error is passed out to the host environment.
- Exceptions occur when either an Oracle error occurs, (this automatically raises an exception) or you explicitly raise an error or a routine that executes corrective action when detecting an error.
- Thus, Exceptions are identifiers in PL/SQL that are raised during the execution of a block to terminate its action.
- There are two classes of exceptions, these are:

1. **Predefined exception:** Oracle predefined errors which are associated with specific error codes. (Oct. 10)
2. **User-defined exception:** Declared by the user and raised when specifically requested within a block. You can associate a user-defined exception with an error code if you wish.

2.4.2 What is Exception Handling ? (Oct. 13)

- PL/SQL provides a feature to handle the Exceptions which occur in a PL/SQL Block known as exception Handling.
- Using Exception Handling we can test the code and avoid it from exit suddenly. When an exception occurs a message which explains its cause is received.
- PL/SQL Exception message consists of three parts.
    1. **Type of Exception**
    2. **An Error Code**
    3. **A message**
- By Handling the exceptions we can ensure a PL/SQL block does not exit suddenly.
- The general syntax for coding the exception section are given below:

```
DECLARE
    Declaration section
BEGIN
    Exception section
EXCEPTION
WHEN ex_name1 THEN
    -Error handling statements
WHEN ex_name2 THEN
    -Error handling statements
```

```
WHEN Others THEN
    -Error handling statements
END;
```
- General PL/SQL statements can be used in the Exception Block.
- When an exception is raised, Oracle searches for an appropriate exception handler in the exception section.
- For example in the above example, if the error raised is 'ex_name1 ', then the error is handled according to the statements under it.
- Since, it is not possible to determine all the possible runtime errors during testing of the code, the 'WHEN Others' exception is used to manage the exceptions that are not explicitly handled. Only one exception can be raised in a Block and the control does not return to the Execution Section after the error is handled.
- If there are nested PL/SQL blocks like this:

```
DECLARE
   Declaration section
BEGIN
   DECLARE
      Declaration section
   BEGIN
      Execution section
   EXCEPTION
      Exception section
   END;
EXCEPTION
   Exception section
END;
```

- In the above case, if the exception is raised in the inner block it should be handled in the exception block of the inner PL/SQL block else the control moves to the Exception block of the next upper PL/SQL Block. If none of the blocks handle the exception the program ends suddenly with an error.
- There are three types of Exceptions:
  1. Named System Exceptions
  2. Unnamed System Exceptions
  3. User-defined Exceptions

1. Named System Exceptions:

- System exceptions are automatically raised by Oracle, when a program violates a RDBMS rule. There are some system exceptions which are raised frequently, so they are pre-defined and given a name in Oracle which are known as Named System Exceptions.

    For example: NO_DATA_FOUND and ZERO_DIVIDE are called Named System exceptions.

- Named system exceptions are:
  (i) Not Declared explicitly,
  (ii) Raised implicitly when a predefined Oracle error occurs,
  (iii) Caught by referencing the standard name within an exception-handling routine.

Exception Name	Reason	Error Number
CURSOR_ALREADY_OPEN	When you open a cursor that is already open.	ORA-06511
INVALID_CURSOR	When you perform an invalid operation on a cursor like closing a cursor, fetch data from a cursor that is not opened.	ORA-01001
NO_DATA_FOUND	When a SELECT...INTO clause does not return any row from a table.	ORA-01403
TOO_MANY_ROWS	When you SELECT or fetch more than one row into a record or variable.	ORA-01422
ZERO_DIVIDE	When you attempt to divide a number by zero.	ORA-01476

For Example: Suppose a NO_DATA_FOUND exception is raised in a procedure, we can write a code to handle the exception as given below:

```
BEGIN
   Execution section
EXCEPTION
   WHEN NO_DATA_FOUND THEN
     dbms_output.put_line ('A SELECT...INTO did not return any row.');
END;
```

2. Unnamed System Exceptions:

- Those system exception for which oracle does not provide a name is known as unamed system exception.
- These exception do not occur frequently. These Exceptions have a code and an associated message.

  There are two ways to handle unnamed system exceptions:
  (i) By using the WHEN OTHERS exception handler, or
  (ii) By associating the exception code to a name and using it as a named exception.

- We can assign a name to unnamed system exceptions using a **Pragma** called **EXCEPTION_INIT.**
- **EXCEPTION_INIT** will associate a predefined Oracle error number to a programmer _defined exception name.

- The general syntax to declare unnamed system exception using EXCEPTION_INIT is:
  ```
  DECLARE
      exception_name EXCEPTION;
      PRAGMA
      EXCEPTION_INIT (exception_name, Err_code);
  BEGIN
  Execution section
  EXCEPTION
     WHEN exception_name THEN
        handle the exception
  END;
  ```
  For Example: Lets consider the product table and order_items table from sql joins. Here product_id is a primary key in product table and a foreign key in order_items table. If we try to delete a product_id from the product table when it has child records in order_id table an exception will be thrown with oracle code number -2292. We can provide a name to this exception and handle it in the exception section as given below.
  ```
  DECLARE
     Child_rec_exception EXCEPTION;
     PRAGMA
      EXCEPTION_INIT (Child_rec_exception, 2292);
  BEGIN
     Delete FROM product where product_id= 104;
  EXCEPTION
     WHEN Child_rec_exception
     THEN Dbms_output.put_line('Child records are present for this
     product_id.');
  END;
  /
  ```

3. **User-defined Exceptions:**
- Apart from system exceptions we can explicity define exceptions based on business rules. These are known as user-defined exceptions.
- Steps to be followed to use user-defined exceptions:
   1. They should be explicitly declared in the declaration section.
   2. They should be explicitly raised in the Execution Section.
   3. They should be handled by referencing the user-defined exception name in the exception section.

For Example: Lets consider the product table and order_items table from sql joins to explain user-defined exception.

- Lets create a business rule that if the total no of units of any particular product sold is more than 20, then it is a huge quantity and a special discount should be provided.

```
DECLARE
  huge_quantity EXCEPTION;
  CURSOR product_quantity is
  SELECT p.product_name as name, sum(o.total_units) as units
  FROM order_tems o, product p
  WHERE o.product_id = p.product_id;
  quantity order_tems.total_units%type;
  up_limit CONSTANT order_tems.total_units%type:= 20;
  message VARCHAR2(50);
  product_rec product_quantity%rowtype;
BEGIN
  FOR product_rec in product_quantity LOOP
    quantity:= product_rec.units;
    IF quantity > up_limit THEN
      message:= 'The number of units of product '||
  product_rec.name ||'is more than 20. Special discounts should
  be provided. Rest of the records are skipped.'
      RAISE huge_quantity;
    ELSIF quantity < up_limit THEN
      message:= 'The number of unit is below the discount limit.';
    END IF;
    dbms_output.put_line (message);
  END LOOP;
  EXCEPTION
    WHEN huge_quantity THEN
      dbms_output.put_line (message);
END;
/
```

2.4.3 Predefined Exception (Oct. 10, 12; April 14)

- The two most common errors originating from a SELECT statement occur when it returns no rows **(WHEN NO_DATA_FOUND)** or more than one row (remember that this is not allowed in PL/SQL select command).

- If no rows are selected from SELECT statement then WHEN NO_DATA_FOUND exception is used and for more than one row **WHEN TOO_MANY_ROWS** exception is used.

- The example below deals with these two conditions.

```
DECLARE
   TEMP_Sal NUMBER(10,2);
BEGIN
   SELECT sal INTO TEMP_sal
   From emp
   WHERE empno>=7698;

    IF TEMP_sal > 1000 THEN
         UPDATE emp SET sal = (TEMP_sal*1.175)
         WHERE empno>=7698;
      ELSE
         UPDATE emp SET sal = 5000
         WHERE empno>=7698;
      END IF;
      COMMIT;
EXCEPTION
   WHEN NO_DATA_FOUND THEN
       Dbms.Output.put_line('Empno does not exists');
   WHEN TOO_MANY_ROWS THEN
      Dbms.Output.put_line('No. of rows selected');
END;
/
SQL> /
```

- The block above will generate an error either there are more than one record with an empno greater than 7698 or emp table does not have a record with empno>=7698. The exception raised from this will be passed to the EXCEPTION section where each handled action will be checked. The statements within the TOO_MANY_ROWS or NO_DATA_FOUND will be executed before the block is terminated.
- But if some other error occurred this EXCEPTION section would not handle it because it isn't defined as a checkable action. To cover all possible errors other than this, use WHEN OTHERS exception.

For example:

```
DECLARE
   TEMP_Sal NUMBER(10,2);

BEGIN
   SELECT sal INTO TEMP_sal
   From emp
   WHERE empno>=7698;
```

```
        IF TEMP_sal > 1000 THEN
              UPDATE emp SET sal = (TEMP_sal*1.175)
              WHERE empno>=7698;
        ELSE
              UPDATE emp SET sal = 5000
              WHERE empno>=7698;
        END IF;
        COMMIT;
EXCEPTION
    WHEN NO_DATA_FOUND THEN
        Dbms.Output.put_line('Empno does not exists');
    WHEN TOO_MANY_ROWS THEN
        Dbms.Output.put_line('No. of rows selected');
    WHEN OTHERS THEN
        Dbms.Output.put_line('SOME ERROR OCCURRED');
END;
```

- This block will trap all errors. If the exception isn't no rows returned or too many rows returned then the OTHERS action will perform the error handling.
- PL/SQL provides two special functions for use within an EXCEPTION section, they are SQLCODE and SQLERRM. SQLCODE is the Oracle error code of the exception, SQLERRM is the Oracle error message of the exception. You can use these functions to detect what error has occurred (very useful in an OTHERS action). This is generally used to store errors occurs in PL/SQL program in table so SQLCODE and SQLERRM should be assigned to variables before you attempt to use them.

For example:
```
DECLARE
    TEMP_Sal NUMBER(10,2);
    ERR_MSG VARCHAR2(100);
    ERR_CDE NUMBER;
BEGIN
    SELECT sal INTO TEMP_sal
    From emp
    WHERE empno>=7698;

    IF TEMP_sal > 1000 THEN
        UPDATE emp SET sal = (TEMP_sal*1.175)
        WHERE empno>=7698;
      ELSE
        UPDATE emp SET sal = 5000
        WHERE empno>=7698;
      END IF;
```

```
      COMMIT;
    EXCEPTION
      WHEN NO_DATA_FOUND THEN
        INSERT INTO ERRORS (CODE, MESSAGE)
      VALUES (99, 'NOT FOUND');
      WHEN TOO_MANY_ROWS THEN
        INSERT INTO ERRORS (CODE, MESSAGE)
      VALUES (99, 'TOO MANY');
      WHEN OTHERS THEN
          ERR_CDE:= SQLCODE;
          ERR_MSG:= SUBSTR(SQLERRM,1,100);

      INSERT INTO ERRORS (CODE, MESSAGE) VALUES(ERR_CDE, ERR_MSG);
    END;
```

- In this case ERRORS table contain fields code and message. According to error occurred in PL/SQL block, the values of code and messge will get stored into an ERRORS table.
- **Predefined Exceptions are:**

  No-data-found: when no rows are returned

  Cursor-already-open: when a cursor is opened in advance

  Storage-error: if memory is damaged

  Program-error: internal problem in PL/SQL

  Zero-divide: divide by zero

  invalid-cursor: if a cursor is not open and you are trying to close it

  Login-denied: invalid user name or password

  Invalid-number: if you are inserting a string datatype for a number datatype which is already declared

  Too-many-rows: if more rows are returned by select statement.

- Predefined exceptions are raised implicitly by the runtime system. For example, if you try to divide a number by zero, PL/SQL raises the predefined exception ZERO_DIVIDE automatically.

2.4.4 User Defined Exceptions   (April 12; Oct 13)

- There are two methods of defining exception by user.
    1. RAISE statement
    2. RAISE_APPLICATION_ERROR statement.

1. RAISE Statement

- If you explicitly need to raise an error then RAISE statement is used and you have to declare an exception variable in declare section.

For example:

```
DECLARE
   TEMP_Sal NUMBER(10,2);
   NEGATIVE_SAL EXCEPTION;
BEGIN
     SELECT sal INTO TEMP_sal
     From emp
     WHERE empno=7698;

     IF TEMP_sal < 0 THEN
         Raise NEGATIVE_SAL;
     ELSE
         UPDATE emp SET sal = 5000
         WHERE empno=7698;
     END IF;
     COMMIT;
EXCEPTION
    WHEN NO_DATA_FOUND THEN
        Dbms_output.put_line('Record NOT FOUND');

    WHEN NEGATIVE_SAL THEN
        Dbms_output.put_line('Salary is negative');
   END;
```

- If the above example find row with a salary less than 0 then PL/SQL raise user_defined Negative_sal exception.

2. RAISE_APPLICTAION_ERROR Statement

- The RAISE_APPLICATION_ERROR takes two input parameters: the error number and error message. The error number must be between –20001 to –20999. You can call RAISE_APPLICATION_ERROR from within procedures, functions, packages and triggers.

For examples:

```
DECLARE
    TEMP_Sal NUMBER(10,2);
BEGIN
    SELECT sal INTO TEMP_sal
    From emp
    WHERE empno=7698;
         UPDATE emp SET sal = TEMP_sal *1.5
         WHERE empno=7698;
```

```
        COMMIT;
EXCEPTION
    WHEN NO_DATA_FOUND THEN
        RAISE_APPLICATION_ERROR (-20100,'Record NOT FOUND');
END;
```

Note that in this case exception variable declaration is not required.

```
DECLARE
    TEMP_sal NUMBER (10, 2);
BEGIN
    SELECT sal INTO TEMP_sal
    from emp
    WHERE empno = 7698;
If temp_sal < 0 then
    Raise_application_error (- 20010, 'Salary is negative');
else
    UPDATE emp
    SET sal = 5000
    WHERE empno = 7698;
end if;
EXCEPTION
    WHEN NO_DATA.FOUND THEN
    DBMS_OUTPUT.PUT_LINE('Record not found');
end;
```

Program 2.17: Accept empno and check whether it is present in emp table or not.

```
Declare
  v_no emp.empno%type;
  v_empno emp.empno%type;
Begin
  v_empno:=&v_empno;

  select empno into v_no
  from emp
  where empno=v_empno;

  if v_no=v_empno then
    dbms_output.put_line('Empno exists');
  end if;
  Exception
    When no_data_found then
        dbms_output.put_line('Empno does not exists');
End;
```

Output:
```
SQL> /
```

```
Enter value for v_empno: 7768
old 5: v_empno:=&v_empno;
new 5: v_empno:=7768;
Empno does not exists
SQL> /
Enter value for v_empno: 7698
old 5: v_empno:=&v_empno;
new 5: v_empno:=7698;
Empno exists
```

Program 2.18: Print name of emp getting second max salary.

```
Declare
   v_name     emp.ename%type;
Begin
   select e2.ename into v_name
   from emp e1, emp e2
   where e1.sal>e2.sal;

   dbms_output.put_line(v_name || 'is getting second max salary');
Exception
   When too_many_rows then
       dbms_output.put_line('More than one Empno getting second
                                                   max salary');
End;
```

Output:
```
SQL> /
More than one Empno getting second max salary.
```

Program 2.19: Accept empno and check whether comm is null or not.
If comm is null raise an exception otherwise display comm.

```
Declare
   v_comm    emp.comm%type;
   v_empno   emp.empno%type;
   check_comm exception;
Begin
   v_empno:=&v_empno;
   select comm into v_comm
   from emp
   where empno=v_empno;

   if v_comm is NULL then
     raise check_comm;
```

```
    else
       dbms_output.put_line('comm = '||v_comm);
    end if;
Exception
    When no_data_found then
       dbms_output.put_line('Empno does not exists');
    When check_comm then
       dbms_output.put_line('Empno getting null comm');
End;
```

Output:
```
SQL> /
Enter value for v_empno: 7566
old 6: v_empno:=&v_empno;
new 6: v_empno:= 7566;
Empno getting null comm

SQL> /
Enter value for v_empno: 7521
old 6: v_empno:=&v_empno;
new 6: v_empno:=7521;
comm = 500
```

2.5 FUNCTIONS (Oct. 10; April 14)

- A function contain a PL/SQL block to perform specific task. It can read a list of values but it will explicitly return a single value which is normally assigned to a variable.

2.5.1 What is a Function ? (Oct. 10)

- A function is a named PL/SQL Block which is similar to a procedure.
- The major difference between a procedure and a function is, a function must always return a value, but a procedure may or may not return a value.

2.5.2 Creating a Function (Oct. 10)

- The General syntax to create a function is:
```
CREATE (OR REPLACE) FUNCTION function_name (parameters]
RETURN return_datatype;
IS
Declaration_section
BEGIN
Execution_section
Return return_variable;
```

```
EXCEPTION
exception section
Return return-variable;
END;
```

1. Return Type: The header section defines the return type of the function. The return datatype can be any of the oracle datatype like varchar, number etc.
2. The execution and exception section both should return a value which is of the datatype defined in the header section.

   For example, let's crete a function called "employer_details_func' similar to the one created in stored proc

```
CREATE OF REPLACE FUNCTION employer_details_func
    RETURN VARCHAR (20);
Is
    emp_name VARCHAR(20);
BEGIN
    SELECT first_name INTO emp_name
    FROM emp_tbl where empID = '100';
    RETURN emp_name;
END;
/
```

- In the example we are retrieving the 'first_name' of employee with empID 100 to variable 'emp_name'.
- The return type f the function is VARCHAR which is declared in line no 2.
- The function returns the 'emp_name' which is of type VARCHAR as the return value in line no. 9.

Program 2.20: Pass empno as a parameter to function and function will return salary.

```
CREATE OR REPLACE FUNCTION  myfunc1
(f_no   IN number)
RETURN number
IS
V_sal    emp.sal%TYPE;
Begin
    Select sal into v_sal
     From emp
      Where emp_no=f_no;
   If  SQL%FOUND  then
       RETURN (v_sal);
    Else
        RETURN 0;
    End if;
END myfunc1;
```

2.5.3 How to Execute a Function?

- A function can be executed in the following ways.
1. A function returns a value we can assign it to a variable.

    ```
    employee_name:= employer_details_func;
    ```

    If 'employee_name' is of datatype varchar we can store the name of the employee by assigning the return type of the function to it.

2. As a part of a SELECT statement,

    ```
    SELECT employer_details_func FROM dual;
    ```

3. In a PL/SQL Statements like,

    ```
    dbms_output.put_line(employer_details_func);
    ```

2.5.4 Deleting a Function

- To delete a function DROP FUNCTION command is used.
- **Syntax:**

    ```
    DROP FUNCTION function_name;
    ```

    For example:

    ```
    DROP FUNCTION myfunc1;
    ```

PROGRAMS

Program 1: Pass a no. to a function and check whether It is divisible by 5 or not.

```
create or replace function f1
(f_no in number)
return number
as
Begin
  if (mod(f_no,5)=0) then
    return 1;
  else
    return 0;
  end if;
End f1;
/
```

Function can be executed using select statement by calling Program as follows:

```
SQL> select f1 (10) from dual;
F1 (10)
--------
    1
```

Calling program:
```
Declare
   no number;
   r number;
Begin
   no:=&no;
   r:=f1(no);
   if(r=1) then
      dbms_output.put_line(no || ' is divisible by 5');
   else
      dbms_output.put_line(no || ' is not divisible by 5');
   end if;
End;
```

Output:
```
SQL> /
Enter value for no: 30
old 5: no:=&no;
new 5: no:=30;
30 is divisible by 5

SQL> /
Enter value for no: 12
old 5: no:=&no;
new 5: no:=12;
12 is not divisible by 5
```

Program 2: Pass two string to a function and print which string is largest.
```
create or replace function f2
(str1 in varchar2,
str2 in varchar2)
return varchar2
as
   L1 number;
   L2 number;
Begin
   L1:=length(str1);
   L2:=length(str2);

   if (L1>L2) then
       return 'First string is largest';
   else if(L2 >L1 ) then
       return 'Second string is largest';
```

```
            else
                return 'Both are equal;
           end if;
       end if;
    End f2;
/
```

Output:
```
    SQL> select f2('smita','chavan') from dual;
    F2('SMITA','CHAVAN')
    ------------------------------
    Second string is largest
    SQL> select f2('hello','hi') from dual;
    F2('HELLO','HI')
    ------------------------
    First string is largest
    SQL> select f2('smita','swati') from dual;
    F2 ('SMITA','SWATI')
    ----------------------------
    Both are equal
```

Program 3: Pass a month to a function and print no. of emp joined in that month.
```
    create or replace function f3
    (f_mon in varchar2)
    return number
    as
       v_count number;
    Begin
         select count(*) into v_count
         from emp
         where to_char(hiredate,'mon')=f_mon;
         return v_count;
    End f3;
/
    SQL> select f3('apr') from dual;
    F3('APR')
    -----------
          2
```

Calling program:
```
    Declare
       v_mon varchar2( 10);
```

```
    r number;
Begin
    v_mon:=&v_mon;
    r:=f3(v_mon);
    if(r>0) then
        dbms_output.put_line('No. of  emp  joined  in  '|| v_mon ||
                                                        '=' || r);
    else
        dbms_output.put_line('No emp is joined in ' ||  v_mon);
    end if;
End;
```

Output:
```
SQL> /
Enter value for v_mon: 'dec'
old 5: v_mon:=&v_mon;
new 5: v_mon:='dec';
No. of emp joined in dec = 1
SQL> /
Enter value for v_mon: 'jan'
old 5: v_mon:=&v_mon;
new 5: v_mon:='jan';
No emp is joined in jan
```

Program 4: Pass a character to a function and return how many emp name(s) start with accepted character.

```
create or replace function f4
(f_ch in varchar2)
return number
as
    v_count number;
Begin
    select count(*) into v_count
    from emp
    where instr(ename,f_ch)=1;
    return v_count;
End f4;
/
```

Output:
```
SQL> select f4('B') from dual;
F4('B')
----------
    1
```

Calling program:
```
Declare
  v_ch varchar2(10);
  r number;
Begin
  v_ch:=&v_ch;
  r:=f4(v_ch);
  if(r>0) then
    dbms_output.put_line('No. of emp having name starting with
    '||v_ch ||'=' || r);
  else
    dbms_output.put_line('No emp name start with ' || v_ch);
  end if;
End;
/
```

Output:
```
SQL> /
Enter value for v_ch: 'C'
old 5: v_ch:=&v_ch;
new 5: v_ch:='C';
No. of emp having name starting with C = 1

SQL> /
Enter value for v_ch: 'E'
old 5: v_ch:=&v_ch;
new 5: v_ch:='E';
No emp name start with E
```

Program 5: Accept a deptno and Pass it to function and check whether it is present in dept table or not. If it present print no. of emp working in that dept.

```
create or replace function f5
(f_no in number)
return number
as
  v_no number;
  v_count number;
Begin
  select deptno into v_no
  from dept
  where deptno=f_no;
  if (v_no=f_no) then
```

```
        select count(*) into v_count
        from emp
        where deptno=f_no;
        return v_count;
    end if;
  Exception
    when NO_DATA_FOUND then
        return -1;
  End f5;
/
```

Output:
```
   SQL> select f5(10) from dual;
   F5(10)
   --------
        5
   SQL> select f5(40) from dual;
   F5(40)
   --------
        0
   SQL> select f5(70) from dual;
   F5(70)
   --------
       - 1
```

Calling program:
```
   Declare
     v_no number;
     r number;
   Begin
     v_no:=&v_no;
     r:=f5(v_no);
     if(r>0) then
        dbms_output.put_line('No. of emp working in dept ' ||
                                                 v_no || ' = ' || r);
     else if(r=0) then
        dbms_output.put_line('Dept ' || v_no || ' exist in dept
            table but no emp working in this dept');
       else
            dbms_output.put_line('Dept ' || v_no ||' does not exist
                                            in dept table ');
       end if;
     end if;
     End;
/
```

Output:

```
SQL> /
Enter value for v_no: 30
old  5: v_no:=&v_no;
new  5: v_no:=30;
No. of emp working in dept 30 = 2

SQL> /
Enter value for v_no: 40
old  5: v_no:=&v_no;
new  5: v_no:=40;
Dept 40 exist in dept table but no emp working in this dept
SQL> /
Enter value for v_no: 60
old  5: v_no:=&v_no;
new  5: v_no:=60;
Dept 60 does not exist in dept table
```

Program 6: Pass a salary to a function and check whether it is greater than max or less than min sal or in between. (use out variable which indicate max or min value)

```
create or replace function f6
(f_sal in number,
f_no out number)
return number
as
  v_max number;
  v_min number;
Begin
  select max(sal) into v_max
  from emp;

  select min(sal) into v_min
  from emp;
    dbms_output.put_line('max sal = ' || v_max);
    dbms_output.put_line('min Sal = ' ||  v_min);
  if (v_max<f_no) then
     f_no:=v_max;
     return 1;
  else if (v_min>f_no) then
     f_no:=v_min;
     return 2;
```

```
        else
            return 0;
        end if;
    end if;
End f6;
/
```

Calling program:
```
    Declare
        v_sal number;
        v_no number;
        r number;
    Begin
        v_sal:=&v_sal;
        r:=f6(v_sal,v_no);

        if(r=1) then
            dbms_output.put_line(v_sal || ' is greater than max Sal
                                                = ' || v_no);
        else if(r=2) then
            dbms_output.put_line(v_sal || ' is less than min sal = '
                                                || v_no);
            else
                dbms_output.put_line(v_sal || ' is in between max and
                                                    min sal');
            end if;
        end if;
    End;
    /
```

Output:
```
    SQL> /
    Enter value for v_sal: 30000
    old 6: v_sal:=&v_sal;
    new 6: v_sal:=30000;
    max sal = 25000
    min sal = 1100
    30000 is grater than max sal = 25000

    SQL> /
    Enter value for v_sal: 200
    old 6: v_sal:=&v_sal;
    new 6: v_sal:=200;
```

```
max sal = 25000 min sal = 1100
200 is less than min sal = 1100

SQL> / Enter value for v_sal: 2000
old 6: v_sal:=&v_sal;
new 6: v_sal:=2000;
max sal = 25000
min sal= 1100
2000 is in between max and min sal
```

Program 7: Pass name to a function and print no. of years of service he has put in.

```
create or replace function f7
(f_name in varchar2)
return number
as
   v_count number;
Begin
   select round((sysdate-hiredate)/365) into v_count
   from emp
   where ename=f_name;
   return v_count;
Exception
     when NO_DATA_FOUND then
         return -1;
End f7;
/
```

Output:

```
SQL> select f7('BLAKE') from dual;
F7('BLAKE')
---------------
   21

SQL> select f7('SEEMA') FROM DUAL;
F7('SEEMA')
----------------
 - 1
```

Calling program:

```
Declare
   v_name varchar2(20);
   r number;
Begin
   v_name:='&v_name';
```

```
        r:=f7(v_name);
        if(r>0) then
            dbms_output.put_line(v_name    ||    '  is    working    in
                        organization since last '|| r || ' years');
        else if(r=-1) then
            dbms_output.put_line(v_name || ' employee does not exist
                                                in emp table');
        end if;
      end if;
End;
/
```

Output:
```
SQL> /
Enter value for v_name: MARTIN
old 5: v_name:='&v_name';
new 5: v_name:='MARTIN';
MARTIN is working in organization since last 21 years
SQL> /
Enter value for v_name: SANDEEP
old 5: v_name:='&v_name';
new 5: v_name:='SANDEEP';
SANDEEP employee does not exist in emp table
```

Program 8: Pass deptno to a function and print details of salesmen working in that dept.
```
create or replace function f8
(f_no in number)
return number
as
  v_count number;
  cursor c_dept is select ename,sal,job,deptno
            from emp
            where deptno=f_no and job='SALESMAN';
Begin
  dbms_output.put_line('Name sal job deptno');
  dbms_output.put_line('------------------------');
  for e_rec in c_dept
  loop
    dbms_output.put_line(e_rec.ename || ' ' || e_rec.sal || ' '
    || e_rec.job || ' ' || e_rec.deptno);
    v_count:=c_dept%rowcount;
```

```
        end loop;
        if(v_count>1) then
            return v_count;
        else
            return -1;
        end if;
    End f8;
```

Calling program:
```
    Declare
      v_no number;
      r number;
    Begin
      v_no:=&v_no;
      r:=f8(v_no);
      if(r>0) then
         dbms_output.put_line('No. of emp working in dept ' || v_no
                                                    || ' = ' || r);
      else if(r=-1) then
         dbms_output.put_line('Dept'|| v_no ||' does not exist in
                                                emp table');
         end if;
      end if;
    End
```

Output:
```
    SQL>/
    Enter value for v_no: 40
    old 5: v_no:=&v_no;
    new 5: v_no:=40;
    Name sal job deptno
    -----------------------
    Dept 40 does not exist in emp table

    SQL> /
    Enter value for v_no: 30
    old 5: v_no:=&v_no;
    new 5: v_no:=30;
```

Name	sal	job	deptno.
MARGIN	1250	SALESMAN	30
TURNER	1500	SALESMAN	30

```
    No. of emp working in dept 30 = 2.
```

2.6 PROCEDURE (April 11)

- Procedures are simply a named PL/SQL block, that executes certain task. A procedure is completely portable among platforms in which Oracle is executed.
- Procedure is similar to a procedure in other programming languages. A procedure has a header and a body.
- The header consists of the name of the procedure and the parameters or variables passed to the procedure.
- The body consists or declaration section, execution section and exception section similar to a general PL/SQL Block.
- A procedure is similar to an anonymous PL/SQL Block but it is named for repeated usage.

2.6.1 Creating a Procedure (April 11)

- A procedure is created using CREATE PROCEDURE command.

Syntax:
```
CREATE [OR REPLACE] PROCEDURE   procedure _name
[(argument [in/out/in out] datatype [,argument [in/out/in out]
                                              datatype......])]
{IS / AS}
[variable declaration]
{PL/SQL block};
```

Note: Square brakets [ ] indicate optional part.

- CREATE PROCEDURE procedure_name will create a new procedure with the given procedure_name. OR REPLACE is an optional clause. It is used to change the definition of an existing procedure.

  If the procedure accept arguments specify argument details as,

  Argument_name IN / OUT / IN OUT datatype

  Argument_name indicate   Variable_name

- **IN** indicate the variable is passed by the calling program to procedure.
- **OUT** indicate that the variable pass value from procedure to calling program.
- **IN OUT** indicate that the variable can pass values both in and out of a procedure.
- Datatype specify any PL/SQL datatype.

Program 2.21: Pass empno as an argument to procedure and modify salary of that emp.

```
CREATE OR REPLACE PROCEDURE myproc1
(p_no  IN  number)           /* argument */
IS
```

```
        v_sal    number(10,2);
   BEGIN
      Select  sal into v_sal
      From emp
      Where empno=p_no;

   If v_sal > 1000 then
      Update emp
      Set sal = v_sal*1.75
      Where empno=p_no;
   Else
      Update emp
      Set sal = 5000
      Where empno=p_no;
   End if;
EXCEPTION
   WHEN NO_DATA_FOUND THEN
      Dbms_output.put_line('Emp_no doesn't exists');
END myproc1;
```

2.6.2 Executing a Procedure

- To execute the stored procedure simply call it by name in EXECUTE command as,

  ```
  SQL> execute myproc1(7768);
  ```
- This will execute myproc1 with the value 7768.
- The second method of calling the procedure is given below:
  Write the following code in an editor.

```
Declare
   C_empno   number;
Begin
   Myproc1(&c_empno);
End;
/
Execute it as
   SQL >/
```

- In this case the value of variable c_empno is accepted from user and then it is passed to myproc1 procedure.
- To see the effect of this procedure use command,

  ```
  SQL>select * from emp;
  ```

Program 2.22: Pass a empno as argument to procedure and procedure will pass job to the calling program.

```
CREATE OR REPLACE PROCEDURE myproc2
(p_no  IN   number, p_job OUT emp.job%TYPE) /* arguments */
IS
    v_job     emp.job%TYPE;
BEGIN
    Select  JOB  into v_job
    From emp
    Where empno=p_no;

    P_job:=v_job;
EXCEPTION
   WHEN NO_DATA_FOUND THEN
       P_job:='NO';
END myproc2;
```

Calling procedure myproc2 using following code:

```
Declare
   C_empno   number;
   C_job     emp.job%TYPE;
Begin
   Myproc2(&c_empno,c_job);
    If c_job='NO' then
       Dbms_output.put_line('Emp_no doesn't exists');
        Else
           Dbms_output.put_line('Job of emp. Is ' || c_job);
        End if;
End;
/
SQL> /
```

Program 2.23: Pass salary to procedure and procedure will pass no. of employee(s) having salary equal to given salary in the same variable. (Use IN OUT variable).

```
CREATE OR REPLACE PROCEDURE myproc3
(p_sal  IN  OUT   emp.sal%TYPE)                      /* arguments */
IS
   v_count   number;
BEGIN
   Select count(*) into v_count
   From emp
   Where sal=p_sal;
   P_sal:=v_count;
```

```
EXCEPTION
   WHEN NO_DATA_FOUND THEN
        P_sal:=0;
END myproc3;
```
Calling procedure myproc3 using following code:
```
Declare
 C_sal     emp.sal%TYPE;
Begin
    C_sal:=&c_sal;
    Myproc3(c_sal);
    If c_sal=0 then
        Dbms_output.put_line('No  employee  is  having  salary  equal
                                                to accepted salary');
          Else
    Dbms_output.put_line('No.  of  emp.  having  salary  =  accepted
                                           salary are  ' || c_sal);
          End if;
End;
/
```

2.6.3 Deleting a Procedure

- To delete a procedure DROP PROCEDURE command is used.

Syntax:
```
DROP PROCEDURE procedure_name;
```
For example:
```
DROP PROCEDURE myproc1;
```

PROGRAMS

Program 1: Pass deptno to procedure and print maximum salary of emp working in that department. If deptno does not exist print message.

```
create or replace procedure p1
(p_deptno in number)
as
  max_sal emp.sal%type;
Begin
    select max(sal) into max_sal
    from emp
    where deptno=p_deptno;

    if(max_sal > 0) then
      dbms_output.put_line('Max salary = ' || max_sal);
    else
```

```
            dbms_output.put_line('Deptno does not exists');
        end if;
End p1;
/
```
- Procedure can be executed using execute statement or by calling program as follows:
```
SQL> execute p1 (90);
Deptno does not exists
SQL> execute p1 (30);
Max salary = 1500
```

Calling program:
```
Declare
    v_deptno emp.deptno%type;
Begin
    v_deptno:=&v_deptno;
    p1(v_deptno);
End;
SQL> /
Enter value for v_deptno: 50
old 4: v_deptno:=&v_deptno;
new 4: v_deptno:=50;
Max salary = 3000
```

Program 2: Pass empno and sal to procedure and print name and sal of employee having empno = accepted empno and modify sal with accepted sal.

```
create or replace procedure p2
(p_no in number,
p_sal in number)
as
    v_name emp.ename%type;
    v_sal emp.sal%type;
Begin
    select ename,sal into v_name,v_sal
    from emp
    where empno=p_no;
    update emp
    set sal=sal+p_sal
    where empno=p_no;
    v_sal:=v_sal+p_sal;
    dbms_output.put_line('Modified salary of '|| v_name ||' is
                                              '|| v_sal);
Exception
    when NO_DATA_FOUND then
        dbms_output.put_line('Empno does not exist!....');
End p2;
/
```

Output:
```
SQL> execute p2(7698, 100);
Modified salary of BLAKE is 3150

SQL> execute p2(111,1000);
Empno does not exist!...
```

Program 3: Pass comm to procedure and set this value of comm of emp having comm as null.

```
create or replace procedure p3
(p_comm in number)

as
Begin
  update emp
  set comm=p_comm
  where comm is null;
End p3;
SQL> execute p3(500);
```

To see the changes in emp table after execution of this procedure use select * from emp;

Program 4: Write a procedure which will accept empno and return (using OUT variable) name of his supervisor.

```
create or replace procedure p4
(p_no in number,
p_name out varchar2)
as
  v_name emp.ename%type;
Begin
  select ename into v_name
  from emp
  where empno =(select mgr
           from emp
           where empno=p_no);
  p_name:=v_name;
Exception
  when NO_DATA_FOUND then
      p_name:='no';
End p4;
/
```

Calling program:
```
Declare
  c_no number;
  c_name varchar2(30);
Begin
  c_no:=&c_no;
  p4(c_no,c_name);

  if(c_name='no') then
     dbms_output.put_line('Empno does not exist! ......... ');
  else
     dbms_output.put_line('Name of supervisor is ' || c_name);
  end if,
End;
```

Output:
```
SQL> /
Enter value for c_no: 7566
old 5: c_no:=&c_no;
new 5: c_no:=7566;
Name of supervisor is KING

SQL> /
Enter value for c_no: 90
old 5: c_no:=&c_no;
new 5: c_no:=90;
Empno does not exist!.....
```

Program 5: Pass deptno to a procedure. Procedure will pass no. of employees working in that dept in same variable. (Use IN OUT variable)

```
create or replace procedure p5
  (p_no in out number)
as
  v_no number;
Begin
  select count(*) into v_no
  from emp
  where deptno =p_no;
  p_no:=v_no;
Exception
  when NO_DATA_FOUND then
       p_no:=0;
End p5;
/
```

Calling program:
```
declare
  c_no number;
begin
  c_no:=&c_no;
  p5(c_no);

  if(c_no=0) then
     dbms_output.put_line('Dept does not exist!.....);
  else
     dbms_output.put_line('No. of emp = ' || c_no);
  end if;
end,
```
Output:
```
SQL> /
Enter value for c_no: 20
old 4: c_no:=&c_no;
new 4: c_no:=20;
No. of emp = 2

SQL> /
Enter value for c_no: 70
old 4: c_no:=&c_no;
new 4: c_no:=70;
   Dept does not exist!.....
```

Program 6: Write a procedure which display name, sal, dname of first 4 highest paid emp.

```
create or replace procedure p6
as
   cursor c1 is select ename,sal,dname
           from emp,dept
           where emp.deptno=dept.deptno
           order by sal desc;
   e_rec c1%rowtype;
Begin
   dbms_output.put line('Name sal dname');
   dbms_output.put_line (' - - - - - - - - -');

   for e_rec in c1
   loop
```

```
        if c1%rowcount<=4 then
          dbms_output.put_line(e_rec.ename || ' ' || e_rec.sal ||
                                            ' ' || e_rec.dname);
        end if;
    end loop;
  End p6;
```

Output:

SQL> execute p6;

Name	sal	dname
KING	5000	ACCOUNTING
BLAKE	3150	ACCOUNTING
SCOTT	3000	RESEARCH
JONES	2975	ACCOUNTING

Program 7: Write a procedure which will list names of employee who are reporting to 'BLAKE'.

```
create or replace procedure p7
as
   cursor c1 is select ename
            from emp
            where mgr = (select empno
                    from emp
                    where ename='BLAKE');
   e_rec c1%rowtype;
Begin
   dbms_output.put_line('Name');
   dbms_output.put_line('-------');

   for e_rec in c1
     loop
        dbms_output.put_line (e_rec.ename);
     end loop;
  End p7;
```

Output:

SQL> execute p7;

Name

WARD
MARTIN
TURNER

Program 8: Pass job to a procedure and Print names and sal of emp whose salary is less than average salary of accepted job.

```
create or replace procedure p8
(p_job in varchar2)
as
   cursor c1 is select ename,sal
         from emp
         where sal <= (select avg(sal)
                  from emp
                  where job=p_job);
   e_rec c1%rowtype;
Begin
   dbms_output.put_line('Name sal');
   dbms_output.put_line('------------');

   for e_rec in c1
   loop
      dbms_output.put_line(e_rec.ename || ' ' || e_rec.sal);
   end loop;
End p8;
/
```

Output:

```
  Name      Sal
  --------  --------
  WARD      1250
  MARTIN    1250
  CLARK     2450
  TURNER    1500
  ADAMS     1100
```

2.7 Cursors   (Oct. 09, 11, 12; April 10, 12, 13)

- Whenever, a SQL statement is issued the Database server opens an area of memory is called Private SQL area in which the command is processed and executed. An identifier for this area is called a cursor.
- When PL/SQL block uses a select command that returns more than one row, Oracle displays an error message and invokes the TOO_MANY_ROWS exception. To resolve this problem, Oracle uses a mechanism called cursor.
- There are two types of cursors.
  1. Implicit cursors and
  2. Explicit cursors.
- PL/SQL provides some attributes which allows to evaluate what happened when the

cursor was last used. You can use these attributes in PL/SQL statements like functions but you cannot use them within SQL statements.

- The SQL cursor attributes are:

    1. **%ROWCOUNT:** The number of rows processed by a SQL statement.
    2. **%FOUND:** TRUE if at least one row was processed.
    3. **%NOTFOUND:** TRUE if no rows were processed.
    4. **%ISOPEN:** TRUE if cursor is open or FALSE if cursor has not been opened or has been closed. Only used with explicit cursors.

What are Cursors ? (Oct. 09, 13; April 11, 12, 14)

- A cursor is a temporary work area created in the system memory when a SQL statement is executed.
- A cursor contains information on a select statement and the rows of data accessed by it. This temporary work area is used to store the data retrieved from the database, and manipulate this data.
- A cursor can hold more than one row, but can process only one row at a time. The set of rows the cursor holds is called the *active* set.

2.7.1 Definition (Oct. 10)

- A cursor is a temporary work area used to store the data retrieved from the database and manipulate this data.

OR

- A cursor is a temporary work area created by system memory when SQL/PL/SQL statements are executed.

Declaring a Cursor:

- Cursors are defined within a DECLARE section of a PL/SQL block with DECLARE command.

Syntax:
```
Cursor cursor_name [(parameters)] [RETURN return_type] IS SELECT
                                                            query.
```

- The cursor is defined by the CURSOR keyword followed by the cursor identifier (Cursor_name) and then the SELECT statement.
- Parameter and return are optional part. When parameters are passed to cursor it is called as **parameterized cursor**.

    For example:
    ```
    DECLARE
         CURSOR   c_deptno   IS   SELECT   ename,sal,deptno FROM EMP;
    ```

Opening a Cursor:

- Cursors are opened with the OPEN statement, this populates the cursor with data.

Syntax:
```
OPEN Cursor_name[parameters];
```
For example:
```
DECLARE
    CURSOR   c_deptno   IS   SELECT   ename,sal,deptno
                                    FROM EMP;
Begin
    Open c_deptno;
End;
```
Parameters is an optional part. It is used in parameterized cursor.

Accessing the cursor rows

- To access the rows of data within the cursor the FETCH statement is used.

For example:
```
DECLARE
    CURSOR   c_deptno   IS   SELECT   ename,sal,deptno FROM EMP;
    V_name      emp.ename%type;
    v_sal       emp.sal%type;
    v_deptno    emp.deptno%type;
Begin
    Open c_deptno;
    FETCH c_deptno INTO v_name,v_sal,v_deptno;
    Dbms_output.put_line(V_NAME ||' '||V_deptno||' '||V_SAL);
End;
SQL > /
SMITH 800    20
```

- The FETCH statement reads the column values for the current cursor row and puts them into the specified variables. This can be as an equivalent to the SELECT INTO command. The cursor pointer is updated to point at the next row. If the cursor has no more rows the variables will be set to null on the first FETCH attempt, subsequent FETCH attempts will raise an exception.
- To process all the rows within a cursor use a FETCH command in a loop and check the cursor NOTFOUND attribute to see if we successfully fetched a row or not as follows:

```
DECLARE
    CURSOR   c_deptno   IS   SELECT   ename,sal,deptno
                                    FROM EMP;
    V_name      emp.ename%type;
    v-sal       emp.sal%type;
    v_deptno    emp.deptno%type;
```

```
Begin
    Open   c_deptno;
    Loop
       FETCH c_deptno INTO v_name,v_sal,v_deptno;
       Exit when c_deptno%NOTFOUND;
            Dbms_output.put_line(V_NAME ||''||V_deptno||''||V_SAL);
    End loop;
    close c_deptno;
End;
```

Closing a Cursor:

- The CLOSE statement releases the cursor and any rows within it, you can open the cursor again to refresh the data in it.

    Syntax:
    ```
    CLOSE Cursor_name;
    ```
    For example:
    ```
    Close c_deptno;
    ```

Using Cursor For.... Loop

- In the cursor FOR loop, the result of SELECT query are used to determine the number of times the loop is executed.
- In a Cursor FOR loop, the opening, fetching and closing of cursors is performed implicitly.
- When you use it, Oracle automatically declares a variable with the same name as that is used as a counter in the FOR command. Just precede the name of the selected field with the name of this variable to access its contents.

    For example:
```
DECLARE
    CURSOR   c_deptno  IS   SELECT ename, sal, deptno  FROM EMP;
Begin
    For x in c_deptno
    Loop
       Dbms_output.put_line(x.ename ||' '||x.deptno||' '||x.SAL);
    End loop;
End;
```

- In above example a Cursor For loop is used, there is no `open` and `fetch` command.
- `For x in c_deptno` implicitly opens the c_deptno cursor and fetches a value into the x variable. Note that x is not explicitly declared in the block.
- When no more records are in the cursor, the loop is exited and cursor is closed. There is no need to check the cursor %NOTFOUND attribute-that is automated via the cursor FOR loop. And also there is no need of close command.

Cursor Variables:

- A cursor variable is a reference type. It can refer to different storage locations as the program runs.
- To use cursor variable, first the variable has to be declared. And the storage has to allocated. It is then opened, fetched and closed similar to a static cursor.

Syntax:

```
TYPE type_name IS REF CURSOR [RETURN return_type];
```

- Where type_name is the name of new reference type and return.type is a record type.

```
DECLARE
..... Defination using Rowtype
TYPE student_R is REF CURSOR RETURN students % ROWTYPE;
..... Define a new record type
TYPE Student_Rec IS RECORD (
    fname       students.f_name%TYPE,
    lname       students_l_name%TYPE);
    variable of new type
    Namerec     Student_REC;

BEGIN
____
____
END;
```

Constrained and Unconstrained Cursor variables

1. **Constrained Variables:**
- When the cursor variables are declared for a specific return type only, then these variables called constrained variables.
- When these variables are later opened, it must be opened for a query whose 'select' list matches the return type of the cursor. Otherwise predefined exception ROWTYPE_MISMATCH is raised.

2. **Unconstrained Variables:**
- An unconstrained cursor variable does not have a RETURN clause. When this variable is later opened, it can be for any query.
- Example of unconstrained variable are given below:

```
TYPE Stock_cur-price IS REF CURSOR;
----- variable of that type
v_cursor var stock_cur_price;
```

```
BEGIN
    _____
    _____
END;
```

3. **Opening a cursor variable for a query:**
- **Syntax:**
    ```
    OPEN cursor_variable FOR select_statement;
    ```
- Where cursor_variable is a previously declared cursor variable and select_statement is the desired query. If the cursor variable is constrained, the select statement must match the return type of the cursor. Otherwise it raised error.
    ```
    OPEN Student_R FOR
        Select * from students;
    ```

4. **Closing the Cursor Variables:**
- The CLOSE statment closes or deactivates the previously opened cursor and makes the active set undefined. After the cursor is closed, user cannot perform any operation on it.
    ```
    CLOSE Cursor_name;
    ```
    where cursor_name is previously opened cursor name.
- It does not necessary to free the storage for the cursor variable itself. It is fixed when the variable goes out of scope.

5. **Restrictions on Using cursor variables:**
- Cursor variable are a powerful feature of allowing different kinds of data to be returned in same variable. But, there are a number of restrictions with their use.
1. PL/SQL collections (index-by-tables, Nested tables and V arrays) cannot store cursor variables. Similarly, database tables and views can not store REF CURSOR columns.
2. The query associated with a cursor-variable in the OPEN-FOR statement can not be FOR UPDATE.
3. Remote subprograms cannot return the value of a cursor variable. They can be passed between client and server side PL/SQL (from oracle forms clients), but not between two servers.
4. You cannot use cursor variables with dynamic SQL in pro*c.

2.7.2 Types of Cursor - Implicit, Explicit Cursor

2.7.2.1 Implicit Cursor   (Oct. 09, 10, 13)
- These are created by default when DML statements like, INSERT, UPDATE, and DELETE statements are executed. They are also created when a SELECT statement that returns just one row is executed.
- When the executable part of a PL/SQL block issues a SQL command, PL/SQL creates an implicit cursor which has the identifier SQL. PL/SQL internally manages this cursor.

Program 2.24: Print no. of rows deleted from emp.

```
DECLARE
      ROW_DEL_NO NUMBER;
BEGIN
      DELETE    FROM EMP;
      ROW_DEL_NO:= SQL%ROWCOUNT;
      DBMS_OUTPUT.PUT_LINE('No.   of    rows   deleted   are:'||
                                                    ROW_DEL_NO);
END;
/
SQL> /
No. of rows deleted are: 14
PL/SQL procedure successully completed
```

Program 2.25: Accept empno and print it's details(using cursor).

```
DECLARE
        V_NO        EMP.EMPNO%TYPE:=&V_NO;
        V_NAME      EMP.ENAME%TYPE;
        V_JOB       EMP.JOB%TYPE;
        V_SAL       EMP.SAL%TYPE;
BEGIN
     SELECT ename,job,sal  INTO  V_NAME,V_JOB,V_SAL
     FROM emp
     WHERE empno=V_NO;

IF SQL%FOUND THEN   /* SQL%FOUND  is true if empno=v_no */
     Dbms_output.put_line(V_NAME ||' '||V_JOB||' '||V_SAL);
Exception
  when no_data_found then
  dbms_output.put_line ('Empno does not exists');
End;
SQL > /
Enter value for v_no: 34
Old 2: v_no emp.empno%type:=&v_no;
New 2: v_no emp.empno%type:=34
Empno does not exists
PL/SQL rpocedure successfully completed

SQL > /
Enter value for v_no: 7369
SMITH CLERK 800
PL/SQL procedure successfully completed.
```

2.7.2.2 Explicit Cursor (Oct. 09, 10)

- If SELECT statements in PL/SQL block return multiple rows then you have to explicitly create a cursor which is called as explicit cursor.
- The set of rows returned by a explicit cursor is called a result set. The row that is being processed is called the current row.
- Oracle uses four commands to handle Cursors. They are:
   1. **DECLARE:** Defines the name and structure of the cursor together with the SELECT statement.
   2. **OPEN:** Executes the query and the number of rows to be returned is determined.
   3. **FETCH:** Loads the row addressed by the cursor pointer into variables and moves the cursor pointer on to the next row ready for the next fetch.
   4. **CLOSE:** Releases the data within the cursor and closes it.

Syntax of explicit cursor:
```
Cursor cursorname is SQL select statement;
```
Cursor can be controlled using following 3 control statements. They are

1. **OPEN:** Open statement identifies the active set...i.e. query returned by select statement.
   Syntax of open cursor:
   ```
   open cursorname;
   ```
2. **FETCH:** Fetch statement fetches rows into the variables...Cursors can be made into use using cursor for loop and fetch statement.
   Syntax of fetch:
   ```
   fetch cursorname into variable1, variable2...;
   ```
3. **CLOSE:** Close statement closes the cursor.
   Syntax of close:
   ```
   close cursorname;
   ```

2.7.3 Parameterised Cursor (April 11; Oct. 12)

- Syntax for declaring a parameterized cursor:
   ```
   CURSOR Cursorname (variable name Data type)
      is <select statement, ....>
   ```
- Opening a parameterized cursor and passing values to the Cursor.
   ```
   OPEN CursorName (value/variable/Expression)
   ```
- **Patameterised cursor** passing parameter to cursor.

Program 2.26: Accept a salary and print name, salary and job of employee having salary less than equal to accepted salary.

```
Declare
  cursor c1(c_sal emp.sal%type) is select * from emp where sal<=c_sal;
```

```
    emp_rec c1%rowtype;
    v_sal emp.sal%type;
Begin
    v_sal:=&v_sal;
    dbms_output.put_line('Name salary job');
    dbms_output.put_line('--------------------');
    for emp_rec in c1(v_sal)
    loop
        dbms_output.put_line(emp_rec.ename || ' ' || emp_rec.sal
        ||' '|| emp_rec.job);
    end loop;
End;
```

Output:
```
SQL> /
Enter value for v_sal: 2000
old 7: open c1(&v_sal);
new 7: open c1 2000);
            Name      Salary      Job
            --------  -------     ---------
            WARD       1250       SALESMAN
            MARTIN     1250       SALESMAN
            TURNER     1500       SALESMAN
            ADAMS      1100       CLERK
```

Program 2.27: Accept job and print details of employees having job as accepted job. Also print the number of employee and name(s) of employee with maximum salary.

```
Declare
    cursor c1 (c_job emp.job%type) is select * from emp where job=cjob;
    emp_rec c1%rowtype;
    v_count number;
    v_job emp.job%type;
    max_sal emp.sal%type;
    name emp.ename%type;
Begin
    v_job:=&v_job;
    select ename,sal into name,max_sal
    from emp
    where job=v_job and sal =(select max(sal)
                    from emp
                    where job=v_job);
```

```
      dbms_output.put_line('Name salary job deptno');
      dbms_output.put_line('----------------------------');
      for emp_rec in c1(v_job)
      loop
         dbms_output.put_line(emp_rec.ename || ' ' || emp_rec.sal || '
         '|| emp_rec.job || ' ' || emp_rec.deptno);
         v_count:=c1%rowcount;
      end loop;
      dbms_output.put_line('No. of employees = ' || v_count);
      dbms_output.put_line(name ||' having max sal =' || max_sal);
   End;
```

Output:
```
SQL>/
Enter value for v_job: 'SALESMAN'
old 9: v_job:=&v_job;
new 9: v_job:='SALESMAN';
          Name      salary      Job         deptno
          --------  --------    ----------  -------
          WARD      1250        SALESMAN    50
          MARTIN    1250        SALESMAN    30
          TURNER    1500        SALESMAN    30
No. of employees = 3
TURNER having max sal = 1500
```

Program 2.28: Accept deptno and employee details who are working in that department. Also print no. of employees.

```
Declare
   cursor c1(c_deptno emp.deptno%type) is select * from emp where deptno=c_deptno;
   emp_rec c1%rowtype;
   v_deptno emp.deptno%type,
   v_count number;
Begin
   dbms_output.put_line('Name salary job deptno');
   dbms_output.put_line ('--------------------'),
   for emp_rec in c1 (&v_deptno)
   loop
      dbms_output.put_line(emp_rec.ename ||' '|| emp_rec.sal ||'
      '|| emp_rec.job ||' '|| emp_rec.deptno),
      v_count:=c1%rowcount;
   end loop;
   dbms_output.put_line('No. of employees = ' || v_count);
End;
```

Output:

```
SQL> /
Enter value for v_deptno: 20
old 7: open c1 (&v_deptno);
new 7: open c1 (20);
           Name      salary     job      deptno
          --------  --------  ---------  -------
           SCOTT      3000    ANALYST      20
           ADAMS      1100    CLERK        20
   No. of employees = 2.
```

PROGRAMS

Program 1: Print the name, salary and deptno of all employees who belongs to deptno 10.

```
Declare
  cursor c1 is select ename,sal,deptno
         from emp
         where deptno=10;
  v_name emp.ename%type;
  v_sal emp.sal%type;
  v_deptno emp.deptno%type;
Begin
  open c1;
  dbms_output.put_line('Name salary deptno');
  dbms_output.put_line('--------------------');
  loop
    fetch c1 into v_name,v_sal,v_deptno;
    exit when c1%notfound;
    dbms_output.put_line(v_name ||' '||v_sal||' '||v_deptno);
  end loop;
  close c1;
End;
```

Output:

```
   SQL> /
  Name    Salary   deptno
 ------  -------  ------
 JONES    2975      10
 BLAKE    3050      10
 CLARK    2450      10
 KING     5000      10
```

Program 2: Print the name, job of employees having job as MANAGER or ANALYST.

```
Declare
   cursor c1 is select ename,job
              from emp
              where job='MANAGER' or job='ANALYST';
   v_name emp.ename%type;
   v_job emp.job%type;
Begin
   open c1;
   dbms_output.put_line('Name job');
   dbms_output.put_line ('----------------');
   loop
      fetch c1 into v_name,v_job;
      exit when c1 %notfound;
      dbms_output.put_line(v_name || ' ' ||v_job);
   end loop;
   close c1;
End;
```

Output:
```
SQL> /
   Name      Job
   ------    ---------
   SONU      ANALYST
   JONES     MANAGER
   BLAKE     MANAGER
   CLARK     MANAGER
   SCOTT     ANALYST
```

Program 3: Write a PL/SQL block to print 3rd, 6th and 7th record from emp.

```
Declare
   cursor c1 is select * from emp;
   emp_rec c1 %rowtype;
Begin
   open c1;
   dbms_output.put_line('Name salary job');
   dbms_output.put_line('--------------------');
   loop
      fetch c1 into emp_rec;
      exit when c1%notfound;
      if(c1%rowcount=3 or c1%rowcount=6 or c1%rowcount=7) then
         dbms_output.put_ line(emp_rec.ename ||' '|| emp_rec.sal ||'
         '|| emp_ rec. job);
      end if;
```

```
        end loop;
     close c1;
   End;
```

Output:

```
SQL> /
   Name     Salary      Job
   ------   -------   ----------
   WARD      1250     SALESMAN
   BLAKE     3050     MANAGER
   CLARK     2450     MANAGER
```

Program 4: Write a PL/SQL block which assign comm=500 for those employee who are getting null comm.

```
   Declare
     cursor c1 is select * from emp
             where comm is null;
     emp_rec c1%rowtype;
   Begin
     dbms_output.put_line('Name salary comm');
     dbms_output.put_line('-------------');
     for emp_rec in c1
     loop
        emp_rec.comm:=500;
        dbms_output.put_line(emp_rec.ename ||' '|| emp_rec.sal ||' '|| emp_rec. comm);
     end loop;
   End;
```

Output:

```
SQL> /
   Name     Salary    Comm.
   ------   -------   ------
   JONES     2975      500
   BLAKE     3050      500
   CLARK     2450      500
   SCOTT     3000      500
   KING      5000      500
   ADAMS     1100      500
```

> **Note:** When cursor for loop is used then open, fetch and close operations are automatically performed.

2.8 TRIGGER (April 10, 11, 14)

- A trigger is PL/SQL code block which is executed by an event which occurs to a database table.
- Triggers are implicitly called (executed) when INSERT, UPDATE or DELETE command is executed.
- A trigger is associated to a table or a view. When a view is used, the base table triggers are normally enabled.
- Triggers are stored as text and compiled at execute time, because of this it is not to include much code in them.
- You may not use COMMIT, ROLLBACK and SAVEPOINT statements within trigger blocks.
- The advantages of using trigger are:
    1. It creates consistency and access restrictions to the database.
    2. It implements the security.

2.8.1 What is a Trigger ? (Oct. 09, 13; April 10, 12, 13)

- A trigger is a PL/SQL block structure which is fired when a DML statements like Insert, Delete, Update is executed on a database table.
- A trigger is triggered automatically when an associated DML statement is executed.

2.8.2 Creating a Trigger (Oct. 09, 12; April 13)

- A trigger is created with CREATE TRIGGER command.
- **Syntax:**
```
CREATE [OR REPLACE] TRIGGER trigger_name
{BEFORE / AFTER / INSTEAD OF}
{DELETE / INSERT / UPDATE [OF column [,column....]}
[OR {DELETE / INSERT / UPDATE [OF column
[,column....]}]
ON {TABLE/VIEW}
FOR EACH   {ROW / STATEMENT}
[WHEN (condition)]
PL/SQL block.
```
- Triggers may be called BEFORE or AFTER the following events. INSERT, UPDATE and DELETE.
    1. The BEFORE trigger is used when some processing is needed before execution of the command.
    2. The AFTER trigger is triggered only after the execution of the associated trigger commands.
    3. INSTEAD OF trigger is applied to view only. Triggers may be **ROW** or **STATEMENT** types.

- **ROW type trigger** which is also called as **ROW** level trigger is executed on all the rows that are affected by the command.
- **STATEMENT type trigger** (STATEMENT level trigger) is triggered only once. For example, if an DELETE command deletes 15 rows, the commands contained in the trigger are executed only once, and not with every processed row.
- The trigger can be activated by a SQL command or by system event or a user event which are called triggering events.

Types of Triggers (Oct. 10, 13; April 10, 12)

- PL/SQL trigger consist of following types:
    1. **TABLE triggers:** Applied to DML commands (INSERT / DELETE / UPDATE)
    2. **SYSTEM EVENT triggers:** Such as startup, shutdown of the database and server error message event.
    3. **USER EVENT triggers:** Such as User logon and logoff, DDL commands (CREATE, ALTER, DROP), DML commands (INSERT, DELETE, UPDATE).
- WHEN clause is used to specify trigger restriction i.e. it specifies what condition must be true for the trigger to be activated.
- PL/SQL block is a trigger action. Thus, every trigger is divided into three components as:
    1. Triggering event,
    2. Triggering restriction, and
    3. Triggering action.

Access the Value of Column Inside a Trigger

- A value of a column of a ROW-LEVEL trigger can be accessed using NEW and OLD variable.
- **Syntax:**   Column_name: NEW
                  Column_name: OLD
- Depending on the commands INSERT, UPDATE and DELETE, the values NEW and OLD will be used as follows:
    1. **INSERT command:** The value of the fields that will be inserted must be preceded by: NEW
    2. **UPDATE command:** The original value is accessed with: OLD and the new values will be preceded by: NEW.
    3. **DELETE command:** The values in this case must be preceded by: OLD.

For example:
```
SQL> create trigger tr_sal
     before insert on emp
     for each row
```

```
begin
if :new.sal=0 then
Raise_application_error('-20010','Salary should be greater than 0');
end if;
end;
SQL> /
Trigger created
```

- When you insert data into an emp table **with salary 0** at that time this trigger will get executed.

2.8.3 Modifying a Trigger

- A trigger can be modified using OR REPLACE clause of CREATE TRIGGER command.

  For example:
  ```
  SQL>create or replace trigger tr_sal
      before insert on emp
      for each row
      begin
      if :new.sal<=0 then
      Raise_application_error('-20010','Salary should be greater than 0');
      end if;
      end;
  SQL> /
  Trigger created
  ```

- When you insert data into an emp table with salary 0 or less than 0 at that time this trigger will get executed.

2.8.4 Enabling/Disabling a Trigger

- To enable or disable a specific trigger, ALTER TRIGGER command is used.
- **Syntax:**
  ```
  ALTER TRIGGER trigger_name ENABLE / DISABLE;
  ```
- When a trigger is created, it is automatically enabled and it gets executed according to the triggering command. To disable the trigger, use DISABLE option as,
  ```
  ALTER TRIGGER tr_sal DISABLE;
  ```
- To enable or disable all the triggers of a table, ALTER TABLE command is used.
- **Syntax:**
  ```
  ALTER TABLE table_name ENABLE / DISABLE ALL TRIGGERS;
  ```
  For example:
  ```
  ALTER TABLE emp DISABLE ALL TRIGGERS;
  ```

2.8.5 Deleting a Trigger

- To delete a trigger, use DROP TRIGGER command.
- **Syntax:**

  DROP TRIGGER trigger_name;

  For example:

  DROP TRIGGER tr_sal;

2.9 PACKAGE (Oct. 10; April 13)

- A package is a collection of related functions, procedures and/or routines. Package may contain subprograms that can be called from trigger, procedure or function.
- Packages are used to group together PL/SQL code blocks which make up a common application or are attached to a single business function.
- A package improves machine performance, because it simultaneously transfers several objects to the memory.
- A *package* is a collection of PL/SQL objects that are grouped together.
- There are a number of benefits to using packages, including information hiding, object-oriented design, top-down design, object persistence across transactions, and improved performance.
- Elements that can be placed in a package include procedures, functions, constants, variables, cursors, exception names, and TYPE statements (for index-by tables, records, REF CURSORs, etc.).

2.9.1 Package Structure

- A package has two sections:
  1. Specification section
  2. Body section.
- Physically, the package specification section and the body section are separate.

1. Specification Section:

- The package specification lists the public interfaces to the blocks within the package body.
- In this section, the names of procedures and functions are declared together with the variable and constant names which are included in the initialization.
- To create a package specification use the CREATE PACKAGE command as follows:
- **Syntax:**

  CREATE [OR REPLACE] PACKAGE package_name
  {IS/AS} PL/SQL_package _spec

- OR REPLACE is optional, it is use to re_create the package specification if it is already exists. If a package specification changes, Oracle recomplies it.

For example:
```
CREATE OR REPLACE  PACKAGE  mypack AS
   PROCEDURE   myproc (p_no in number);
   FUNCTION   myfun (f_no in number)
   RETURN number;
END mypack;
```
- In this example of package(mypack) a procedure (myproc) and a function (myfun) are declared. The END of the package is indicated as END package_name.

2. Package Body:

- The package body contains the PL/SQL blocks which defines procedures and functions referenced in the specification section.
- The package body is created with the CREATE PACKAGE BODY command as follows:
- **Syntax:**
  ```
  CREATE [OR REPLACE] PACKAGE BODY package_name
  {IS/AS} PL/SQL_package_body
  ```
- To create a package body we now specify each PL/SQL block that makes up the package, note that we are not creating these blocks separately (no CREATE OR REPLACE is required for the procedure and function definitions).

For example:
```
CREATE OR REPLACE PACKAGE BODY mypack AS
-- Procedure mypack

PROCEDURE  myproc
   (p_no in number)
IS
   Temp_sal number(10,2);
BEGIN
     Select  SAL into Temp_sal
       From emp
       Where empno=p_no;

   If Temp_sal > 1000 then
        Update emp
        Set  SAL=(Temp_sal*1.75)
        Where empno=p_no;
   Else
        Update emp
        Set  SAL=5000
        Where empno=p_no;
```

```
        End if;
    Exception
        When NO_DATA_FOUND then
            Dbms_output.put_line('Empno does not exists');
    End myproc;
    _*************
    --Function myfun
    FUNCTION myfun
    (f_no in number)
    RETURN number
    IS
      v_sal number(10,2);
    BEGIN
        Select SAL into v_sal
        From emp
        Where empno=f_no;
    If   SQL%FOUND then
             RETURN(v_sal);
    Else
             RETURN 0;
    End if;
    END myfun;


    END mypack;
```

- The procedure in package is executed using EXECUTE command as:
  Execute mypack.myproc(7789);
- And the function is execute using SELECT command like:
  Select mypack.myfun(7698) from dual;

For example:

```
CREATE OR REPLACE PACKAGE time_pkg IS
    FUNCTION  GetTimestamp  RETURN DATE;
    PRAGMA RESTRICT_REFERENCES (GetTimestamp, WNDS);

    PROCEDURE ResetTimestamp;
END time_pkg;
CREATE OR REPLACE PACKAGE BODY time_pkg IS
    StartTimeStamp    DATE:= SYSDATE;
    -- StartTimeStamp is package data
```

```
FUNCTION GetTimestamp RETURN DATE IS
BEGIN
   RETURN StartTimeStamp;
END GetTimestamp;

PROCEDURE ResetTimestamp IS
BEGIN
   StartTimeStamp:= SYSDATE;
END ResetTimestamp;

END time_pkg;
```

Package Data

- Data structures declared within a package specification or body, but outside any procedure or function in the package are *package data*.
- The scope of package data is your entire session; it spans transaction boundaries, acting as global for your programs.
- Keep the following guidelines in mind as you work with package data:
    - The state of your package variables is not affected by COMMITs and ROLLBACKs.
    - A cursor declared in a package has global scope. It remains OPEN until you close it explicitly or your session ends.
    - A good practice is to *hide* your data structures in the package body and provide "get and set" programs to read and write that data. This technique protects your data.

2.9.2 Package Initialization

- The first time a user references a package element, the entire package is loaded into the SGA of the database instance to which the user is connected. That code is then shared by all sessions that have EXECUTE authority on the package.
- Any package data are then instantiated into the session's UGA (User Global Area), a private area in either the SGA or PGA (Program Global Area). If the package body contains an initialization section, that code will be executed.
- The initialization section is optional and appears at the end of the package body, beginning with a BEGIN statement and ending with the EXCEPTION section (if present) or the END of the package.
- The following package initialization section runs a query to transfer the user's minimum balance into a global package variable.
- Programs can reference the packaged variable (via the function) to retrieve the balance, rather than executing the query repeatedly.

```
CREATE OR REPLACE PACKAGE usrinfo
IS
   FUNCTION minbal RETURN VARCHAR2;
END usrinfo;
/

CREATE OR REPLACE PACKAGE BODY usrinfo
IS
   g_minbal NUMBER;  -- Package data
   FUNCTION minbal RETURN VARCHAR2
      IS BEGIN RETURN g_minbal; END;
BEGIN  -- Initialization section
   SELECT minimum_balance
      INTO g_minbal
      FROM user_configuration
      WHERE username = USER;
EXCEPTION
   WHEN NO_DATA_FOUND
   THEN g_minbal:= NULL;
END usrinfo;
```

PROGRAMS

Program 1: Write a package which consists of 1 procedure and 1 function; Pass a no. to procedure and print factorial of it. Pass name to function and print the no. of employees reporting to him.

Note: In case of package first package specification is created and then the package body is created which consist of actual code.

```
create or replace package pack1
as
  procedure p1(p_no in number);
  function f1(f_name in varchar2)
        return number;
end pack1;
SQL>/

Package created.

create or replace package body pack1
as
  procedure p1
```

```
        (p_no in number)
    as
        fact number:= 1;
        i number;
    Begin
        for i in 1..p_no
        loop
            fact:=fact*i;
            end loop;
                dbms_output.put_line(p_no || '!=' || fact);
    End p1;
    function f1
    (f_name in varchar2)
    return number
    as
        v_count number;
    Begin
        select count(*) into v_count
        from emp
        where mgr = (select empno
                    from emp
                    where ename=f_name);
        return v_count;
    End f1;
end pack1;

SQL>/
Package body created.
```

Note: Procedures in Package can be executed by using execute command or by calling program. Functions in package can be executed be select statement or by calling program.

Output:

```
SQL> execute pack1.p1(5);
5!= 120
SQL> select pack1.f1('KING') from dual,
PACK1.F1 ('KING')
-----------------------
        3
```

Calling program:

```
Declare
    no number;
    name varchar2(20);
    cnt number;
```

```
begin
  no:=&no;
  pack1.p1(no);
  name:=&name;
  cnt:=f1(name);
  if cnt=0 then
      dbms_output.put_line('No emp reporting to '|| name);
  else
      dbms_output.put_line('No. of emp reporting to '|| name||
                                                   'are' || cnt);
  end if;
end;
```

Output:
```
SQL>/
Enter value for no: 3
old 6: no:=&no;
new 6: no:=3;
Enter value for name: 'KING'
old 8: name:=&name;
new 8: name:='KING';
3!=6
No. of emp reporting to KING are 3

SQL>/
Enter value for no: 4
old 6: no:=&no,
new 6: no:=4;
Enter value for name: 'WARD'
old 8: name:=&name;
new 8: name:='WARD';
4!=24
No emp reporting to WARD
```

Program 2: Write a package which consists of two procedures and 1 function. Pass a name to first procedure and Print the details of supervisor to whom he is reporting Pass a year to second procedure and print details of emp joined in that year. Write a function which print details of emp who are having sal greater than min sal of 'ANALYST' and return those no. of emp.

```
create or replace package pack2
as
  procedure p1(p_name in number);
  procedure p2(p_no in number);
```

```
    function f1 return number;
end pack2;
/

create or replace package body pack2
as
  procedure p1
  (p_name in number)
as
  e_det emp%rowtype;

Begin
    select * into e_det
    from emp
    where empno = (select mgr
             from emp
             where ename=p_name);
    dbms_output.put_line(e_det.ename ||' '|| e_det.sal ||' '||
                                                    e_det.job);
End p1;
--************
procedure p2
(p_no in number)
as
cursor c_emp is select * from emp
          where to_char(hiredate,'yy')=p_no;
e_det emp%rowtype;
v_count number:=0;
Begin
    dbms_output.put_line('Name sal hiredate job');
    dbms_output.put_line('----------------------------');
    for e_det in c_emp
    loop
      dbms_output.put_line(e_det.ename ||' '|| e_det.sal ||' '||
      e_det.hiredate ||' '|| e_det.job);
      v_count:=c_emp%rowcount;
    end loop;
    if(v_count=0) then
        dbms_output.put_line('No emp joined in this year');
    end if;
```

```
End p2;
--***************
function f1 return number
as
    cursor c_emp is select * from emp
                where sal >(select min(sal)
                        from emp
                        where job='ANALYST');
    e_det emp%rowtype;
    v_count number;
Begin
    dbms_output.put_line('Name sal job');
    dbms_output.put_line('---------------');
    for e_det in c_emp
    loop
       dbms_output.put_line(e_det.ename   ||'  '||  e_det.sal   ||'
                                                     '|| e_det.job);
       v_count:=c_emp%rowcount;
    end loop;
    return v_count;
  End f1;
end pack2;
/
```

Output:
```
SQL> execute pack2.p1('KING');
KING is not reporting to anyone

SQL> execute pack2.p1('WARD');
BLAKE 3150 MANAGER

SQL> execute pack2.p2(87);
Name sal hiredate job
-----------------------------
SCOTT 3000 19-APR-87 ANALYST
ADAMS 1100 23-MAY-87 CLERK

SQL> execute pack2.p2(90);
Name sal hiredate job
```

```
------------------------------
No emp joined in this year.

SQL> select pack2.f1 from dual;
    F1
------------------
     4
```

Note: In case of this function it returns number that is displayed when Select command is used. To see all details of emp or output of dbms command you have to use calling program as follows:

Calling program (for function):
```
Declare
   cnt: number;
begin
   cnt =pack2.f1;
   dbms_output.put_line('No. of emp = '|| cnt);
end;
```

Output:
```
SQL> /
Name sal job
--------------------
BLAKE 3150 MANAGER
KING 5000 PRESIDENT
No. of emp = 2
```

Program 3: Write a package which works as a calculator.
```
create or replace package pack3
as
   procedure p1(p_n1 in number, p_n2 in number, p_op in varchar2);
   end pack3;
/
Package created.
create or replace package body pack3
as
   procedure p1
     (p_n1 in number,
```

```
       p_n2 in number,
       p_op in varchar2)
    as
       result number;
    Begin
       if (p_op='+') then
            result:=p_n1 + p_n2;
       elsif (p_op='-') then
            result:=p_n1 - p_n2,
       elsif (p_op='*') then
            result:=p_n1 * p_n2;
       elsif (p_op='/') then
            result:=p_n1/p_n2;
       end if;
       dbms_output.put_line('Result='|| result);
    exception
       When ZERO_DIVIDE then
       dbms_output.put_line('Divide by zero error occurs since
                                        second no. is 0');
    end p1;
End pack3;
/
```

Output:
```
SQL> execute pack3.p1 (3,4,'+');
Result = 7

SQL> execute pack3.p1 (40,20,'-');
Result = 20
SQL> execute pack3.p1 (4,5,'*');
Result = 20

SQL> execute pack3.p1 (30,5,'/');
Result = 6

SQL> execute pack3.p1(3,0,'/');
Divide by zero error occurs since second no. is 0.
```

Practice Questions

1. What is PL/SQL ?
2. State advantages of PL/SQL.
3. With neat diagram describe PL/SQL engine.
4. Enlist various features of PL/SQL.
5. With suitable diagram describe PL/SQL block.
6. Describe the following terms:
   (a) %type,   (b) %rowtype
7. What is an exception ?
8. What is exception handling ?
9. Explain the following exceptions.
   (a) Predefined,   (b) User defined
10. With suitable example describe parameterized cursor.
11. Name four predefined exceptions.
12. Which are the two classes of exception ?
13. What is the use of exception section in PL/SQL block ?
14. Which are the parts of PL/SQL block ?
15. What is the difference between a unary operator and a binary operator ?
16. What is the difference between FOR and WHILE Loops ?
17. Write a loop to calculate a factorial.
18. Write a code to display following series.
    (a) 10 9 8 ---- 1
    (b) 2 4 6 8 ---- 20
19. What are the four steps to using an explicit cursor ?
20. What are the cursor attributes and what is their purpose ?
21. Explain briefly package.
22. Explain package structure.
23. Write short notes on:
    (a) Specification section,   (b) Package body.
24. Explain briefly Trigger.
25. How to create a procedure ?
26. How to create a function ?
27. Explain how to access the value of column inside a Trigger.
28. Give the syntax of Modifying a trigger.
29. Explain briefly how to enabled and disable a trigger.
30. Write a procedure to change the salary to 1000 of emp having location as NEW YORK.
31. Write a procedure that set the commission as 500 for those employee having commission as NULL.
32. Write a procedure to print the name of employee who is senior person in the organisation.
33. Write a procedure to print departmentwise total salary.

34. Write a function which will return name of employee who is senior person and working in department 10.
35. Write a function which will print department name in which maximum employees were working.
36. Which function used to convert character type date to oracle date ?
37. How to remove padded spaces to the right of a string in oracle ?

University Question & Answers

October 2009

1. What is Cursor? Which are various types of cursor? **[2 M]**
Ans. Please refer to Section 2.8.1.

2. Give proper syntax of trigger. **[2 M]**
Ans. Please refer to Section 2.8.2.

3. Explain advantages and disadvantages of PL/SQL. **[4 M]**
Ans. Please refer to Section

(a) Consider the following relational database :
doctor (doct_no, doct_name, address, city, area)
hospital (hosp_no, hosp_name, hosp_city)
doc_hosp (doct_no, hosp_no)
Write a script of cursor to print list showing the doctorwise list of hospitals.

(b) Consider the following relational database :
movie (m_no, m_name, rel_year)
actor (a_no, a_name)
mov-act (m_no, a_no, rate)
Define a trigger before insert or update of each row of movie that movies released after 2009 be entered into movie table.

(c) Consider the following relational database :
publisher (p_no, p_name, p_addr)
book (b_no, b_name, price)
pub-book (p_no, b_no)
Write a script, which will take publisher name as parameter and will display books published by the publisher.

(d) Consider the following relational database :
dept (d_no, d_name, loc)
employee (e_no, e_name, e_addr, e_salary, d_no)
Write a function that will accept d_name as a parameter and return no. of employees, working in that department.

(e) Write a package, which consists of one procedure and one function. Pass a number to procedure and print whether a number is odd or even. Pass employee number to function and print salary of that employee. For this consider the following relation :
employee (e_no, e_name, e_addr, salary)

April 2010

1. What is Cursor? Which are various attributes of cursor? [2 M]
Ans. Please refer to Section 2.7.

2. What is trigger? Explain any two types of triggers. [4 M]
Ans. Please refer to Section 2.8.1.

3. Explain different data type in PL/SQL. [4 M]
Ans. Please refer to Section 2.2.

4. Explain for an if Loop used in PL/SQL with proper example.
Ans. Please refer to Section 2.40 point (3).

Q.4 Attempt any Four : (16)

(a) Consider the following relational database :
Dept (deptno, deptname)
Emp (empno, empname, designation, salary, deptno)
Write a script using cursor to give raise in salary by 15% for all the employees earning less than 15,000 and 19% for all employees earning more than or equal to 15,000.

(b) Consider the following relational database :
Item (itemno, itemname, qty)
Supplier (sno, sname, address, city, phno)
It-Su (itemno, sno, rate, discount)
Define a trigger before updatation on discount field, if the difference in the old discount and new discount to be entered is 15%, raise an exception and display corresponding message.

(c) Consider the following relational database :
Company (c_no, c_name, c_addr, c_city, c_share_value)
Person (p_no, p_name, p_addr, p_city, p_phone_no)
CP (c_no, p_no, no_of_shares)
Write a function, which will take company name as parameter and will find names of persons who are shareholders of the company.

(d) Consider the following relational database :
Publisher (p_no, p_name, p_addr)
Book (book_no, book_name, price, p_no)
Write a script, which will accept book number entered by user and print details of book.

(e) Write a package, which consists of one procedure and one function. Pass a number to procedure and print whether a number is positive or negative pass roll number of student to function and print percentage of that student. For this consider the following relation :
Student (roll_no, name, addr, total, per)

October 2010

1. What is difference between %type and %rowtype. **[2 M]**
Ans. Please refer to Sections 2.3.14 and 2.3.2.

2. List steps involved in explicit cursor. **[2 M]**
Ans. Please refer to Section 2.7.8.

3. List any four predefined exceptions. **[2 M]**
Ans. Please refer to Section 2.4.3.

4. Give proper syntax of PL/SQL. **[2 M]**
Ans. Please refer to Section 2.1.5.

5. What is PL/SQL? Give PL/SQL block structure and explain its detail. **[2 M]**
Ans. Please refer to Sections 2.1.1 and 2.1.5.

(a) Consider the following relational database :
doctor (doct_no, doct_name, doct_city)
hospital (hosp_no, hosp_name, hosp_city)
doct_hosp (doct_no, hosp_no)
Write a script using cursor to print hospitalwise list of doctors.

(b) Consider the following relational database :
department (dept_no, dept_name)
employee (emp_no, emp_name, designation, salary, dept–no)
Define a trigger that will take care of the constraint that employee salary should not be less than zero.

(c) Consider the following relational database :
publisher (pub_no, pub_name, pub_city)
book (book_no, book_name, price)
pub_book (pub_no, book_no)
Write a procedure which will take publisher name as parameter and will display books published by that publisher.

(d) Consider the following relational database :
customer (cust_no, cust_name, cust_city)
account (acc_no, acc_type, balance, cust_no)
Write a function which will take acc_type as a parameter and will return total number of accounts of given acc_type.

(e) Write a package which consists of one procedure and one function. Pass a number as parameter to a procedure and print whether a number is even or odd. Pass per_no of person as a parameter to a function and return ph_no of that person. For this consider the following relation:
Person (Per_no, Per_name, Per_addr, Per_city, Ph_no)

April 2011

1. List modes of trigger and it's syntax. [2 M]
Ans. Please refer to Section 2.8.
2. Give proper syntax of procedure in PL/SQL. [4 M]
Ans. Please refer to Section 2.6.1.
3. What is cursor? Explain all attributes of cursor with suitable example. [4 M]
Ans. Please refer to Section 2.7.1.
   (a) Consider the following relational database:
   Publisher (Pub_no, Pub_name, Pub_city)
   Book (Book_no, Book_name, Book_price)
   Pub—Book (Pub_no, Book_no)
   Write a function which will take publisher name as a parameter and will return total number of books published by given publisher.
   (b) Consider the following relational database: Customer (Cust_no, Cust_name, Cust_city) Account (Acc_no, Acc_type, Balance, Cust_no)
   Write a procedure which will take Acc_type as a parameter and will display customer name having accounts of given Acc_type.
   (c) Consider the following relational database:
   Doctor (doc_no, doc_name, doc_city)
   Hospital (hosp_no, hosp_name, hose_city)
   Doct_Hosp (doc_no, hosp_no)
   Write a script using cursor to print doctorwise list of hospitals visited.
   (d) Consider the following relational database:
   Department (dept–no, dept_name)
   Employee (emp_no, emp_name, designation, salary, dept_no)
   Define a trigger that will take care of the constraint that employees salary should not be less than zero.
   (e) Write a package, which consists of one procedure and one function. Pass a number as parameter to a procedure and print whether a number is positive or negative. Pass Roll_no of student as a parameter to a function and return percentage of that student. For this consider the following relation.
   Student (Roll_no, Stud_name, Stud_addr, Stud_percentage)

October 2011

1. What is cursor? List attributes of cursor. [2 M]
Ans. Please refer to Section 2.7.
2. Explain with different control structure used in PL/SQL with proper example. [4 M]
Ans. Please refer to Section 2.3.3.2.
3. What is PL/SQL give PL/SQL block structure. [2 M]
Ans. Please refer to Sections 2.1.1 and 2.1.5.

April 2012

1. Define PL/SQL. What is use of PL/SQL. **[2 M]**
Ans. Please refer to Section 2.1.1.

2. What is structure of PL/SQL blocks ? **[2 M]**
Ans. Please refer to Section 2.1.5.

3. What is exception handling? Explain predefined and user defined exception with example. **[4 M]**
Ans. Please refer to Sections 2.4.2, 2.4.3 and 2.4.4.

4. What is trigger ? What are the types of trigger. **[2 M]**
Ans. Please refer to Sections 2.8.1 page 2.94 point.

5. What is curser? Explain different attributes used in it. **[4 M]**
Ans. Please refer to Section 2.2.

(a) Consider the following Relational Database:
Department (D_no, D_name, Location)
Employee (Eno, Ename, Edesg, Esalary, D_no_
Write a cursor to display the department details of employee "Mr. Joshi".

(b) Consider the following Relational Database:
Item(Itemno, Itemname, Qty)
Supplier (Supplierno, Suppliername, Address, City, Phno)
I_S(Itemno, supplierno, Rate, Discount)
Define a trigger before updation on discount field, if the difference in the old discount and new discount be is entered is > 15% raise an exception and display corresponding message.

(c) Consider the following Relational Database:
Game (Game_no, Game_name, Team_size, Name of coach)
Player (Player_no, Player_name, Player_city)
Game_Player (Game_no, Player_no)
Write a function which will take game name as a parameter and return total number of players playing that game.

(d) Consider the following Relational Database:
Publisher (P_no, P_name, P_addr);
Book (B_no, B_name, Price, P_no);
Write a script, which will update the book details of book number entered by user. Raise exception if the given book number is not present or if the price of the price of the book is greater than 500.

(e) Write a package, which consist of one procedure and one function; pass a number to procedure and print addition of two numbers. Pass city name as a parameter to function and display number of hospitals located in that city for this consider following relation:
Hospital (Hno, Hname, Hcity)

October 2012

1. Give the proper syntax of Trigger. **[2 M]**
Ans. Please refer to Section 2.8.1.

2. Which are different attributes of cursor. **[2 M]**
Ans. Please refer to Section 2.7.

3. Explain follwoing pre-defined exceptions: **[4 M]**
   no_data_found, zero_divide, too_many_rows, dup_val_on_index.
Ans. Please refer to Section 2.4.3.

4. What is parameterized cursor? Explain it with example. **[2 M]**
Ans. Please refer to Section 2.7.

   (a) Consider the following Relational Database :
   Doctor (d–no, d_name, d_city)
   Hospital (h_no, h_name, h_city)
   Doc_Hosp (d–no, l h_no)
   Write a function, which will count number of doctors visiting to 'Poona' Hospital.

   (b) Consider the following Relational Database
   Book (b_no, b_name, pub_name, price)
   Author (a–no, a–name)
   Book-Auth (b_no, a_no)
   Write a procedure to display details of all books written by `Mr. Mohite.'

   (c) Consider the following Relational Database
   Customer (c_no, c_narne, c – city)
   Loan (1 _no, l _amt, .no_of years, c_no)
   Define a trigger that restricts updation of Loan Amount.

   (d) Consider the following Relational Database
   Employee (e_no, e – name, city, dept name)
   Project (p_no, p_name, status)
   Emp_Proj (e_no, p_no, no–of days)
   Write a cursor to display details of all projects having status `Completed'.

   (e) Write a package which consist of one procedure and one function. For this consider the following Relational Database
   Customer (cust—no, cust—name, cust_city)
   Account (acc—no, acc_type, balance, cust—no)
   (i) Pass account number as a parameter to a procedure and display account details.
   (ii) Pass customer number as a parameter to a function and return total number of accounts of given customer.

April 2013

1. What is cursor? What are the types of cursor? [2 M]
Ans. Please refer to Section 2.7.

2. What are the different data types in PL/SQL? [2 M]
Ans. Please refer to Section 2.2.

3. What is Trigger? Explain it with proper syntax and example. [4 M]
Ans. Please refer to Section 2.8.

4. What is package in PL/SQL? Explain with example. [4 M]
Ans. Please refer to Section 2.9.

5. Write a note on exception handling. [4 M]
Ans. Please refer to Section 2.4.

(a) Consider the following relational database
   Doctor (dno, dname, deity)
   Hospital (hno, hname, hcity)
   Doct — Hosp (dno, hno)
   Write a function to return count of number of hospitals located in Pune city.

(b) Consider the following relational database
   Book (bno, bname, pubname, price)
   Author (ano, aname)
   Book — Author (bno, ano)
   Define a trigger that restricts insertion or updation of books having price less than 0.

(c) Consider the following relational database
   Customer (cno, cname, ccity)
   Loan (lno, lamt, no_of years, cno)
   Write a procedure to display total loan amount from Pune city.

(d) Consider the following relational database
   Employee (eno, ename, city, deptname)
   Project (pno, pname, status)
   Employee_ Project (eno, pno, no_of days)
   Write a cursor to display departmentwise details of employee working in the department.

(e) Write a package which consist of one procedure and one function. For this consider following relational database
   Movie (mno, mname, releaseyear) Actor (ano, aname)
   Movie — Actor (mno, ano)
   (i) Pass movie number as a parameter to a procedure and display movie details.
   (ii) Pass actor number as a parameter to a function and return total number of movies in which given actor is acting.

October 2013

1. What is Trigge? List tow types of Trigger. [2 M]
Ans. Please refer to Section 2.8.
2. What is difference between % type and % row type? [2 M]
Ans. Please refer to Section 2.3.1.
3. What is PL/SQL? Explain different datatypes in PL/SQL. [4 M]
Ans. Please refer to Section 2.2.
4. What is cursor? Explain various attributes of cursor with example. [4 M]
Ans. Please refer to Section 2.7.
5. What is exception handling? Explain user defined exception with example. [4 M]
Ans. Please refer to Section 2.4.

   (a) Consider the following Relational Database :

   Customer (cno, cname, city)

   Account (ano, acc – type, balance, cno)

   Define a trigger that restricts insertion or updation of account having balance less than 100.

   (b) Consider the following Relational Database :

   Book (bno, bname, pubname, price)

   Author (ano, aname)

   Book-Author (bno, ano)

   Write a cursor to display authorwise their book details.

   (c) Consider the following Relational Database :

   Party (party code, party name)

   Politician (pno, pname, description, partycode)

   Write a function which will take partycode as a parameter and return total number of politicians of a given party.

   (d) Consider the following Relational Database :

   Student (rollno, name, class, totalmarks)

   Teacher (tno, tname)

   Student-Teacher (rollno, tno, subject)

   Write a procedure to display details of all students of class 'FY'.

   (e) Write a package, which consists of one procedure and one function. Pass a number as a parameter to a procedure and print whether a number is odd or even. Pass employee number as a parameter to a function and print salary of that employee. For this consider the following relation

   Employee (eno, ename, eaddr, salary).

April 2014

1. What is cursor? **[2 M]**
Ans. Please refer to Section 2.7.
2. List any two data types in PL/SQL. **[2 M]**
Ans. Please refer to Section 2.2.
3. Explain Trigger with proper proper syntax and suitable example. **[4 M]**
Ans. Please refer to Section 2.8.
4. Explain function in PL/SQL with proper syntax and suitable exmaple. **[4 M]**
Ans. Please refer to Section 2.5.
5. Write a note on predefine exception. **[4 M]**
Ans. Please refer to Section 2.4.3.

(a) Consider the following Relational Database :
Supplier (sid, sname, saddr)
Parts (pid, pnmae, pdesc)
Supp_Part (sid, pid, cost)
Define a trigger that restricts insertion or updation of Supp_Part having cost <= 0.

(b) Consider the following Relational Database:
Employee (eid, ename, eaddr)
Project (pid, prname, budget)
Emp_Yroj (eid, pid, duration)
Write a cursor to display projectwise list of employees working on project.

(c) Consider the following Relational Database :
Medical (mno, mname, city)
Drug (dno, dname, company, price)
Medial_Drug (mno, dno, quantity)
Write a procedure to display details of drugs available in medical number `123'.

(d) Consider the following Relational Database :
Bill (bill no, bill_date, bill amt)
Item (item_no, item_name, price)
Bill_Item(bill_no, item_no, quantity)
Write a function which will take bill_no as a parameter and return total number of items included in a given b I 11.

(e) Write a package which consists of one procedure and one function. Pass a number as a parameter to a procedure and print whether a number is positive or negative. Pass customer number as a parameter to a function and return mobile number of that customer, for this consider the relation
Customer(cno, ename, caddy, cmob_no)

Chapter 3...
Transaction Management

Contents ...

This chapter gives Transaction Management concepts such as:

3.1 INTRODUCTION
3.2 TRANSACTION CONCEPT
3.3 TRANSACTION PROPERTIES
    3.3.1 Significance of ACID Properties
3.4 TRANSACTION STATES
    3.4.1 Schedule
3.5 CONCURRENT EXECUTION
3.6 SERIALIZABILITY
    3.6.1 Conflict Serializability
    3.6.2 View Serializability
3.7 RECOVERABILITY
    3.7.1 Recoverable Schedule
    3.7.2 Cascadless Schedule

3.1 INTRODUCTION   (Oct. 09, 10, 11, 13; April 10, 11, 12, 14)

- Collection of operations that forms a single logical unit of work is called **transaction**.
- A transaction accesses and possibly updates various data items. After every transaction, the database should be in a consistent state.
- Usually a transaction is the result of execution of a user program, written in a high-level data manipulation language or programming language.
- Every transaction is delimited by statements or function calls of the form begin transaction and end transaction.
- A computer system is an electronic device and it is subject to failures of various types.
- During the execution of a transaction if some failure occurs, the transaction may result in some inconsistent state of database.
- Hence, the reliability of DBMS is linked to the reliability of computer system, and some solution must be there to deal with such computer system failures.

- Recovery system, the main component of Transaction management/Processing unit, deals with such failures. It makes the database fault tolerant.
- Number of transactions can be executed at the same time and they may be accessing the same database. Such concurrent access to the database, may result in some inconsistent state of database.
- Concurrency control/ management unit of transaction management preserves the consistency of database in case of concurrent accesses.
- This chapter deals with the following topics:
  1. Basic concepts of transaction,
  2. Concurrency control, and
  3. Recovery system.

3.2 TRANSACTION CONCEPTS (Oct. 10, April 11)

- A transaction is a program unit whose execution accesses and possibly updates the contents of a database.
- If the database was in consistent state before a transaction, then on execution of transaction, the database will be in a consistent state.
- In day-to-day life, a transaction can be defined as "an act of giving something to a person and receiving something from that person in return."
- E.g. If a customer wants to buy a commodity from a shopkeeper, the customer first pays an amount for that commodity and then receives the commodity from the shopkeeper in return. Here a customer cannot receive a commodity without paying amount. Similarly, after receiving an amount, the shopkeeper has to hand over the commodity to customer. It means that, omission of any step will result into invalid transaction.
- Clearly, a transaction is an atomic (not splittable) unit. Either all instructions from transaction should be completed or none of the instruction should be completed.

3.3 TRANSACTION PROPERTIES (Oct. 09, 10, 11, 12; April 10, 12, 13, 14)

- To ensure the integrity of data, database system maintains following properties of transaction.
  1. **Atomicity:** Atomicity property ensures that at the end of the transaction, either no changes have occurred to the database or the database has been changed in a consistent manner. At the end of a transaction, the updates made by the transaction will be accessible to other transactions and processes outside the transaction.
  2. **Consistency:** Consistency property of transaction implies that if the database was in consistent state before the start of a transaction, then on termination of a transaction, the database will also be in a consistent state.

3. **Isolation:** Isolation property of transaction indicates that action performed by a transaction will be hidden from outside the transaction until the transaction terminates. Thus each transaction is unaware of other transactions executing concurrently in the system.

4. **Durability:** Durability property of a transaction ensures that once a transaction completes successfully (commits), the changes it has made to the database persist, even if there are system failures.

These four properties are often called ACID (Atomicity, Consistency, Isolation, and Durability) properties of transaction.

3.3.1 Significance of ACID Properties

- Consider a banking system consisting of several accounts and a set of transactions that accesses and updates those accounts. Here consider that the database resides on disk, but some portion of database is temporarily stored in main memory.
- Following are the functions to access the database.
- **read (X):** Which transfers the data item X from the database to a local buffer, belonging to the transaction that executed the read operation.
- **write (X):** Which transfers the data item X from the local buffer of the transaction that executed the write back to the database.
- Let T_i be a transaction that transfers ₹ 50 from account A to account B. This transaction can be defined as:

    T_i :   Read (A);

    A := A – 50;

    write (A);

    Read (B);

    B:= B + 50;

    write (B).

- Let us now consider the significance of ACID properties.
- **Consistency:** Here, consistency requirement is that the sum of accounts A and B must be unchanged. It can be easily verified that if database is consistent before an execution of transaction and the database remains consistent after the execution of transaction. This task may be fascilitated by atomic testing of integrity constraints.
- **Atomicity:** Suppose that just before the execution of transaction T_i, the values of account A and B are ₹ 100 and ₹ 200 respectively. If a failure has occurred during the execution of transaction T_i and that prevented T_i from completing its execution successfully. Suppose that failure happened after the write (A) operation was executed but before the write (B) operation was executed. In this case, the values of accounts A and B reflected in database

are ₹ 50 and ₹ 200. But now A + B is no longer preserved and the database is in inconsistent state.
- But if the atomicity property is provided, all actions of the transaction are reflected in the database or none are reflected i.e. the database contents are ₹ 100 and ₹ 200 or ₹ 50 and ₹ 250.
- **Durability:** The durability assures that once transaction completes successfully, all updates that it carried out on the database persist even if there is a system failure. We can guarantee durability by ensuring that either:
  1. The updates carried out by a transaction have been written to disk before the transaction completes.
  2. Information about updates carried out by the transaction and written to disk is sufficient to enable the database to reconstruct the updates when the database system is restarted after failure.
- **Isolation:** Even if the consistency and atomicity properties are ensured for each transaction, if several transactions are executed concurrently, their operations may interleave in some undesirable way. The isolation property ensures that the concurrent execution of transactions results in system state that is equivalent to a state that could have been obtained by execution of one transaction at a time.
- Each of these properties are ensured by components of transaction management unit.

3.4 TRANSACTION STATES (Oct. 09, 10, 13; April 10)

- Following are the possible states of a transaction during its execution.
  1. **Active:** Transaction is active when it is executing. This is the initial state of transaction.
  2. **Partially committed:** When a transaction completes its final statement, it enters in partially committed state.
  3. **Failed:** If the system decides that the normal execution of the transaction can no longer proceed, then transaction is termed as failed.
  4. **Committed:** When the transaction completes its execution successfully it enters committed state from partially committed state.
  5. **Aborted:** To ensure the atomicity property, changes made by failed transaction are undone i.e. the transaction is rolled back. After rollback, that transaction enters in aborted state.
- A state is said to be terminated if it is committed or aborted.

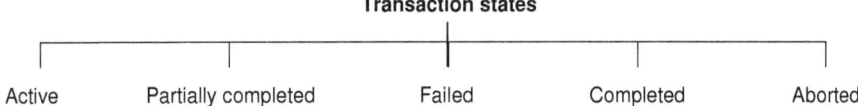

- The state diagram corresponding to transaction states is:

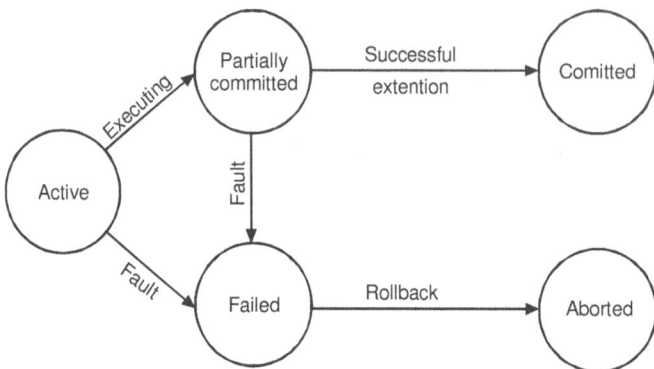

Fig. 3.1: State diagram of Transaction

- A transaction always starts with active state. It remains in active state till all commands of that transaction are executed.
- When it completes executing the last command of that transaction, it enters partially committed state and when the transaction execution is successfully completed, and enters in committed state.
- But, if some failure occurs in active state or partially committed state transaction enters failed state. When the transaction is in failed state, it rollsback that transaction and enters in aborted state.
- When the transaction is in aborted state, the system has two options:
1. If the transaction was aborted as a result of some hardware or software error (software error which is not created because of some internal logic of transaction), then such transaction can be restarted and that transaction is considered to be a new transaction.
2. If the transaction was aborted because of some internal logical error which can be corrected only by rewriting of the application program or because of the input was bad or the desired data were not found in the database, then system can kill such transactions.

3.4.1 Schedule (Oct. 09, 13; April 12, 14)

- Schedule represents the chronological order in which instructions are executed in the system.
- Two schedule types are serial schedule and concurrent schedule.
    1. **Serial Schedule:** It consists of a sequence of instructions from various transactions where the instructions belonging to one single transaction appear together in that

schedule. Thus, for a set of n transactions, there exist n ! different valid serial schedules.

2. **Concurrent Schedule:** When several transactions are executed concurrently, the corresponding schedule is called concurrent schedule. Several execution sequences are possible since the various instructions from both transactions may now be interleaved. In general it is not possible to predict exactly how many instructions of a transaction will be executed before CPU switches to other transaction. Thus, the number of possible concurrent schedules for a set of n transactions is much larger than n !

- **Examples of Schedules:** Consider the banking system of several accounts and a set of transactions that accesses and updates those accounts. Let T_1 and T_2 be two transactions. Assume initial balances of A & B are 1000 and 2000 respectively.

    T_1: Transfers ₹ 50 from account A to account B.

    T_1 :   read (A);
    A = A – 50;
    write (A);
    read (B);
    B = B + 50;
    write (B).

    T_2: Transfers 10% of balance from account A to B.

    T_2 :   read (A);
    temp: = A . 0.1;
    A:= A – temp;
    write (A);
    read (B);
    B:= B + temp;
    write (B).

    For T_1 and T_2, two serial schedules are possible:

1. **<T_1, T_2> Serial Schedule:** It will execute transaction T_1 first and then T_2.

    After executing both transactions, account balance of A is ₹ 855 and account balance of B is ₹ 2145. i.e. <T_1 T_2> preserves A + B i.e. the database are consistent.

Table 3.1: Schedule 1

T₁	T₂
read (A)	
A:= A − 50	
write (A)	
read (B)	
B:= B + 50	
Write (B)	
	read (A)
	temp:= A . 0.1
	A:= A − temp
	write (A)
	read (B)
	B:= B + temp
	write (B)

2. **<T₂, T₁> Serial Schedule:** It executes T₂ first and then T₁.

Table 3.2: Schedule 2

T₁	T₂
	read (A)
	temp:= A . 0.1
	A:= A − temp
	write (A)
	read (B)
	B:= B + temp
	write (B)
read (A)	
A:= A − 50	
write (A)	
read (B)	
B:= B + 50	
write (B)	

- Here, after executing both the transactions, values of A and B are ₹ 850 and ₹ 2150 respectively. In this case also A + B is constant and it preserves the consistency.
- For T₁ and T₂, number of concurrent schedules is possible. But, not all the transactions are consistency preserving.
- A concurrent schedule for T₁ and T₂ is given in Table 3.3.

3. **Consistent concurrent schedule for T_1 and T_2:** This concurrent schedule preserves the consistency of database and A + B is constant.

Table 3.3: Schedule 3

T_1	T_2
read (A)	
A:= A − 50	
write (A)	
	read (A)
	temp:= A * 0.1
	A:= A − temp
	write (A)
read (B)	
B:= B + 50	
write (B)	
	read (B)
	B:= B + temp
	write (B)

4. **Inconsistent concurrent schedule for T_1 and T_2:**

Table 3.4: Schedule 4 (concurrent schedule)

T_1	T_2
read (A)	
A:= A − 50	
	read (A)
	temp:= A * 0.1
	A:= A − temp
	write (A)
	write (B)
write (A)	
read (B)	
B:= B + 50	
write (B)	
	B:= B + temp
	write (B)

3.5 CONCURRENT EXECUTION (April 13)

- The DBMS interleaves the actions of different transactions to improve performance, in terms of increased throughput or improved response times for short transactions, but not all interleaving should be allowed.
- Ensuring transaction isolation while permitting such concurrent execution is difficult but is necessary for performance reasons. First, while one transaction is waiting for a page to be read in from disk, the CPU can process another transaction. This is because I/O activity can be done in parallel with CPU activity in a computer. Overlapping I/O and CPU activity reduces the amount of time disks and processors are idle, and increases system throughput (the average number of transactions completed in a given time). Second, interleaved execution of a short transaction with a long transaction usually allows the short transaction to complete quickly. In serial execution, a short transaction could get stuck behind a long transaction leading to unpredictable delays in response time, or average time taken to complete a transaction.

T_1	T_2
R (A)	
W (A)	
	R (A)
	W (B)
R (C)	
W (C)	

3.6 SERIALIZABILITY (Oct. 09, 10, 13; April 10, 11, 12, 14)

- For a transaction always a serial schedule results in a consistent database and not every concurrent schedule can result in consistent database.
- But a concurrent schedule results in a consistent state if its result is equivalent to a serial schedule of that transaction. Such concurrent schedule is known as serializable.
- A **serializable schedule** is defined as:

  Given (an interleaved execution) a concurrent schedule for n transactions; the following conditions hold for each transaction in the set.

  1. All transactions are correct i.e. if any one of the transactions is executed on a consistent database, the resulting database is also consistent.
  2. Any serial execution of the transactions is also correct and preserves the consistency of the database.

- There are two forms of serializability
  (i) Conflict serializability and
  (ii) View serializability,

3.6.1 Conflict Serializability (Oct. 09, 10, 12)

- Consider that T_1 and T_2 are two transactions and S is a schedule for T_1 and T_2. I_i and I_j are two instructions. If I_i and I_j refer to different data items, then I_i and I_j can be executed in any sequence.
- But, if I_i and I_j refer to same data items then the order of two instructions may matter. Here, I_i and I_j can be a read or write operation only. Hence, following 3 conditions are possible.

    (i) I_i = read (A)

    I_j = read (A)

    The order of I_i and I_j does not matter because both are reading the data.

    (ii) I_i = read (A) I_j = write (A)

    I_i = write (A) I_j = read (A)

    Here, if read (A) is executed before write (A) then it will read the original value of A otherwise it will read that value of A which is written by write (A). Hence, the order of I_i and I_j matters.

    (iii) I_i = write (A) I_j = write (A)

    Here, order of I_i and I_j does not affect either T_i or T_j. But the database is changed, and it makes difference for next read.

- We say that I_i and I_j conflict if they are operated by different transactions on the same data item and at least one of them is write operation. i.e. only in case 1, I_i and I_j do not conflict.
- Consider an example of concurrent schedule 5.

Table 3.5: Concurrent schedule 5

T_1	T_2
read (A)	
write (A)	
	read (A)
	write (A)
read (B)	
write (B)	
	read (B)
	write (B)

- Here, write (A) of T_1 conflicts with read (A) of T_2, similarly write (B) of T_1 conflicts with read (B) of T_2. But write (A) of T_2 does not conflict with read (B) of T_1 because both are accessing different data items.
- If I_i and I_j are two consecutive instructions of schedule S and if they do not conflict, then we can swap the order of I_i and I_j, to produce new schedule S'. We say that S and S' are equivalent since all instructions appear in the same order except for I_i and I_j whose order does not matter.
- Equivalent schedule for a schedule given in Table 3.5 can be obtained by following swap.
- Swap write (A) of T_2 with read (B) of T_1.

Table 3.6: Schedule 6 (Schedule after swapping instructions)

T_1	T_2
Read (A)	
write (A)	
	read (A)
read (B)	
	write (A)
write (B)	
	read (B)
	write (B)

- Similarly swap the following in schedule given in Table 3.6.
    1. read (B) instruction and read (A) instruction of T_1 and T_2 respectively.
    2. write (B) instruction and write (A) instruction of T_1 and T_2 respectively.
    3. write (B) instruction and read (A) instruction of T_1 and T_2 respectively.
- The final schedule S' after these swapping is given below:

Table 3.7: Schedule 7

T_1	T_2
read (A)	
write (A)	
read (B)	
write (B)	
	read (A)
	write (A)
	read (B)
	write (B)

- Which is a serial schedule of T_1 and T_2. Thus concurrent schedule S is transferred to serial schedule S' by a series of swaps of non-conflicting instructions and schedules S and S' are conflict equivalent.
- We say that a schedule S is conflict serializable, if it is conflict equivalent to a serial schedule. Consider the schedule shown in Table 3.8.

Table 3.8: Schedule 8

T_1	T_2
read (Q)	
	write (Q)
read (Q)	

- This schedule is not conflict serializable, since it is not conflict equivalent to any serial schedule $<T_1, T_2>$ or $<T_2, T_1>$.
- There may be any two schedules which are not conflict equivalent but produce same outcome. Schedule given in Table 3.9 is not conflict serializable.

Table 3.9: Schedule 9 (Concurrent schedule)

T_1	T_5
read (A) A:= A − 50 write (A)	
	read (B) B:= B − 10 write (B)
read (B) B:= B + 50 write (B)	
	read (A) A:= A + 10 write (A)

- Result of above schedule is same as serial schedule $<T_1, T_5>$, but this is not conflict serializable, since, in above schedule write (B) of T_5 conflicts with read (B) of T_1. Thus, we cannot move all instructions of T_1 before those of T_5 by swapping consecutive non-conflicting instructions.

3.6.2 View Serializability

- Consider two schedules S and S', where same set of transactions participate in both schedules.
- The schedules S and S' are said to be view equivalent if the following three conditions are satisfied:
1. For each data item Q if transaction T_i reads the initial value of Q in schedule S, then transaction T_i in schedule S' must also read the initial value of Q.
2. For each data item Q if transaction T_i executes read (Q) in schedule S, and that value was produced by transaction T_j (if any), then transaction T_i in schedule S', must also read the value of Q that was produced by T_j transaction.
3. For each data item Q, the transaction that performs the final write (Q) operation in schedule S must perform the final write (Q) operation in schedule S'.
- A schedule S is view serializable if it is view equivalent to a serial schedule.
- Example of view equivalence: Schedule 1 is not view equivalent to schedule 2 since, in schedule 1 the value of account A read by transaction T_2 was produced by T_i, whereas this is not the case in schedule 2. Schedule 1 is view equivalent to schedule 3, because values of account A and B read by transaction T_2 were produced by T_1 in both schedules.
- Example of view serializable schedule: A schedule given in Table 3.10 is view serializable schedule.

Table 3.10: Schedule 10

T_3	T_4	T_6
read (A)		
	write (A)	
write (A)		
		write (A)

This schedule is view equivalent to serial schedule $<T_3, T_4, T_6>$.

Note: Transactions T_4 and T_6 perform write (A) operations without having performed a read (A) operation. Writes of this form are called blind writes.

- Every conflict serializable schedule is view serializable, but there are view serializable schedules that are not conflict serializable.
- A view serializable schedule in which blind write appear is not a conflict serializable.
- Schedule 10 is view serializable but it is not conflict serializable.

Testing for Serializability

- A serializability schedule gives same result as some serial schedule.
- A serial schedule always gives correct result. i.e. a schedule that is serializable schedule is always correct.
- Hence, we must show that schedules generated by concurrency control scheme are serializable. This section deals with methods for determining conflict and view serializability.

1. Conflict Serializability: (Oct. 10)

- There is an algorithm to establish the serializability of a given schedule for a set of transactions.
- This algorithm uses a directed graph called precedence graph, constructed from given schedule.
- **Precedence graph:** It consists of a pair G = (V, E) where,
    V – set of vertices.
- The set of vertices consists of all transactions participating in the schedule.
    E – the set of edges.
- The set of edges consists of all edges $T_i \rightarrow T_j$ for which one of the following three conditions hold:
  1. T_i executes write (Q) before: T_j executes read (Q)
  2. T_i executes read (Q) before: T_j executes write (Q)
  3. T_i executes write (Q) before: T_j executes write (Q)
- A precedence graph is said to be acyclic if there are no cycles in the graph otherwise it is a cyclic graph.

Algorithm: Conflict serializability

   Step 1 : Construct a precedence graph G for given schedule S.

   Step 2 : If the graph G has a cycle, schedule S is not conflict serializable.

- If the graph is acyclic, then find, using the topological sort given below, a linear ordering of transactions, so that if there is arc from Ti to Tj in G, Ti precedes Tj.
- Find a serial schedule as follows:
  (i)   Initialize the serial schedule as empty.
  (ii)   Find a transaction T_i, such that there are no arcs entering T_i, T_i is the next transaction in the serial schedule.
  (iii)   Remove T_i and all edges emitting from T_i. If the remaining set is non-empty, return to (ii), otherwise the serial schedule is complete.

Examples:

1. **Given schedule is:**

Table 3.11

T_{11}	T_{12}	T_{13}
Read (A)		
	Read (B)	
A := f_1 (A)		
		Read (C)
	B := f_2 (B)	
	write (B)	
		C := f_3 (C)
		write (C)
write (A)		
	Read (A)	
	A := f_4 (A)	
Read (C)		
	Write (A)	
C := f_5 (C)		
Write (A)		
		B := f_6 (B)
		write (B)

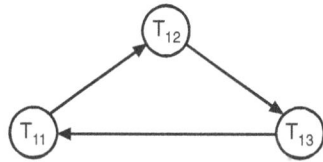

Fig. 3.2 : Precedence graph for the schedule

- This graph contains cycle. Hence, the schedule is not conflict serializable.

2. The given schedule is:

Table 3.12

T_{14}	T_{15}	T_{16}
Read (A)		
A:= f_1 (A)		
Read (C)		
write (A)		
A:= f_2 (C)		
	Read (B)	
write (C)		
	Read (A)	
		Read (C)
	B:= f_3 (B)	
	write (B)	
		C:= f_4 (C)
		Read (B)
		write (C)
	A:= f_5 (A)	
	write (A)	
		B:= f_6 (B)
		write (B)

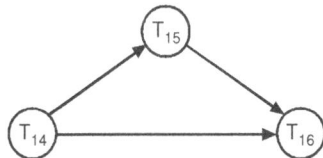

Fig. 3.3: The precedence graph for the given schedule

- The graph is acyclic. The conflict equivalent serial schedule for given schedule can be obtained using step 2 of algorithm.
- T_{14} is the transaction with no arcs entering in T_{14}. Hence T_{14} is the first transaction in serial schedule. Remove T_{14} and all edges emitting from T_{14}.
- T_{15} is the next schedule, since it has no incoming edges. Remove T_{15} and edges emitting from T_{15}.
- T_{16} is the last schedule. Hence the serial schedule which is conflict equivalent to given schedule is:

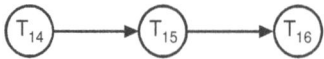

Fig. 3.4: Precedence graph

- Hence, the schedule is conflict serializable.
3. Consider schedule 3, the precedence graph for it is given as:

Fig. 3.5: Precedence graph for schedules

- Since, T_1 executes write (A) and write (B) before T_2 executes read (A) and read (B).
- This graph is acyclic and the conflict equivalent serial schedule is $T_1 \rightarrow T_2$. Hence, schedule 3 is conflict serializable.
4. Consider schedule 4, the precedence graph for it is:

Fig. 3.6: Precedence graph for schedules

which is a cyclic graph and hence it is not conflict serializable.

5. Consider the precedence graph given in Fig. 3.7.

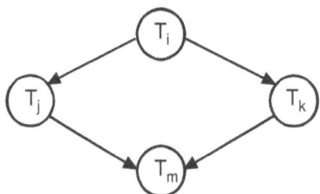

Fig. 3.7: Precedence graph

- The graph is acyclic. The conflict equivalent serial schedule is equivalent to this are:

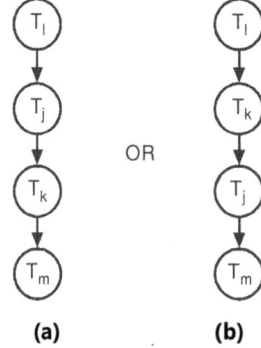

(a) (b)

Fig. 3.8: Precedence graph

- Hence, the schedule corresponding to precedence graph in Fig. 3.8 is conflict serializable.

6. Consider the precedence graph in Fig. 3.9.

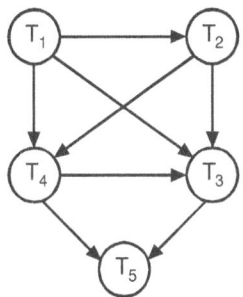

Fig. 3.9: Precedence graph

- The graph is acyclic. The serial schedules that are conflict equivalent to given schedule are:

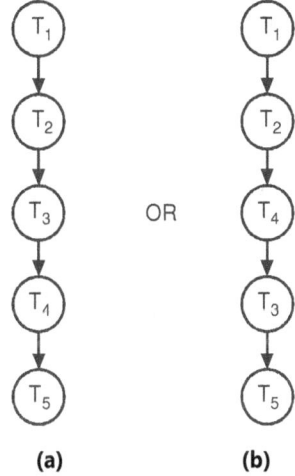

Fig. 3.10: Precedence graph

- Hence the schedule corresponding to given precedence graph is conflict serializable.

2. View Serializability

- Testing for view serializability is complicated. It has been shown that testing for view serializability is itself NP-complete.
- Thus there exists no algorithm to test for view serializability. However concurrency control schemes can still use sufficient conditions for view serializability.
- That is if sufficient conditions are satisfied, the schedule is view serializable schedule. But there may be view serializable schedules that do not satisfy the sufficient conditions.

3.7 RECOVERABILITY   (Oct. 09. April 10)

3.7.1 Recoverable Schedule   (Oct. 10, 13)

- A recoverable schedule is one where for each pair of transactions T_i and T_j such that T_j reads a data item previously written by T_i, the commit operation of of T_i appears before the commit operation of T_j. Otherwise the schedule is non-recoverable.
- Consider the schedule given in Table 3.13. Transaction T_9 reads the data written by T_8. commit of transaction T_8 occurs after commit of transaction T_9. Hence, it is a non-recoverable schedule.

Table 3.13

T_8	T_9
Read(A)	
Write(A)	
	Read(A)
Read(B)	

3.7.2 Cascadeless Schedules   (Oct. 10, 13)

- Even if a schedule is recoverable, to recover correctly from the failure of a transaction T_i, we may have to rollback the transaction.
- Consider the partial schedule shown below:

T_{10}	T_{11}	T_{12}
Read(A)		
Read(B)		
Write(A)		
	Read(A)	Read(A)
	Write(A)	

- Transaction T_{10} writes a value of A that is read by transaction T_{11}. Transaction T_{11} writes a value of A that is read by transaction T_{12}. Suppose that at a point transaction T_{10} fails. T_{10} must be rolled back. Since, T_{11} is dependent on T_{10}, T_{11} must be rolled back. Since, T_{12} is dependent on T_{11}, T_{12} must be rolled back.
- This concept, in which a single transaction failure results in a series of transaction rollbacks, is called **cascading rollback.**
- A **cascadeless schedule** is one where, for each pair of transactions T_i and T_j such that T_j reads a data item previously written by T_i, the commit operation of T_i appears before commit operation of T_j.

Practice Questions

1. Define Transaction ?
2. With suitable diagram explain different states of transaction.
3. Enlist ACID properties of transaction.
4. What is a transaction ?
5. Explain the term Schedule.
6. What is serializability ?
7. With suitable example describe conflict serializability.
8. With suitable example describe view serializability.
9. What are the main different between view at conflict serializability.
10. Describe following schedules:
    (a) Cascadeless schedule
    (b) Recoverable schedule
    (c) Non-Recoverable schedule
11. Explain recoverable and Cascadeless schedules in detail.
12. Explain following states of transaction: Partially committed, failed, Aborted, Active.
13. What is the need for concurrent execution of transactions ?
14. Explain when schedule is conflict serializable when it is view serializable ? Test if the given schedule is view serializable.

T_3	T_4	T_5
read(Q)		
	write(Q)	
write(Q)		
		write(Q)

15. Explain state diagram of transaction.
16. Differentiate between serial and serializable schedule.
17. What is transaction concept ?
18. Give the properties of transaction.
19. Explain: View serializability.
20. What is the test for conflict serializability ?
21. What is the test view serializability ?
22. What is recoverable schedule ? Why it is desirable ?

University Question & Answers

October 2009

1. What is schedule? Give it's types of schedules. [2 M]

Ans. Please refer to Section 3.4.1.

2. List properties of transaction. [2 M]

Ans. Please refer to Section 3.3.

3. What is transaction? Explain states of transaction. [4 M]

Ans. Please refer to Sections 3.1 and 3.4.

4. Consider the following non-serial schedule. Is this schedule serializable to a serial schedule <T1, T2> ?

T1	T2
Read (X) X = X – N	
	Read (X) X = X + N
Write (X) Read (Y)	
	Write (X)
Y = Y + N Write (Y)	

April 2010

1. List states of transaction. [2 M]

Ans. Please refer to Section 3.4.

2. What is serializability. [2 M]

Ans. Please refer to Section 3.6.

3. What is transaction? Explain properties of transaction. [2 M]

Ans. Please refer to Sections 3.1 and 3.3.

(a) Consider the following transaction. Give two non-serial schedules serializable that are serizlizable:

T0	T1
Read (x)	Read (y)
x = x − 70	y = y + 10
Write (x)	Write (y)
Read (y)	Read (z)
y = y + 70	z = z − 5
Write (y)	Read (x)
	Write (z)
	x = x − 15
	Write (x)

(a) Consider the following transaction. Find out non-serial schedule which is serializable to serial schedule <T1, T2, T3> :

T1	T2	T3
Read (x)	Read (z)	Read (x)
Read (z)	z = z + 10	Read (y)
x = x + z	Read (y)	y = y − x
Write (x)	y = y + z	Write (y)
	Write (z)	
	Write (y)	

October 2010

1. What is transaction? List properties of transaction. **[2 M]**

Ans. Please refer to Sections 3.1 and 3.3.

2. What is serializability? Explain conflict serializabilty? **[4 M]**

Ans. Please refer to Sections 3.6.1 and 3.6.2.

3. Consider the following transaction. Give two non-serial schedules that are serializable:

T_1 T_2

read (x)   read (x)

x = x − m   x = x + n

write (x)   write (x)

read (y)

y = y + m

write (y)

4. Consider the following transaction. Find out a non-serial schedule which is serializable to serial schedule <T_1, T_2, T_3>

T_1	T_2	T_3
read (x)	read (z)	read (y)
x = x + 100	read (y)	read (z)
write (x)	y = y + z	y = y + 50
read (y)	write (y)	write (y)
y = y – 100	read (x)	z = z + y
write (y)	x = x – z	write (z)
	write (x)	

April 2011

1. What is serializability? List types of serializability? **[2 M]**

Ans. Please refer to Section 3.6.

2. What is transaction ? Explain sates of transaction with the help of diagram. **[4 M]**

Ans. Please refer to Sections 3.1 and 3.4.

3. Consider the following transaction. Give two non-serial schedules that are serializable.

T_1	T_2
read (A)	read (x)
A = A + 5	x = x – 10
write (A)	write (x)
read (B)	read (B)
read (C)	B = B – 20
B = B + 10	write (B)
write (B)	
C = C + 15	
write (C)	

4. Consider the following transaction. Find out a non-serial schedule which is serializable to serial schedule. <T_1, T_2, T_3>

T_1	T_2	T_3
read (x)	read (x)	read (z)
read (y)	read (z)	read (y)
y = y – x	x = x + z	y = y + z
write (y)	write (x)	write (y)

October 2011

1. What is transaction? Explain ACID properties of transaction. [4 M]
Ans. Please refer to Section 3.1.4.

2. List states of transaction. [4 M]
Ans. Please refer to Section 3.4.

3. Consider the following transactions. Find outs two concurrent schedule, which will be serializable to serial schedule <T_1, T_2> :

T1	T2
Read (A)	Read (B)
A : = A – 70	B : = B + 10
Write (A)	Write (B)
Read (B)	Read (C)
B : = B + 70	C : = C + 50
Write (B)	Write (C)

4. Consider the following non-serial schedule. Is this schedule serializable to a serial schedule (T_1, T_2)?

T1	T2
Read (X)	
X : = X – N	
	Read (X)
	X : = X + N
Write (X)	
Read (Y)	
	Write (X)
Y : = Y + N	
Write (Y)	

April 2012

1. What is transaction ? List states of transaction. [2 M]
Ans. Please refer to Section 3.1 and 3.4.

2. What is serializability. [2 M]
Ans. Please refer to Section 3.6.

3. Explain ACID properties of transaction in detail. [4 M]
Ans. Please refer to Section 3.3.

4. What is schedule? Give types of schedules. [4 M]
Ans. Please refer to Section 3.4.1.

5. Consider the following Non-serial Schedule :

T₁	T₂
Read (X)	
X : = X – N	
	Read (X)
	X : = X + N
Write (X)	
Read (Y)	
	Write (X)
Y : = Y + N	
Write (Y)	

Is this schedule serializable to a serial schedule <T₁, T₂> ?

6. Consider the following transactions :

T₀	T₁
Read (A)	Read (A)
A : = A – 70	t : = A * 0.1
Write (A)	A = A – t
Read (B)	Write (A)
B : = B + 70	Read (B)
Write (B)	B = B + t
	Write (B)

Give at least two serial schedules.

October 2012

1. What is cascadeless schedule? [2 M]
Ans. Please refer to Section 3.7.2.

2. What is transaction? List properties of transaction. [2 M]
Ans. Please refer to Section 3.1 and 3.3.

3. Explain all possible sequence of states through which a transaction may pass. [4 M]
Ans. Please refer to Section 3.1 and 3.4.

4. Explain conflict serializability using precedences graph. [4 M]
Ans. Please refer to Section 3.6.1.

5. Consider the following Transaction. Give two non-serial schedules that the serializable :

T₁	T₂
Read (X)	Read (Y)
X = X − 1000	Y = Y + 5000
Write (X)	Write (Y)
Read (Y)	Read (Z)
Y = Y + 1000	Z = Z + 5000
Write (Y)	Write (Z)

6. Consider the following transactions. Give two non-serial schedules that are serializable.

T₁	T₂
Read (X)	Read (Y)
X = X + 10	Y = Y − 10
Write (X)	Write (Y)
Read (Y)	Read (Z)
Y = Y + 20	Z = Z − 20
Write (Y)	Write (Z)
Read (Z)	
Z = Z + 30	
Write (Z)	

Give at least two serial schedules.

April 2013

1. List the ACID properties. Explain the usefulness of each. **[2 M]**

Ans. Please refer to Section 3.3.

2. Explain problems in concurrent execution of Transaction. **[4 M]**

Ans. Please refer to Section 3.5.

3. Consider the following Transaction. Give two non-serial schedules that the serializable :

T₁	T₂
Read (X)	Read (Z)
X = x + 100	Read (X)
Write (X)	X = x − z
Read (Y)	Write (X)
Read (Z)	Read (Y)
Y = y + z	Y = y − 100
Write (Y)	Write (Y)

4. Consider the following transactions. Give two non-serial schedules that are serializable.

T$_1$	T$_2$
Read (Y)	Read (X)
Read (a)	Read (a)
Y = y + a	X = x + a
Write (Y)	Write (X)
	Read (Y)
	Y = y + a
	Write (Y)

October 2013

1. What is serializability? List the types of serializability. **[2 M]**
Ans. Please refer to Section 3.6.

2. What is schedule? List the type of schedule. **[2 M]**
Ans. Please refer to Section 3.4.1.

3. What is transaction? Explain state of transaction by granting locks?. **[4 M]**
Ans. Please refer to Section 3.4.

4. Explain recoverable schedule and cascadeless schedule with example. **[4 M]**
Ans. Please refer to Section 3.7.

5. Consider the following Transaction. Give two non-serial schedules that the serializable :

T$_1$	T$_2$
Read (A)	Read (B)
A = A − 1000	B = B + 100
Write (A)	Write (B)
Read (B)	Read (C)
B = B − 100	C = C + 100
Write (B)	Write (C)

6. Consider the following transactions. Give two non-serial schedules that are serializable.

T$_1$	T$_2$
Read (x)	Read (x)
x = x + 10	x = x − 10
Write (x)	Write (x)
Read (y)	Read (y)
y = y + 20	y = y − 20
Write (y)	Write (y)
z = z + 30	
Write (z)	

April 2014

1. What is transaction? **[2 M]**

Ans. Please refer to Section 3.1.

2. List type of serializability. **[4 M]**

Ans. Please refer to Section 3.6.

3. Explain properties of transaction. **[2 M]**

Ans. Please refer to Section 3.3.

4. What is schedule? Explain type of schedule with example. **[4 M]**

Ans. Please refer to Section 3.4.1.

5. Consider the following Transaction. Give two non-serial schedules that are serializable to serial schedule $<T_1, T_2, T_3>$.

T_1	T_2	T_3
Read (a)	Read (c)	Read (b)
a = a + 100	Read (b)	b = b + 100
Write (a)	b = b + c	Write (b)
Read (b)	Write (b)	Read (a)
b = b – 100	Read (a)	c = c – 100
Write (b)	a = a – c	Write (c)
	Write (a)	

6. Consider the following transactions. Give two non-serial schedules that are serializable to serial schedule $<T_1, T_2>$.

T_1	T_2
Read (c)	Read (c)
Read (a)	Read (a)
a = a – c	a = a + c
Write (a)	Write (a)
Read (b)	
b = b – c	
Write (b)	

Chapter 4...

Concurrency Control

Contents ...

This chapter gives concurrency control concepts in RDBMS such as:

4.1 INTRODUCTION
4.2 LOCK BASED PROTOCOL
    4.2.1 Locks
    4.2.2 Granting of Locks
    4.2.3 Two Phase Locking Protocol
4.3 TIMESTAMP BASED PROTOCOL
    4.3.1 Timestamp
    4.3.2 Timestamp ordering protocol
    4.3.3 Thomas's Write Rule
4.4 VALIDATION BASED PROTOCOL
    4.4.1 Multiple Granularity
    4.4.2 Multiversion Schemes
    4.4.3 Multiversion Time Stamp Ordering
    4.4.4 Multiversion Two-Phase Locking
    4.4.5 Optimistic Technique
4.5 DEADLOCK HANDLING
    4.5.1 Deadlock Prevention
    4.5.2 Deadlock Detection
    4.5.3 Deadlock Recovery

4.1 INTRODUCTION

- If all schedules in a concurrent environment are restricted to serializable schedule, the result will be consistent with some serial execution of transactions and will be considered correct.
- But there some disadvantages of serializability.
    1. It limits the degree of concurrency.
    2. testing for serializability of a scheme is computationally expensive.
    3. Testing for serializability of a scheme is an after-the-fact technique and it is impractical.

- This section deals with some concurrency control schemes. These schemes ensure that the schedules produced by concurrent transaction are serializable.
- Following are the concurrency control schemes :
  1. Lock-based protocol,
  2. Time-stamp based protocol,
  3. Validation based protocol,
  4. Multiple granularity, and
  5. Multiversion schemes.

4.2 LOCK-BASED PROTOCOL

- Serializability can easily be ensured if access to database is done in mutually exclusive manner i.e. if one transaction is accessing a data item, no other transaction can modify that data item.
- The most common method to implement mutual exclusion is to use locks.

4.2.1 Lock (Oct. 09, April 10, 14)

- Consider that database is made up of data-items. A lock is a variable associated with each data item. Manipulating the value of lock is called locking.
- The value of lock is used in locking schemes to control the concurrent access and to manipulate the associated data items.

  Following are the two types or modes of locks.
  1. **Shared :** If a transaction T_i has obtained a shared mode lock (denoted by S) on item A, then T_i can read but it cannot write A.
  2. **Exclusive :** If a transaction T_i, has obtained an exclusive mode lock (denoted by X) on item A, then T_i can both read and write A.

- Depending on the type of the operation, the transaction requests a lock in an appropriate mode on data item.
- The request is made to the concurrency-control manager, and the transaction can proceed with operation only after the concurrency-control manager grants the lock to that transaction.

4.2.1.1 Compatibility Function

- Given a set of lock modes, the compatibility function can be defined as :
- Let A and B represent arbitrary lock modes. Suppose that a transaction T_i requests a lock of mode A on item Q on which transaction T_j currently holds a lock of mode B.
- If transaction T_i can be granted a lock on Q immediately, in spite of presence of the lock of mode B, then we say that mode A is compatible with B. Such a function can be

represented conveniently by a matrix. Compatibility of two modes of lock is given in compatibility matrix.

	S	X
S	true	false
X	false	false

4.2.1.2 Comp Lock-compatibility Matrix

- If comp (A, B) is true it means that A is compatible with B. Notice that shared mode (S) is compatible with shared mode (S).
- At any time, several shared-mode locks can be held simultaneously on a particular data item.
- A transaction requests a shared lock on data item Q by executing the lock-S(Q) instruction and an exclusive lock is requested through lock-X(Q) instruction. A data item Q can be unlocked via the unlock (Q) instruction.
- Transaction T_i can unlock the data item Q by executing unlock (Q) instruction. But transaction must hold a lock on a data item, as long as it accesses the data item.
- Locking protocols indicate when a transaction may lock and unlock each of the data items. Each transaction must follow the set of rules specified by locking protocols.
- Locking protocols restrict the number of possible serializable schedules. This section deals with only those locking protocols which allow conflict serializable schedules.

4.2.1.3 Starvation of Locks   (April 10, 11, 13; Oct. 13)

- Suppose that transaction :
    T_2 - has a shared mode lock on data item, and
    T_1 - requests an exclusive mode lock on same data item.
- Clearly T_1 has to wait for T_2 to release the shared mode lock.
- Meanwhile, suppose that,
    T_3 - request a shared mode lock on same data item.
- This lock request is compatible with the lock granted to T_2, so T_3 may be granted the shared mode lock.
- At this point, T_2 may release the lock but still T_1 has to wait for T_3. But again there may be a new transaction T_4 requesting a shared mode lock on the same data-item.
- It is possible that there is a sequence of transactions that each requests a shared mode lock on same data item and T_1 never gets the exclusive mode lock on the data item. The transaction T_1 may never make progress and is said to be starved.

- Starvation of transactions can be avoided by granting locks as follows. When a transaction T_i requests a lock on a data item Q in a particular mode M, the lock is granted provided that :
   1. There is no other transaction holding a lock on Q in a mode that conflicts with M.
   2. There is no other transaction that is waiting for a lock on Q and that made its lock request before T_i.

4.2.2 Granting of Lock   (Oct. 13)

- When a request is queued, no other request which would conflict with the request in queue is granted. For example, assume program A has locked a data entry in data set X, and program B wants to lock data set X and data set Y. Program B's request is queued. When program C requests to lock a data entry in data set Y, that request is queued because program B is waiting to lock data set Y.
- When using DBLOCK wait modes, the programmer should be careful to avoid possible deadlock conditions. If a program makes multiple resource requests using the commands DBLOCK, LOCK# or REQUEST, a potential deadlock can occur if another program is also making requests for the same resources. For example, suppose program A holds resource 1 and is queued waiting for resource 2 which is held by program B. If program B makes a wait request for resource 1, a deadlock situation occurs. Programs requesting the same resources can avoid deadlock by making their resource requests in the same order.
- The following table summarizes the conditions for granting a lock:

Lock Mode Requested	Locking Mode Held				
	None	Access	Read	Write	Exclusive
Access or Checksum	Lock Granted	Lock Granted	Lock Granted	Lock Granted	Request Queued*
Read	Lock Granted	Lock Granted	Lock Granted	Request Queued*	Request Queued*
Write	Lock Granted	Lock Granted	Request Queued*	Request Queued*	Request Queued*
Exclusive	Lock Granted	Request Queued*	Request Queued*	Request Queued*	Request Queued*

- Deadlock Detection: Deadlocks tend to be rare and typically involve very few transactions. This observation suggests that rather than taking measures to prevent deadlocks, it may be better to detect and resolve deadlocks as they arise. In the detection approach, the DBMS must periodically check for deadlocks. When a transaction Ti is suspended because a lock that it requests cannot be granted, it must wait until all transactions Tj that currently hold conflicting locks release them. The lock manager maintains a structure called a waits-for-graph to detect deadlock cycles. The nodes correspond to active transactions, and there is an edge from Ti to Tj if (and only if) Ti is waiting for Tj to release a lock. The lock manager adds edges to this graph when it queues lock requests and removes edges when it grants lock requests. Detection versus Prevention: In prevention-based schemes, the abort mechanism is used preemptively in order to avoid deadlocks. On the other hand, in detection-based schemes, the transactions in a deadlock cycle hold locks that prevent other transactions from making progress. System throughput is reduced because many transactions may be blocked, waiting to obtain locks currently held by deadlocked transactions. This is the fundamental trade-off between these prevention and detection approaches to deadlocks: loss of work due to preemptive aborts versus loss of work due to blocked transactions in a deadlock cycle. We can increase the frequency with which we check for deadlock cycles, and thereby reduce the amount of work lost due to blocked transactions, but this entails a corresponding increase in the cost of the deadlock detection mechanism. A variant of 2PL called Conservative 2PL can also prevent deadlocks. Under Conservative 2PL, a transaction obtains all the locks that it will ever need when it begins, or blocks waiting for these locks to become available. This scheme ensures that there will not be any deadlocks, and, perhaps more importantly, that a transaction that already holds some locks will not block waiting for other locks. The trade-off is that a transaction acquires locks earlier. If lock contention is low, locks are held longer under Conservative 2PL. If lock contention is heavy, on the other hand, Conservative 2PL can reduce the time that locks are held on average, because transactions that hold locks are never blocked.

4.2.3 Two-Phase Locking Protocol (Oct. 09; April 13)

- This protocol requires that each transaction issue a lock and unlock requests in two phases :
    - **(1) Growing phase:** A transaction may obtain locks, but may not release any lock. (April 11, 14; Oct. 12)
    - **(2) Shrinking phase:** A transaction may release locks, but may not obtain any new locks. Initially the transaction is in growing phase. In this it acquires locks as needed. Once, the transaction releases a lock, it enters the shrinking phase and it can issue no more lock requests. (April 11, 14; Oct. 12)
- The point in the schedule where the transaction has obtained its final lock (the end of its growing phase) is called the lock point of the transaction. The transactions can be ordered according to lock points.
- This ordering gives the serializability ordering for transaction. This serial schedule is conflict equivalent i.e. the two-phase locking protocol ensures conflict serializability.

- **Example :** Following two transactions are two phase transactions.

  T_3 :   lock-X (B);
  read (B);
  B : = B – 50;
  write (B);
  lock-X(A);
  read (A);
  A : = A + 50;
  write (A);
  Unlock (B);
  Unlock (A).

  T_4 :   lock-S (A);
  read (A);
  lock-S (B);
  read (B);
  display (A + B);
  Unlock (A);
  Unlock (B).

- The unlock instructions do not need to appear at the end of the transaction.
- Two phase locking does not ensure freedom from deadlock. Transactions T_3 and T_4 are two phase, but they are deadlocked in the schedule.

Table 4.1

T_3	T_4
Lock-X (B)	
read (B)	
B := B – 50	
write (B)	
	lock- S (A)
	read (A)
	lock-S (B)
Lock-X (A)	
read (A)	
A := A + 50	
write (A)	
unlock (B)	
unlock (A)	
	read (B);
	display (A + B);
	unlock (A);
	unlock (B)

Cascading rollback may occur under two phase locking.

4.2.3.1 Variations on Two-Phase Locking

1. **Strict Two-Phase Locking Protocol : (Strict 2PL)**

   Cascading rollbacks can be avoided by a modification of two phase locking called strict two phase locking protocol.

   It requires that in addition to locking being two-phase, all exclusive-mode locks taken by a transaction must be held until that transaction commits.

   This requirement ensures that any data written by an uncommitted transaction are locked in exclusive mode until the transaction commits, preventing any other transaction from reading the data.

2. **Rigorous Two-Phase Locking Protocol : (Rigorous 2PL)**

   It requires that all locks to be held until the transaction commits.

   With rigorous two-phase locking, transactions can be serialized in the order in which they commit. Most database system implement strict or rigorous two-phase locking.

3. **Two-Phase Locking with Lock Conversion :**

   Basic two phase locking is modified and lock conversions are allowed. We shall provide a mechanism for upgrading a shared lock to an exclusive lock and downgrading an exclusive lock to shared lock.

   Upgrade (Q) : Convert shared lock lock-S (Q) to exclusive lock lock-X (Q). **(April 11; Oct. 13)**
   Downgrade (Q) : Convert exclusive lock lock-X (Q) to shared lock lock-S (Q).
   (April 11; Oct. 13)

   - Lock conversion can not be allowed to occur arbitrarily. Upgrading can take place in growing phase and downgrading can take place in only the shrinking phase.
   - Two phase locking with lock conversion generates conflict serializable schedule.

   Example : Consider the following two transactions with only read and write operations :

   T_8 : read (a_1);
   read (a_2);
   read (a_3);
   read (a_4);
   read (a_5);
   write (a_1)

   T_9 : read (a_1)
   read (a_2)
   display ($a_1 + a_2$)

   - If we employ two phase locking with lock conversion, the schedule can be given as :
   - Automatic generation of appropriate lock and unlock instructions for a transaction is also possible.
   - When a transaction issues a read (a) operation, the system issues lock-S(a) instruction followed by read (a) operation.

- When a transaction T_i issues a write (Q) operation, the system checks to see whether T_i already holds a shared lock on Q. If it does, then the system issues an upgrade (Q) instruction, followed by the write (Q) instruction.
- Otherwise the system issues lock-X(Q) instruction followed by write (Q) operation.

Table 4.2

T_8	T_9
lock-S (a_1)	
read (a_1)	
	lock-S (a_1)
	read (a_1)
lock-S (a_2)	
read (a_2)	
	lock-S (a_2)
	read (a_2)
lock-S (a_3)	
lock-S (a_4)	
	display ($a_1 + a_2$)
	unlock (a_1)
	unlock (a_2)
lock-S (a_5)	
read (a_5)	
upgrade (a_1)	
write (a_1)	

4.2.3.2 Graph - Based Protocols

- Graph-based protocol is not a two phase locking protocol and it requires prior knowledge of how each transaction will access the database.
- To acquire such prior knowledge it uses data graph.
  Let $D = \{d_1, d_2, ..., d_n\}$ is the set of all data items. If $d_i \rightarrow d_j$, then any transaction accessing both d_i and d_j must access d_i before accessing d_j. This partial ordering may be a result of either the logical or physical organization of data or it may be imposed solely for the purpose of concurrency control.
- The partial ordering implies that the set D may be viewed as a directed acyclic graph, called database graph. For simplicity we shall consider only those graphs which are rooted trees.

- A simple protocol called tree-protocol, which is restricted to exclusive locks is stated here.
- Each transaction T_i can lock (lock-X(Q)) a data item at most once and observe the following rules.
    1. The first lock by T_i may be on any data item.
    2. Subsequently, a data item Q can be locked by T_i only if the parent of Q is currently locked by T_i.
    3. Data item may be unlocked at any time.
    4. A data item that has been locked and unlocked by T_i cannot subsequently be relocked by T_i.
- All schedules that are legal under the tree protocol are conflict serializable.
- **Example :** Consider the database graph in Fig. 4.1. The following four transactions follow the tree protocol on this graph.

T_{10}: lock-X (B);
lock-X (E);
lock-X (D);
unlock (B);
unlock (E);
lock-X (G);
unlock (D);
unlock (G).

T_{11}: lock-X (D);
lock-X (H);
unlock (D);
unlock (H).

T_{12}: lock-X (B);
lock-X (E);
unlock (E);
unlock (B).

T_{13}: lock-X (D);
lock-X (H);
unlock (D);
unlock (H).

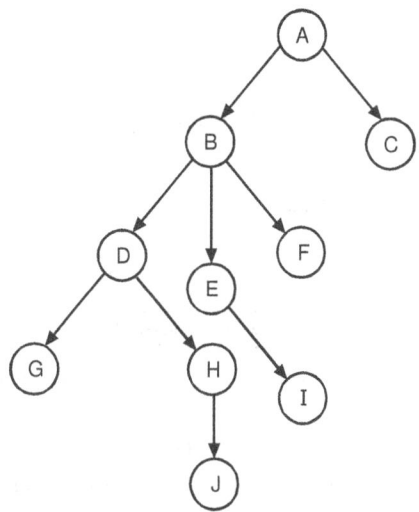

Fig. 4.1 : Database Graph

- The schedule following tree protocol is given below :

Table 4.3

T₁₀	T₁₁	T₁₂	T₁₃
lock-X (B)			
	lock-X (D)		
	lock-X (H)		
	unlock (D)		
lock-X (E)			
lock-X (D)			
unlock (B)			
unlock (E)			
		lock-X (B)	
		lock-X (E)	
	unlock (H)		
lock-X (G)			
unlock (D)			
			lock-X (D)
			lock-X (H)
			unlock (D)
			unlock (H)
		unlock (E)	
		unlock (B)	
unlock (G)			

- This schedule is conflict serializable. Tree protocol ensures conflict serializability and it is free from deadlocks.

Advantages

- Tree locking protocol has an advantage over two phase locking protocol :
    1. Unlocking may occur earlier. Earlier unlocking may lead to shorter waiting times and an increase in concurrency.
    2. It is deadlock free and hence no rollbacks are required.

Disadvantages

- But it has one disadvantage that in some cases, a transaction may have to lock data items that it does not access.
- **Example :** A transaction that needs to access data items A and J in the database graph given in Fig. 4.1 must lock not only A and J but also data items B, D and H.
- This additional locking results in increased locking overhead, the possibility of additional waiting time and potential decrease in concurrency.
- Further, without prior knowledge of what data item will need to be locked, transactions will have to lock the root of tree and that can reduce the concurrency greatly.

4.3 TIMESTAMP BASED PROTOCOL

- This protocol decides the ordering of transactions in advance to determine the serializability order. For this it uses time-stamp ordering scheme.

4.3.1 Timestamp

- With each transaction T_i in the system, a fixed value called timestamp is associated, denoted by TS (T_i). This timestamp is assigned by database system before T_i starts execution.
- If transaction T_i is assigned a timestamp TS (T_i) and a new transaction T_j enters the system, then TS $(T_i) < T_s (T_j)$. There are two simple methods for implementing timestamp scheme.
    1. Use the value of system clock as the timestamp i.e. a transaction's timestamp is equal to the value of system clock, when the transaction enters the system.
    2. Use a logical counter that is incremented after a new timestamp has been assigned. i.e. a transaction's timestamp is equal to the value of the counter when the transaction enters the system.
- Timestamp of transaction determines the serializability order.
- If TS $(T_i) <$ TS (T_j) then the system must ensure that the resultant schedule is equivalent to serial schedule in which T_i appears before T_j.
- To implement this scheme, two timestamp values are associated with each data item Q.

- **W-Timestamp (Q):** It denotes the largest timestamp of any transaction that executed write (Q) successfully.
- **R-Timestamp (Q):** It denotes the largest timestamp of any transaction that executed read (Q) successfully.
- Whenever, a new read(Q) or write(Q) instruction is executed, these timestamps are updated.

4.3.2 Timestamp Ordering Protocol

- Timestamp ordering protocol ensures that any conflicting read and write operations are executed in timestamp order.
- This protocol works as follows :
    1. **Suppose that transaction T_i issues read (Q).**
        (a) If TS (T_i) < W-Timestamp (Q), then T_i needs to read a value of Q that was already overwritten. Hence, the read operation is cancelled, and T_i is rolledback.
        (b) If TS (T_i) ≥ W-Timestamp (Q), then the read operation is executed, and R-Timestamp (Q) is set to maximum of R-Timestamp (Q) and TS (T_i).
    2. **Suppose that T_i issues write (Q).**
        (a) If TS (T_i) < R-Timestamp (Q) then the value of Q that T_i is producing was needed previously and the system assumed that value would never be produced. Hence, the write operation is cancelled, and T_i is rolled back.
        (b) If TS (T_i) < W-timestamp (Q), then T_i is attempting to write an outdated value of Q. Hence, this write operation is cancelled, T_i is rolled back.
        (c) Otherwise the write operation is executed and W-timestamp is set to TS (T_i).
- A transaction T_i, that is rolled back by the concurrency control scheme as a result of either a read or write operation being issued, is assigned a new timestamp and is restarted.
- **Example :** Consider the given transactions T_{14} and T_{15}.

    T_{14} : read (B);
    read (A);
    display (A + B)
    T_{15} : read (B);
    B := B − 50;
    write (B);
    read (A);
    A := A + 50;
    write (A);
    display (A + B).

- Concurrent schedule for the two transactions is given below.
- Here, we consider that TS (T_{14}) < TS (T_{15}). The schedule given in Table 4.4 is possible under the timestamp protocol.

Table 4.4

T_{14}	T_{15}
read (B)	
	read (B)
	B : = B – 50
	write (B)
read (A)	
	read (A)
display (A + B)	
	A : = A + 50
	write (A)
	display (A + B)

1. read (B) of T_{14} is executed because TS (T_{14}) ≥ W-timestamp (B) and it sets R-Timestamp (B) = TS (T_{14}).
2. read (B) of T_{15} is executed because TS (T_{15}) ≥ W-timestamp (B) and it sets R-Timestamp (B) = TS (T_{15}).
3. write (B) of T_{15} is executed because TS (T_{15}) = R-Timestamp (B).

   Similarly, read (A) of T_{14} and write (A) of T_{15} are executed.

4.3.3 Thomas's Write Rule

- Consider the schedule given in Table 4.5.

Table 4.5

T_{16}	T_{17}
read (Q)	
	write (Q)
write (Q)	

- Apply Timestamp-ordering protocol to given schedule.
- Since, T_{16} starts before T_{17}, TS (T_{16}) < TS (T_{17}), read (Q) of T_{16} and write (Q) operations succeed. When T_{16} attempts its write (Q) operation, we observe that,
- TS (T_{16}) < W-Timestamp (Q), since W_timestamp (Q) = TS (T_{17}) According to Timestamp protocol, write (Q) must be rejected, T_{16} will be rolled back.

- Timestamp ordering protocol rolls back the transaction T_{16}, but the value of write (Q) Operation of T_{16} is already written by write (Q) of T_{17}, and the value that write (Q) of T_{16} is attempting to write will never be read. i.e. we can ignore the write (Q) of T_{16}.
- This leads to a modification of Timestamp-ordering protocol. This modified protocol operates as follows :

1. **Suppose that transaction T_i issues read (Q) :**
   (a) If TS (T_i) < W-Timestamp (Q), then T_i needs to read a value of Q that was already over written. Hence, the read operation is rejected, and T_i is rolled back.
   (b) If TS (T_i) ≥ W-timestamp (Q), then read operation is executed, and R-timestamp (Q) is set to the maximum of R-timestamp (Q) and TS (T_i).

2. **Suppose that transaction T_i issues write (Q) :**
   (a) If TS (T_i) < R-Timestamp (Q) then the value of Q that T_i is producing was previously needed, and it was assumed that the value would never be produced. Hence, the write operation is cancelled, and T_i is rolled back.
   (b) If TS (T_i) < W-timestamp (Q), then T_i is attempting write an outdated value of Q. Hence, the write operation can be ignored.
   (c) Otherwise, the write operation is executed, and W-timestamp (Q) is set to TS (T_i).

   i.e. here if TS (T_i) < W-Timestamp (Q), then we ignore the obsolute write operation. This modification to timestamp ordering protocol is called Thomas write rule.
- Thomas write rule for schedule 8 given in table results in a serial schedule < T_{16}, T_{17} > which is view equivalent to given schedule.

4.4 VALIDATION BASED PROTOCOL   (Oct. 12)

- We assume that each transaction T_i executes in two or three phases depending on read only operation or an update operation.
- Following are the three phases of execution.
   1. **Read phase :** During this phase, the execution of transaction T_i takes place. The values of various data item are read and stored in variable local to T_i. All write operations are performed on local variables, without updates of actual database.
   2. **Validation phase :** It performs a validation test to determine whether it can copy the results of write operations stored in temporary local variables to database without causing violation of serializability.
   3. **Write phase :** If transaction T_i succeeds in validation phase, then write phase, actually updates the database, otherwise T_i is rolled back. Each transaction must go through the three phases in the order shown. The three phases of concurrently executing transaction can be interleaved.

- Three different timestamps are associated with transaction T_i to determine when the various phases of transaction T_i take place.

  Start (T_i) : The time when T_i started its execution.

  Validation (T_i) : The time when T_i finished its read phase and started its validation phase.

  Finish (T_i) : The time when T_i finished its write phase.

  Timestamp of transaction T_i is TS (T_i) = validation (T_i)

- If TS (T_j) < TS (T_k) then any resultant schedule must be equivalent to a serial schedule in which transaction T_j appears before transaction T_k.

- The validation test of validation phase for transaction T_j requires that, for all transactions TS with TS (T_i) < TS (T_j), one of the following two conditions must hold.

  1. Finish (T_i) < Start (T_j), since if T_i completes its execution before T_j started, then the serializability order is maintained.
  2. The set of data items written by T_i does not intersect with the set of data items read by T_j, and T_i completes its write phase before T_j starts its validation phase i.e.

     Start (T_j) < Finish (T_i) < Validation (T_j)

- This condition ensures that writes of T_i and T_j do not overlap.
- Since, the write of T_i does not affect read of T_j and since, T_j cannot affect the read of T_i, the serializability order is maintained.
- **Example :** Consider again the transactions T_{14} and T_{15}. A schedule produced using validation is given in Table 4.6.

Table 4.6

T_{14}	T_{15}
read (B)	
	read (B)
	B := B – 50
	read (A)
	A := A + 50
read (A)	
<Validate>	
display (A + B)	
	<Validate>
	write (B)
	write (A)

4.4.1 Multiple Granularity

- In the concurrency control schemes described, we have used each individual data item as the unit on which synchronization is performed.
- But in some cases it would be advantageous to group several data items, and to treat them as one individual synchronization unit.
- **For example :** If a transaction T_i needs to access the entire database, and locking protocol is used, then it must lock each data item in the database. It would be better if T_i could issue a single lock request to lock the entire database. Similarly, if transaction T_i needs to access only one record in the database, it should not be required to lock the entire database.

  i.e. we need a mechanism to allow the system to define multiple levels of granularity.
- We can make one by allowing data items to be of various sizes and defining a hierarchy of data granularities where the small granularities are nested within larger ones. Such a hierarchy can be represented by tree.
- As an illustration consider the tree of Fig. 4.2.
    - The highest level represents the entire database.
    - Below that are nodes of type area.
    - Each area in turn has nodes of type file as its children. Each area contains exactly those files that are its child nodes. No file is in more than one area.
    - Each file has nodes of type record. The file consists of those exactly records that are its child nodes and no record can be present in more than one file. Each node in the tree can be locked individually.

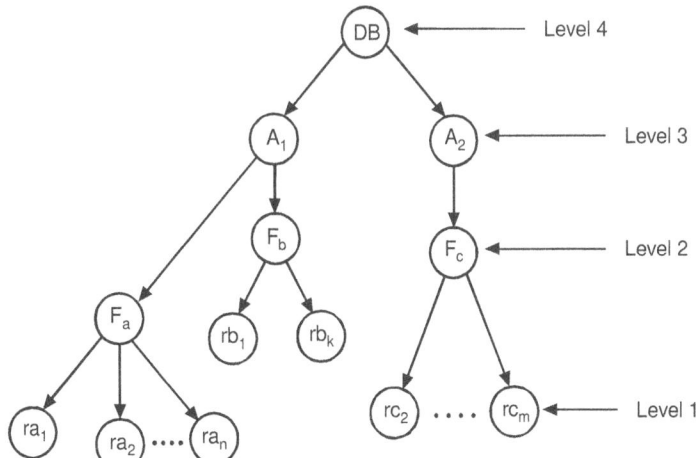

Fig. 4.2 : Hierarchy which is represented by Tree

- Following are modes of lock used in multiple granularity schemes.
  1. Shared mode lock (S)
  2. Exclusive mode lock (X)
  3. Intension-shared mode lock (IS)
  4. Intension-exclusive mode lock (IX)
  5. Shared and Intension-exclusive mode lock-S (SIX).
- When transaction locks a node in shared or exclusive mode, the transaction also has locked all the descendants of that node in the same lock mode.
- If a node is locked in intension-shared mode, then explicit locking is being done at lower level of the tree, but with only shared mode locks.
- If a node is locked in intension-exclusive mode, then explicit locking is being done at a lower level, with exclusive-mode or shared mode locks.
- If a node is locked in shared and intension-exclusive mode, the subtree rooted by that node is locked explicitly in shared mode and that explicit locking is being done at a lower level with exclusive-mode locks.
- The compatibility matrix is given below :

Table 4.7: Compatibility matrix

	IS	IX	S	SIX	X
IS	true	true	True	true	false
IX	true	true	false	false	false
S	true	false	true	false	false
SIX	true	false	false	false	false
X	false	false	false	false	false

- Multiple granularity locking protocol that follows ensures serializability.
- Each transaction Ti can lock a node Q, using the following rules :
  1. The lock compatibility function given in Table 4.7 must be observed.
  2. The root of the tree must be locked first, and can be locked in any mode.
  3. A node Q can be locked by T_i in S or IS mode only if the parent of Q is currently locked by T_i in either IX or IS mode.
  4. A node Q can be locked by T_i in X, SIX or IX mode only if the parent of Q is currently locked by T_i in either IX or SIX mode.
  5. T_i can lock a node only if it has not previously unlocked any node.
  6. T_i can unlock a node Q only if none of the children of Q are currently locked by T_i.
- **Example :** Consider the tree given in Fig. 4.2 and following transactions.
  1. Suppose that transaction T_{18} reads record ra_2 in file F_a.
     Then T_{18} needs to lock, the database area A_1 and file F_a in IS mode and to lock ra_2 in S mode.

2. Suppose that transaction T_{19} modifies record ra_9 in file F_a.

   Then T_{19} needs to lock the database area A_1 and file F_a in IX mode and finally to lock ra_9 in X mode.

3. Suppose that transaction T_{20} reads all records in file F_a.

   Then T_{20} needs to lock the database area A_1 in IS mode and finally to lock file F_a in S mode.

4. Suppose that transaction T_{21} reads the whole database. It can do so after locking the database in S mode.

- **Advantages and Disadvantages :**
  1. This protocol ensures concurrency and reduces lock overhead.
  2. It is particularly useful in applications that include a mix of :
     - Short transactions that access only a few data items
     - Long transactions that produce reports from an entire file or set of files.
  3. Deadlock is possible in this protocol, since it is in 2PL protocol.
- But there are techniques to reduce deadlock frequency to eliminate deadlock entirely.

4.4.2 Multiversion Schemes

- The concurrency control schemes discussed so far ensure serializability by either delaying an operation or aborting the transaction that issued the operation.
- A read operation may be delayed because appropriate value has not been written yet or it may be cancelled because the value that it was supposed to read has already been overwritten.
- These difficulties can be avoided if old copies of data item were presented in system. In multiversion database systems, each write (Q) operation creates a new version of Q. When a read (Q) operation is issued, the system selects one of the versions of Q to be read.
- Concurrency control scheme ensures that selection of version to be read is done and in such a manner that ensures serializability. Following are the two schemes to ensure serializability in multiversion database systems.

4.4.3 Multiversion Time Stamp Ordering

- In this scheme with each transaction a unique static timestamp denoted by TS (T_i) is associated. With each data item Q, a sequence of versions <$Q_1, Q_2, ... Q_m$> is associated.
- Each version Q_k contains three fields :
  1. **Content :** The value of version Q_k.
  2. **R-Timestamp (Q_k) :** The largest timestamp of any transaction that successfully read version Q_k.
  3. **W-Timestamp (Q_k) :** The timestamp of transaction that created version Q_k.

- A new version Q_k of data item Q is created by a transaction by issuing write (Q) operation.
    - The content field holds the value written by T_i.
    - The w-timestamp and R-Timestamp are initialized to TS (T_i).
    - The R-Timestamp is updated wherever a transaction T_j reads the contents of Q_k and R-Timestamp (Q_k) < TS (T_j).
- Multiversion Timestamp scheme operates as follows :
  Suppose that transaction T_i issues a read (Q) or write (Q) operation.
  Let Q_k denote the version of Q whose write timestamp is the largest write timestamp less than or equal to TS (T_i).
    1. If transaction T_i issues a read (Q), then the value returned is the content of version Q_k.
    2. If transaction T_i issues a write (Q), and if TS (T_i) < R - Timestamp (Q_k), then transaction T_i is rolled back. Otherwise if TS (T_i) = W-Timestamp (Q_k), the contents of Q_k are overwritten, otherwise a new version of Q is created.

  Rule 1 : It is transaction reads the most latest version that comes before it in time.

  Rule 2 : It is if T_i attempts to write a version that some other transaction would have read then we cannot allow that write to succeed. Versions of Q that are no longer needed are removed based on the following rule :
- Suppose that there are two versions Q_k and Q_j of a data item and that both versions have a W-Timestamp less than the timestamp of the oldest transaction T_i in the system. Then the older of the two versions Q_k and Q_j will not be used again and can be deleted.
- **Advantages and Disadvantages :**
    1. In multiversion timestamp ordering scheme, a read request never fails and is never made to wait.
    2. Reading of a data item requires updating of R-timestamp field, resulting in two potential disk accesses.
    3. Conflicts between transactions are handled through rollbacks, rather than through waits.

4.4.4 Multiversion Two-Phase Locking

- Multiversion two-phase locking scheme combines the advantages of multiversion concurrency control with two phase locking.
- This protocol differentiates between read-only transactions and update transactions. Update transactions perform rigorous two-phase locking i.e. they keep all locks upto the end of the transaction.
- Thus, they can be serialized according to their commit order. Each data item has a single timestamp. The timestamp in this case is not a real clock based timestamp. But rather it is counter, which is called ts-counter. It is incremented during commit processing.

- Read-only transactions follow the multiversion timestamp ordering scheme. Timestamp is assigned to read-only transactions by reading the current value of ts-counter before they start execution.
- Thus, when a read-only transaction issues a read (Q) request, the value read is the content of the version whose timestamp is the largest timestamp less than or equal to TS.

1. **Update transactions :**
   (i) When an update transaction reads an item, it gets a shared lock on the item, and reads the latest version of that item.
   (ii) When an update transaction wants to write a item, it first gets exclusive lock on the item and then creates a new version of the data item. The timestamp of the new version is initialized set to a value ∞, which value is greater than that of any possible time stamp.
   (iii) When update transaction T_i completes its actions, it carries out commit processing :
   - First T_i sets the timestamp on every version it has created to 1 more the value of ts-counter; then T_i increments ts-counter by 1. Single update transaction is allowed to perform commit processing at a time.

2. **Read-only transactions :**
   (i) Read-only transactions that start after T_i increments ts-counter, can see the values updated by T_i.
   (ii) Read-only transactions that start before T_i increments ts-counter, can see the values before updated by T_i.

- Versions are deleted in a manner similar to that of multiversion timestamp ordering.

4.4.5 Optimistic Technique

- Optimistic techniques are based on the assumption that conflict is rare and that is more efficient to allow transactions to proceed without imposing delays to ensure serializability.
- When a transaction wishes to commit a check is performed to determine whether conflict has occurred. If there has been a conflict the transaction must be rolled back and restarted.
- There are two or three phases of an optimistic concurrency control protocol, depending on whether it is a read only or an update transaction :

1. **Read Phase :** This extends from the start of the transaction until immediately before the commit. The transaction reads the values of all data items it needs from the database and stores them in local variables. Updates are applied to a local copy of data, not to the database itself.

2. **Validation Phase :** This follows the read phase. Checks are performed to ensure that the serializability is not violated if the transaction updates are applied to the database.

- For a read only transaction this consists of checking that the data values read are still current values for the corresponding data item. If no interference occurred then the transaction is committed otherwise it is aborted.
- For a transaction that updates, validation consists of determining whether the current transaction leaves the database in a consistent state, with serializability maintained. If not then the transaction is aborted and restarted.

3. **Write Phase :** This follows the successful validation phase for update transaction. During this phase, the updates made to the local copy are applied to the database.

- The validation phase examines the reads and writes of transactions that may cause interference. Each transaction T is assigned a timestamp at the start of its execution, start(t), one at the start of the validation phase validation(t), and one at its finish time finish(t).
- To pass the validation test, one of the following must be true :
    1. All transactions S with earlier timestamps must have finished before transaction T started; that is finish(S)<start(T).
    2. If transaction T starts before an earlier one S finishes :
        (i) The set of data items written by the earlier transaction are not the ones read by the current transaction.
        (ii) The earlier transaction completes its write phase before the current transaction enters its validation phase, that is start(T)<finish(TS)< validation(T)

4.5 DEADLOCK HANDLING   (Oct. 09, 10; April 10, 11)

- A system is in deadlock state if there exists a set of transactions such that every transaction in the set is waiting for another transaction in the set.
- If $\{T_0, T_1, ..., T_n\}$ is the set of transactions such that T_0 is waiting for a data item that is held by T_1 and T_1 is waiting for a data item that is held by T_2 ... and T_{n-1} is waiting for a data item that is held by T_n.
- T_n is waiting for a data item that is held by T_0. Hence, none of the transactions can make progress in such situation. That is the system is in deadlock state.
- There are three methods for dealing with deadlock problems :
    1. Deadlock prevention.
    2. Time-out based schemes.
    3. Deadlock detection and deadlock recovery.

4.5.1 Deadlock Prevention   (Oct. 09, 11, 13; April 10, 12)

- There are two approaches to deadlock prevention.
    1. It ensures that cyclic waits can be avoided by ordering the requests for locks or requiring all locks to be acquired together.

2. It performs transaction rollbacks instead of waiting for a lock, whenever the wait could potentially result in a deadlock.
- Following are the schemes under first approach. Lock all the data items before a transaction begins its execution. But there are two main disadvantages of using this protocol.
    1. It is often hard to predict, before the transaction, what data items need to be locked.
    2. Data item utilization may be very low, since many of the data items may be locked but unused for a long time.
- Another scheme is to impose a partial ordering of all data items, and transaction can lock the data items only in that order. Using tree protocol, this scheme can be implemented.
- Following are the schemes for second approach. The second approach uses preemption and transaction rollbacks.
- When a transaction T_2 requests a lock that is held by a transaction T_1, the lock granted to T_1, may be preempted by rolling back of T_1 and granting of lock to T_2.
- To control the preemption, we assign a unique timestamp to each transaction. These timestamps will be used to decide whether the transaction should wait or rollback. Locking is used for concurrency control. If a transaction is rolledback, it retains the old timestamp when restarted.
- Two different deadlock prevention schemes using timestamps under the second approach are :

1. **Wait-Die :** Scheme is based on non-preemptive technique. When a transaction T_i requests a lock on a data item currently held by T_j, T_i is allowed to wait only if it has a timestamp smaller than that of T_j. Otherwise T_i is rolled back (die).

    Example : $TS(T_i) = 5$
    $TS(T_j) = 10$
    $TS(T_k) = 15$

    If T_i requests a lock on a data item held by T_j then T_i will wait since $TS(T_i) < TS(T_j)$. If T_k requests a lock on a data item held by T_j, then T_k will be rolled back since $TS(T_k) > TS(T_j)$.

2. **Wound-wait :** This scheme is based on preemptive technique. When a transaction T_i requests a lock on a data item, currently held by T_j, T_i is allowed to wait only if it has a timestamp larger than that of T_j. Otherwise T_j is rolled back (T_j is wounded by T_i).

    Example : Consider the timestamps given in previous example for T_i, T_j and T_k transactions.

    If T_i requests a lock on data item held by T_j, then T_j will be rolled back.
    $$TS(T_i) < TS(T_j)$$

If T_k requests a lock on a data item held by T_j, then T_k will wait since,

$$TS(T_k) > TS(T_j)$$

- Comparison of wait-die and wound-wait schemes :
  1. Both the wait-die and wound-wait schemes avoid starvation.
  2. In wait-die scheme, an older transaction must wait for younger one to release the data item. Whereas in wound-wait scheme the older transaction never waits for a younger transaction.
  3. Number of rollbacks in wait-wound scheme are fewer as compared to wait-die scheme.
  4. Major problem in both the schemes is unnecessary rollbacks.

Time out Based Schemes

- In this approach deadlock handling is based on lock time-outs. A transaction that has requested a lock waits for at most a specified amount of time. If the lock has not been granted within that time, the transaction is said to time out and it rolls back itself and restarts.
- If there was a deadlock, one or more transactions involved in deadlock will time-out and rollback allowing others to complete their execution.

Advantages and Disadvantages :
1. It is easy to implement.
2. It works well if transactions are short and if long waits are likely to be due to deadlocks.
3. It is difficult to decide how long a transaction must wait before time-out.
   Very long wait results in unnecessary delays once a deadlock has occurred.
   Very short wait results in transaction rollbacks even when there is no deadlock, leading to wasted resources.
4. Starvation is the possibility with this scheme.

4.5.2 Deadlock Detection   (April 11, 14)

- This is one method for dealing with deadlock. It allows the system to enter a deadlock state, and then try to recover using deadlock detection and dead-lock recovery scheme.
- If the probability that system enters deadlock state is relatively low, this method is efficient.
- An algorithm that examines the state of the system is executed periodically to determine whether a deadlock has occurred.
- If it has occurred then the system must attempt to recover from the deadlock.
- Following are the requirements for deadlock detection and recovery :
  1. Keep information about the current allocation of data items to transactions, as well as any outstanding data item requests.

2. Provide an algorithm that uses this information to find out whether the system has entered a deadlock state.
3. Recover from the deadlock when detection algorithm finds out that a deadlock exists.

- Deadlocks can be detected using a directed graph called wait for graph.
- The wait for graph consists of a pair G = (V, E) where V is a set of vertices and E is a set of edges. The set of vertices consists of all transactions in the system. Each element in the set E of edges is an ordered pair $T_i \rightarrow T_j$.
- A directed edge $T_i \rightarrow T_j$ in graph imply that T_i is waiting for transaction T_j to release the data item.
- The edge $T_i \rightarrow T_j$ is removed when T_j is no longer holding a data item needed by transaction T_i.
- A deadlock exist in the system if the wait for graph for that system contain a cycle (or loop).
- Consider the wait graph given in Fig. 4.3.

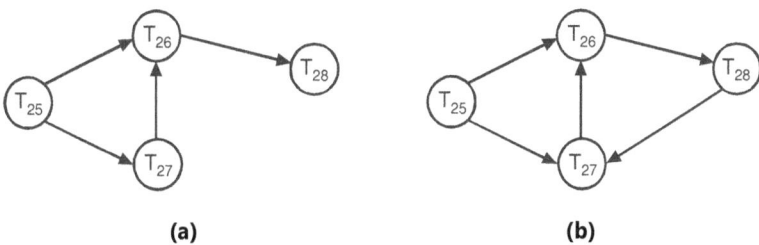

Fig. 4.3 : Wait Graph

Transaction T_{25} is waiting for T_{26} and T_{27}.

Transaction T_{26} is waiting for T_{28}.

Transaction T_{27} is waiting for T_{26}.

- The graph contains no cycle. Hence, the system is not in deadlock state.

But now consider the Fig. 4.3 (b). It contains a loop,

$$T_{26} \rightarrow T_{28} \rightarrow T_{27} \rightarrow T_{26}$$

- Hence, the system is in deadlock state. In this way using this algorithm deadlocks can be detected. Depending on the frequency of deadlock occurrence, the deadlock detection algorithm should be executed.

4.5.3 Deadlock Recovery (Oct. 10, 12)

- The most common solution to recover from deadlock is to rollback one or more transactions to break the deadlock.
- A transaction can be recovered using following three actions.

1. **Selection of victim :** Determine which transaction to rollback. Those transactions that will incur the minimum cost will be rolled back. The cost of rollback can be decided by following factors.
    (i) How long the transaction has computed and how much longer the transaction will compute before it completes the assigned task ?
    (ii) How many data items it has used ?
    (iii) How many more data items it needs to complete ?
    (iv) How many transactions will be involved in the rollback ?
2. **Rollback :** One method to rollback a transaction is to abort transaction and restart it. The other more effective method is to rollback the transaction only as far as necessary to break the deadlock. But this require additional information about all the running transactions. **(Oct. 11)**
3. **Starvation :** It may happen that the same transaction is always selected as victim. This results in starvation. The most common solution is to include the number of rollbacks in the cost factor.

Practice Questions

1. What is meant by concurrency control ?
2. Explain two-phase lock protocol with example.
3. Explain timestamp-based and lock-based protocols.
4. When do deadlocks happen, how to prevent them, and how to recover if deadlock takes place ?
5. State the rules for a timestamp based concurrency control protocol and demonstrate its working.
6. Briefly define any one locking protocol.
7. How to detect a deadlock ?
8. Describe procedure for deadlock recovery.
9. What do you mean by deadlock handling ?
10. What is a lock ?
11. Describe Thomas write rule in detail.
12. What is timestamp ?
13. Explain validation based protocols.
14. Briefly define any one timestamp protocol in detail.
15. Discuss the problems with concurrency. Describe any two methods based on locks to control concurrency.
16. What measures are required for recovery of a database using log based recovery methods ?
17. Explain two phase locking protocol.

University Question & Answers

October 2009

1. Define LOCK. List different types of LOCK. **[2 M]**
Ans. Please refer to Section 4.2.1.

2. Define deadlock. **[2 M]**
Ans. Please refer to Section 4.5.

3. Explain deadlock prevention methods **[4 M]**
Ans. Please refer to Section 4.5.1.

4. Define the following terms. **[4 M]**
   (i) Upgrading and down grading.
   (ii) Growing phase
   (iii) Shrinking phase
   (iv) Lock point

Ans. Please refer to Section 4.2.3.

5. The following is a list of events in an interleaved execution if set of transaction T0, T1, T2 with two phase locking protocol :

Time	Transaction	Code
t1	T0	Lock (A, X)
t2	T1	Lock (B, S)
t3	T2	Lock (A, S)
t4	T0	Lock (C, X)
t5	T1	Lock (D, X)
t6	T0	Lock (D, S)
t7	T1	Lock (C, S)
t8	T2	Lock (B, S)

Construct a wait for graph according to above request. Is there deadlock at any instance? Justify.

6. Following is the list of events in an interleaved execution if set T1, T2, T3 and T4 have 2PL (two phase lock). Is there a deadlock ? If yes, which transaction are involved in deadlock.

Time	Transaction	Code
t1	T1	Lock (A, X)
t2	T2	Lock (B, S)
t3	T3	Lock (A, S)
t4	T4	Lock (B, S)
t5	T1	Lock (B, X)
t6	T2	Lock (C, X)
t7	T3	Lock (D, S)
t8	T4	Lock (D, X)

April 2010

1. Define LOCK. List different types of LOCKS. [4 M]
Ans. Please refer to Section 4.2.1.
2. Define Growing phase. [2 M]
Ans. Please refer to Section 4.2.3.
3. Define starvation. [2 M]
Ans. Please refer to Section 4.2.1.3.
4. What is deadlock? How to prevent deadlock. [4 M]
Ans. Please refer to Sections 4.5 and 4.5.1.
5. Following is the list of events in an interleaved execution of set T1, T2, T3 and T4, assuming 2PL (two phase lock). Is there a deadlock ? If yes, which transactions are involved in deadlock :

Time	Transaction	Code
t1	T1	Lock (A, X)
t2	T2	Lock (C, S)
t3	T3	Lock (A, S)
t4	T4	Lock (C, S)
t5	T1	Lock (B, X)
t6	T2	Lock (C, X)
t7	T3	Lock (D, X)
t8	T4	Lock (D, S)

6. The following is the list of events in an interleaved execution of set of transaction T0, T1, T2 with two phase locking protocol :

Time	Transaction	Code
t1	T0	Lock (A, X)
t2	T1	Lock (B, S)
t3	T0	Lock (A, S)
t4	T1	Lock (C, X)
t5	T2	Lock (D, X)
t6	T0	Lock (D, S)
t7	T1	Lock (C, S)
t8	T2	Lock (B, S)

Construct a wait for graph according to above request. Is there deadlock at any instance ? Justify.

October 2010

1. What is precedence graph? Explain it's use. [2 M]
Ans. Please refer to Section 4.2.1.

2. What is deadlock? Explain how deadlock is recovered. [4 M]
Ans. Please refer to Section 4.5. and 4.5.2.

3. Following is the list of events in an interleaved execution of sets T_1, T_2, T_3 and T_4 assuming 2PL (two phase lock). Is there a deadlock ? If yes, which transactions are involved in deadlock ?

Time	Transaction	Code
t_1	T_1	Lock (A, X)
t_2	T_2	Lock (B, S)
t_3	T_3	Lock (A, S)
t_4	T_4	Lock (B, S)
t_5	T_1	Lock (B, X)
t_6	T_2	Lock (C, X)
t_7	T_3	Lock (D, S)
t_8	T_4	Lock (D, X)

4. Following is the list of events in an interleaved execution of sets T_1, T_2, T_3 and T_4 assuming 2PL (two phase lock). Is there a deadlock ? If yes, which transactions are involved in deadlock?

Time	Transaction	Code
t_1	T_1	Lock (A, S)
t_2	T_2	Lock (B, X)
t_3	T_3	Lock (C, X)
t_4	T_4	Lock (A, S)
t_5	T_1	Lock (C, X)
t_6	T_2	Lock (A, S)
t_7	T_3	Lock (D, X)
t_8	T_4	Lock (B, S)

April 2011

1. What is Deadlock ? Explain how deadlock is detected. [4 M]
Ans. Please refer to Sections 4.5 and 4.5.2.

2. Define growing phase and shrinking here phase. [2 M]
Ans. Please refer to Section 4.2.3. points (1 and 2).

3. Define the following terms :
   (i) Upgrading, (ii) Downgrading, (iii) Lock point, (iv) Starvation. [4 M]
Ans. Please refer to sections 4.2.3.1 and 4.2.1.3.

4. Following is the list of events in an interleaved execution if set T_1, T_2, T_3 and T_4, assuming 2PL. Is there a deadlock ? If yes, which transactions are involved in deadlcok ?

Time	Transaction	Code
t_1	T_1	Lock (A, X)
t_2	T_2	Lock (C, S)
t_3	T_3	Lock (A, S)
t_4	T_4	Lock (C, S)
t_5	T_1	Lock (B, X)
t_6	T_2	Lock (C, X)
t_7	T_3	Lock (D, X)
t_8	T_4	Lock (D, S)

5. Following is the list of events in an interleaved execution if set T_1, T_2, T_3, T_4 assuming 2PL. Is there a deadlock ? If yes, which transactions are involved in deadlock

Time	Transaction	Code
t_1	T_1	Lock (A, X)
t_2	T_2	Lock (B, X)
t_3	T_3	Lock (C, S)
t_4	T_4	Lock (A, S)
t_5	T_1	Lock (C, X)
t_6	T_2	Lock (A, S)
t_7	T_3	Lock (D, X)
t_8	T_4	Lock (B, S)

October 2011

1. Explain strict two phase locking protocol with example. **[4 M]**
Ans. Please refer to Section 4.2.3.

2. Define lock. List different types of lock. **[2 M]**
Ans. Please refer to Section 4.2.1.

3. Define rollback. **[2 M]**
Ans. Please refer to Section 4.5.3 point (2).

4. Explain deadlock prevention methods. **[4 M]**
Ans. Please refer to Section 4.5.1.

5. The following is a list of events in an interleaved execution if set of transaction T_0, T_1, T_2 with two phase locking protocol:

Time	Transaction	Code
t_1	T_0	Lock (A, X)
t_2	T_1	Lock (B, X)
t_3	T_2	Lock (C, S)
t_4	T_0	Lock (A, S)
t_5	T_1	Lock (C, X)
t_6	T_0	Lock (A, S)
t_7	T_1	Lock (D, X)
t_8	T_2	Lock (B, S)

Construct a wait for graph according to above request. Is there deadlock at any instance? Justify.

April 2012

1. Define lock. List different types of locks. [2 M]
Ans. Please refer to Section 4.2.1.

2. Explain two phase locking protocol with example. [4 M]
Ans. Please refer to Section 4.2.3.

3. What is deadlock? How to prevent deadlock. [4 M]
Ans. Please refer to Sections 4.5 and 4.5.1.

4. Following is the list of events in an interleaved execution if set T_1, T_2, T_3 and T_4 assuming 2PL. Is there a Deadlock?

Time	Transaction	Code
t_1	T_1	Lock (A, X)
t_2	T_2	Lock (B, S)
t_3	T_3	Lock (A, S)
t_4	T_4	Lock (B, S)
t_5	T_1	Lock (B, X)
t_6	T_2	Lock (C, X)
t_7	T_3	Lock (D, S)
t_8	T_4	Lock (D, X)

5. Following is the list of events in an interleaved execution if set T_1, T_2, T_3 and T_4 assuming 2PL. Is there a Deadlock? If yes, which transactions are involved in Deadlock?

Time	Transaction	Code
t_1	T_1	Lock (A, X)
t_2	T_2	Lock (B, X)
t_3	T_3	Lock (C, S)
t_4	T_4	Lock (A, S)
t_5	T_1	Lock (C, X)
t_6	T_2	Lock (A, S)
t_7	T_3	Lock (D, X)
t_8	T_4	Lock (B, S)

October 2012

1. Define growing phase and shrinking phase. [2 M]
Ans. Please refer to Section 4.2.3. points (1 and 2)

2. What is deadlock? How deal-lock is recovered? [4 M]
Ans. Please refer to Sections 4.5 and 4.5.3.

3. Explain validation-based protocol. [4 M]
Ans. Please refer to Section 4.4.

4. Following is a list of events in an interleaved execution of set T_1, T_2, T_3 and T_4 assuming 2PL (Two Phase Lock). Is there a Deadlock? If yes, which transactions are involved in Deadlock?

Time	Transaction	Code
t_1	T_1	Lock (B, S)
t_2	T_2	Lock (A, X)
t_3	T_3	Lock (C, S)
t_4	T_4	Lock (B, S)
t_5	T_1	Lock (A, S)
t_6	T_2	Lock (C, X)
t_7	T_3	Lock (A, S)
t_8	T_4	Lock (C, X)

5. Following is the list of events in an interleaved execution of set T_1, T_2, and T_3 assuming 2PL (Two Phase Lock). Is there a Deadlock? If yes, which transactions are involved in Deadlock?

Time	Transaction	Code
t_1	T_1	Lock (A, S)
t_2	T_2	Lock (B, S)
t_3	T_3	Lock (C, S)
t_4	T_1	Lock (C, S)
t_5	T_2	Lock (D, X)
t_6	T_1	Lock (D, S)
t_7	T_2	Lock (A, X)
t_8	T_3	Lock (B, X)

April 2013

1. What is deadlock? [2 M]
Ans. Please refer to Section 4.2.1.
2. Define starvation. [2 M]
Ans. Please refer to Section 4.2.1.3.
3. What is Two phase locking protocol? Explain its two phases. [4 M]
Ans. Please refer to Sections 4.2.3.

4. Following is the list of events in an interleaved execution of set T_1, T_2, T_3 and T_4 assuming 2PL (Two Phase Lock). Is there a Deadlock? If yes, which transactions are involved in Deadlock?

Time	Transaction	Code
t_1	T_1	Lock (A, X)
t_2	T_2	Lock (B, X)
t_3	T_3	Lock (A, S)
t_4	T_4	Lock (B, S)
t_5	T_1	Lock (B, S)
t_6	T_3	Lock (D, X)
t_7	T_2	Lock (D, S)
t_8	T_4	Lock (C, X)

5. Following is the list of events in an interleaved execution of set T_1, T_2, T_3 and T_4 assuming 2PL. Is there a Deadlock? If yes, which transactions are involved in Deadlock?

Time	Transaction	Code
t_1	T_1	Lock (A, X)
t_2	T_2	Lock (B, S)
t_3	T_3	Lock (A, S)
t_4	T_4	Lock (B, S)
t_5	T_1	Lock (B, X)
t_6	T_2	Lock (C, S)
t_7	T_3	Lock (D, S)
t_8	T_4	Lock (D, X)

October 2013

1. Define i) Upgrading ii) Down grading. [2 M]
Ans. Please refer to Section 4.2.3.1.

2. What is starvation? How to avoid starvation of transaction by granting lock? [4 M]
Ans. Please refer to Section 4.2.1.3.

3. Explain deadlock prevention method. [4 M]
Ans. Please refer to Section 4.5.1.

4. Following is the list of events in an interleaved execution if set T_1, T_2, T_3 and T_4 assuming 2PL. Is there a Deadlock? If yes, which transactions are involved in deadlock?

Time	Transaction	Code
t_1	T_1	Lock (A, X)
t_2	T_2	Lock (C, S)
t_3	T_3	Lock (A, S)
t_4	T_4	Lock (C, S)
t_5	T_1	Lock (B, X)
t_6	T_2	Lock (C, X)
t_7	T_3	Lock (D, X)
t_8	T_4	Lock (D, S)

5. Following is the list of events in an interleaved execution if set T_1, T_2, T_3 and T_4 assuming 2PL. Is there a Deadlock? If yes, which transactions are involved in Deadlock?

Time	Transaction	Code
t_1	T_1	Lock (A, X)
t_2	T_2	Lock (B, S)
t_3	T_3	Lock (A, S)
t_4	T_4	Lock (B, S)
t_5	T_1	Lock (B, X)
t_6	T_2	Lock (C, X)
t_7	T_3	Lock (D, S)
t_8	T_4	Lock (D, X)

April 2014

1. Define i) growing phase ii) Shrinking phase [2 M]

Ans. Please refer to Section 4.2.3 Point (1 and 2).

2. What is deadlock? Explain deadlock detection method. [2 M]

Ans. Please refer to Section 4.5.2.

3. Define lock? Explain different types of lock. [4 M]

Ans. Please refer to Sections 4.2.1.

4. Following is the list of events in an interleaved execution of set T_1, T_2, T_3 and T_4 assuming 2PL (Two Phase Lock). Is there a Deadlock? If yes, which transactions are involved in Deadlock?

Time	Transaction	Code
t_1	T_1	Lock (A, X)
t_2	T_2	Lock (B, S)
t_3	T_3	Lock (A, S)
t_4	T_1	Lock (C, X)
t_5	T_2	Lock (D, X)
t_6	T_1	Lock (D, S)
t_7	T_2	Lock (C, S)

5. Following is the list of events in an interleaved execution of set T_1, T_2, T_3 and T_4 assuming 2PL. Is there a Deadlock? If yes, which transactions are involved in Deadlock?

Time	Transaction	Code
t_1	T_1	Lock (A, X)
t_2	T_2	Lock (B, X)
t_3	T_3	Lock (A, S)
t_4	T_4	Lock (B, S)
t_5	T_1	Lock (B, S)
t_6	T_2	Lock (D, S)
t_7	T_3	Lock (C, S)
t_8	T_4	Lock (C, X)

Chapter 5...

Recovery System

Contents ...

This Chapter Gives Recovery System Concepts Such As:

5.1 INTRODUCTION
    5.1.1 Failures and Errors
    5.1.2 Recovery System

5.2 FAILURE CLASSIFICATION
    5.2.1 Transaction Failure
    5.2.2 System Crash
    5.2.3 Disk Failure

5.3 STORAGE STRUCTURES
    5.3.1 Storage Types
    5.3.2 Data Access

5.4 RECOVERY & ATOMICITY
    5.4.1 Log Based Recovery
    5.4.2 Deferred Database Modification
    5.4.3 Immediate Database Modification
    5.4.4 Checkpoints

5.5 RECOVERY WITH CONCURRENT TRANSACTION
    5.5.1 Transaction Rollback
    5.5.2 Restart Recovery

5.6 REMOTE BACKUP SYSTEM
    5.6.1 Guidelines for Backup Strategy
    5.6.2 Remote Backup Systems

5.1 INTRODUCTION

- A computer system is subject to failure of various types. If some failure occurs during the execution of a transaction, it results in inconsistent database.

- Recovery system is an integral part of database system. It is responsible for restoration of the database to a consistent state that existed before the occurrence of the failure.

5.1.1 Failures and Errors (Oct. 11)

- A system is reliable if it works as per its specifications and produces correct set of output values for a given set of input values.
- The failure of a system occurs when the system does not work according to its specifications and fails to deliver the service for which it was intended.
- An error in the system occurs when a component of a system assumes a state that is not desirable. A fault is detected either when an error is propagated from one component to another or the failure of the component is observed.
- There are two types of failures:
  1. Failure that results in loss of information.
  2. Failure that does not results in loss of information.

5.1.2 Recovery System

- A computer system is electrical device, and causes different failures.
- There are various causes of failure, including power failure, software error, disk crash, a fire in the machine room etc. In each of these failure cases, information may be lost.
- Therefore, the database system must take actions in advance to ensure the durability and atomicity properties of transaction.
- An integral part of a database is a recovery scheme i.e. responsible for the restoration of the database to a consistent state that existed before the occurrence of the failure.

5.2 FAILURE CLASSIFICATION (Oct. 09, 10, 11, 12; April 13)

- There are different types of failure that may occur in a system, each of failure needs to be dealt with in a different manner.
- The simplest type of failure to deal with is one that does not result in the loss of information or data in the system.
- The failures that are more difficult or critical to deal with are those, that result in loss of information or data (content).

5.2.1 Transaction Failure

- There are two types of errors that may lead to transaction failure. They are:
  (i) **System Error:** The system has entered an undesirable state as a result of which a transaction cannot continue with its normal execution. The transaction, however, can be re-executed at a later time.
  (ii) **Logical Error:** The transaction can no longer continue with its normal execution, owing the some internal condition, such as data not found, bad input or resource limit overflow exceeded.

5.2.2 System Crash

- There is a hardware bug or error in the database software or the operating system that causes the loss of the content of volatile storage and leads transaction processing to a halt.
- The content of non-volatile storage remains undamaged and is not corrupted.

5.2.3 Disk Failure

- In disk failures disk block losses its content as a result of either a head failure during a data transfer operation. Copies of the data on other disks on tertiary media, such as tapes, disks etc., are used to recover from the failure.
- To find out how the system should recover from failure or crash, we need to recognize the failure modes of those devices used for storing data.
- Next, we must consider how these failure modes or crash modes affect the contents or information of the database. We can then use algorithms to ensure database consistency and transaction atomicity despite failures.
- These algorithms are known as recovery algorithms, although they have two parts, one is actions taken following a failure to recover the database contents or data to a state that ensures database transaction atomicity, durability and consistency and other actions taken during normal transaction processing to ensure that enough information exists to allow recovery from failures.

> **Note:**
> 1. Transaction failure does not result in loss of information.
> 2. System crash loses the contents of volatile storage but it does not corrupt the non-volatile storage contents. (This is known as fail-stop assumption).
> 3. Disk failure loses the data stored on disk. Copies of data on other disks or archival backups on tertiary media such as tapes are used to recover from the failure.

5.3 STORAGE STRUCTURE

- How to ensure the durability and atomicity properties of a transaction, for a better understanding we must know concepts of storage media and their access methods.

Stable – Storage Implementation

- For implementation of stable storage, we need to replicate the needed information/data in several non-volatile storage media with independent failure modes and to update the information in a controlled manner to make sure that failure during data transfer does not damage the needed information or data.

- Block transfer between disk storage and memory can result in:
    1. **Successful completion:** The transferred information/data arrived safely at its destination/output.
    2. **Total failure:** The failure occurred sufficiently early during the transfer process that the destination (output) block remains undamaged.
    3. **Partial failure:** A failure occurred in the middle of transfer process and the destination (output) block has incorrect information.
- If a data-transfer failure occurs, the system detects it and invokes a recovery procedure to restore the block to a consistant state.
- For this process, the system must keep up two physical blocks for each logical database block. In the case of mirrored disks, both blocks are at the same location.
- In the case of remote backup, one of the blocks is local, while the other block is at a remote site.
- An output operation is executed as follows:
    1. Write the information onto the first physical block.
    2. When the first write completes successfully, write the same information on to the second physical block.
    3. The output is completed only after the second write completes successfully.
- During the recovery process, each pair of physical blocks is examined or noted.
- If both blocks are the same and no discoverable error exists, then no further actions are necessary.
- If one block contains a discoverable error, then we replace its content or data with the content or data of the second block.
- If both blocks contains no discoverable error, but they differ in content or data, then we replace the content or data of the first block with the value of the second block.
- This type of recovery procedure makes sure that a write to stable storage either succeeds completely or results in no change.
- The protocols for writing out a block to a remote site are similar to the protocols for writing blocks to a mirrored disk system.
- User can extend this procedure easily to allow the use of a randomly large number of copies of each block of stable storage.
- Although a large number of copies reduce the probability of a failure to even lower than with two copies, it is usually reasonable to simulate stable storage with only two copies.

5.3.1 Storage Types   (April 10, 11, 13, 14; Oct. 12, 13)

- There are different types of storage media according to their relative capacity; speed and resilience to failure which distinguish them.

    1. **Stable storage:** Information in stable storage is never lost. The stable storage is theoretically impossible to obtain, it can be closely approximated by techniques that make data loss extremely unlikely.

    2. **Non-volatile storage:** Information stored in this storage survives system crashes or failures. Example, disk and magnetic tapes. Tapes are used for archival storage whereas disks are used for on-line storage. Both however, are subject to failure which may result in loss of information. Today non-volatile storage is slower than volatile storage by several orders of magnitude. In database systems, disks are used for most non-volatile storage. Other non-volatile media are normally used only for backup data.

    3. **Volatile storage:** Information stored in this storage does not usually survive system crashes or failures. Example, main memory access. Access to this storage is extremely fast, both because of the speed of the memory access itself and because it is possible to access any data item in volatile storage directly.

5.3.2 Data Access

- The database system is stored permanently on non-volatile storage. They are partitioned into fixed-length storage units called blocks.
- Blocks are the units of data transfer to and from disk and contain several data items. We shall assume that no data item spans more than two blocks.
- Transactions input information/data from the disk to main memory and then output the information back onto the disk.
- The I/O operations are done in block units. The blocks stored on the disk are referred to as *physical blocks*; the blocks stored temporarily in main memory are referred to as buffer blocks.
- The area of memory where blocks stored temporarily is called the *disk buffer*.
- Block movements between main memory and disk are initiated through two operations. They are:

    1. **Input (B):** It transfers the physical block B to main memory.

    2. **Output (B):** It transfers the buffer block B to the disk and replaces the appropriate physical block there.

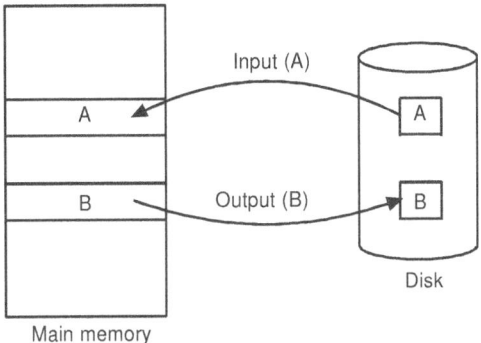

Fig. 5.1: Block storage operations

- Each T_i transaction has a private work area in which copies of all the data items updated and accessed by T_i are kept. This work area to T_i is created when the transaction is initiated; it is removed when the transaction either aborts or commits.

- Each data item x kept in the work area of T_i transaction is denoted by x_i. T_i transaction interacts with the database system by transferring data to and from its work area to the system buffer. We transfer data using two operations one is read (X) and other is write (X).

1. **Read (X):** It assigns the value of data item X to the local variable x_i. This read (X) is executed as follows:

    (a) If the block B_x on which X stored is not in main memory, then issue input (B_x).

    (b) Assign to x_i the value of X from the buffer block.

2. **Write (X):** It assigns the value of local variable x_i to data item X in the buffer block. Write (X) operation is executed as follows:

    (a) If block B_x on which X stored is not in main memory, then issue input (B_x).

    (b) Assign the value of x_i to X in buffer B_X.

- A buffer block is finally written out to the disk either because the buffer manager needs the memory space for other processes or the database system wishes to reflect the change to B on the disk.

- When a transaction needs to access a data item X for the first time, it must execute read (X) operation. All updates to X are then performed on X_i. After the transaction accesses X for the final time, it must execute write (X) to reflect the change to X in the database it self.

- The output (B_X) operation for the B_X buffer block on which X is stored does not need to take effect immediately after write (X) is executed, since the block B_X may contain other data items that are still being accessed.

5.4 RECOVERY AND ATOMICITY

- Consider banking system and transaction T_i that transfers ₹ 1000 from account X to account Y, with initial values of X and Y being ₹ 5000 and ₹ 10000 respectively.

- Suppose that a system crash has occurred during the execution of transaction T_i, after output (Y_A) has taken place, but before output (Y_B) was executed, where Y_A and Y_B denote the buffer blocks on which X and Y are stored. Since, the memory contents were lost, user do not know the fate of the transaction; thus, we could use one of two possible recovery procedures.

- **Re-execute T_i:** This procedure will result in the value of X becoming ₹ 3000, rather than ₹ 4000. Thus, the system enters an inconsistent state.

- **Do not re-execute T_i:** The current system state is value of ₹ 4000 and ₹ 10000 for X and Y respectively. Thus, the system enters an inconsistent state.

- To achieve our goal of atomicity, we must first output information describing the updations of stable storage, without modifying the database itself. As we shall see, this procedure will allow us to output all the updations made by a committed transaction, despite failures.

Recovery Algorithms

- The algorithms which ensure database consistency and transaction atomicity despite failures are known as recovery algorithms and they have two parts:

   1. Actions taken during normal transaction processing to make sure that enough information exists to allow recovery from failures.

   2. Actions taken following a failure to recover the database contents to a state that ensures database consistency, transaction atomicity and durability.

Recoverable Schedule

- A recoverable schedule is defined as a schedule where for each pair of transactions T_i and T_j such that T_j reads a data item previously written by T_i, the commit operation of T_i appears before the commit operation of T_j.

- If some failure occurs during the execution of a transaction and database is in some inconsistent state following are two simple recovery procedures.

    1. **Re-execute:** Execute the same transaction. But because of previous incomplete execution of that transaction, the database is already in an inconsistent state. Hence it results in an inconsistent database.

    2. **Do not re-execute:** If we do not re-execute the transaction, the database will remain in same inconsistent state. The atomicity property (perform either all or no database modifications) is not achieved. To achieve the goal of atomicity, information about

modifications must be stored to stable storage before modifying the database. In this procedure, if some failures occur and modification information is complete then system can reexecute the transaction. Otherwise system will not reexecute the transaction.

- Following are the two schemes to achieve the recovery from transaction failures:
  1. Log-based recovery
  2. Shadow paging.

5.4.1 Log-based Recovery (April 10, 14; Oct. 12)

- It assumes that transactions are executed serially, i.e. only one transaction is active at a time. It uses a structure called log to store the database modifications.
- There are two techniques for using log to achieve the recovery and ensure atomicity in case of failures.
  1. Deferred database modification
  2. Immediate database modification.
- **Deferred modification technique** ensures transaction atomicity by recording all database modifications in the log, but deferring (delaying) the execution of all write operations of transaction until the transaction partially commits.
- The **immediate update technique** allows database modifications to be output to the database while the transaction is still in the active state. Data modifications written by active transactions are called uncommitted modifications. If a failure occurs during execution, the system must use the old value field of log records.

$$\boxed{\text{Log}}$$

- Log is a structure used to store the database modifications.
- It is a sequence of log records and maintains a record of all the update activities in the database.
- There are several types of log records to record significant events during transaction processing.

  1. **Start of transaction:**
     denoted as; $<T_i \text{ start}>$

  2. **Update log:**
     It describes a single database write and it is denoted as:
     $$<T_i, X_j, V_1, V_2>$$
     where, $T_i \rightarrow$ Transaction identifier
     $X_j \rightarrow$ Data item identifier
     $V_1 \rightarrow$ Old value of X_j
     $V_2 \rightarrow$ New value of X_j after the write operation.

3. **Transaction commits:**

   denoted as: $<T_i\ commit>$

4. **Transaction abort:**

   denoted as: $<T_i\ abort>$

   Log is stored in stable storage.

5.4.2 Deferred Database Modification (Oct. 10, 11; April 13)

- Deferred database modification technique stores the database modifications in the log.
- Execution of write operation is done when transaction is in partially committed state.
- According to transaction state diagram, a transaction is in partially committed state when transaction completes executing the last instruction. Execution of transaction T_i proceed as follows:
- Before T_i starts its execution record, a record $<T_i\ start>$ is written to log. Write (X) operation of T_i results in writing a new record $<T_i, X, V_2>$ to the log.

   Note: It doesn't write V_1 - old value of X.

- When T_i partially commits a record $<T_i\ commit>$ is written to log. When T_i partially commits, the records associated with it in the log are used in executing the deferred writes. If system crashes before the transaction completes its execution or if the transaction aborts, then the information on the log is ignored.
- If some failure occurs while updating the database using log records, the log record is written in some stable storage, hence, the transaction can resume its database modification. Using log the system can handle any failure that results in loss of information on volatile storage. The recovery scheme uses the following recovery procedure.
- **redo (T_i):** It sets the value of all data items updated by transaction T_i to the new values. The set of data items and their respective new values can be found in the log. The redo operation must be idempotent i.e. executing it several times must be equivalent to executing it once.
- A transaction **can** execute redo (T_i) if the log contains both the record $<T_i\ start>$ and the record $<T_i\ commit>$.
- **Example:** Consider the transaction T_i, it transfers ₹ 50 from account A to account B. Original values of account A and B are ₹ 1000 and ₹ 2000 respectively. This transaction is defined as:

```
T_0  : read (A);
       A:= A - 50;
       write (A);
```

```
            read (B);
            B:= B + 50;
            write (B).
```
- Consider the second transaction T_1 that withdraws ₹ 100 from account C. This transaction is defined as: (Assume that original values of account C is 700)
```
      T₁  : read (C);
            C:= C - 100;
            write (C).
```
- These two transactions are executed serially $<T_0, T_1>$.

- The log containing relevant information on these two transactions is given below:
```
            <T₀ start>
            <T₀, A, 950>
            <T₀, B, 2050>
            <T₀ commit>
            <T₁ start>
            <T₁, C, 600>
            <T₁ commit>
```

- It shows the log that result from the complete execution of T_0 and T_1.

- The actual output can take place to database system in various orders. One such order is given below:

```
            log                         Database
            <T₀ start>
            <T₀, A, 950>
            <T₀, B, 2050>
            <T₀ commit>
                                        A = 900
                                        B = 2050
            <T₁ start>
            <T₁, C, 600>
            <T₁ commit>                 C = 600
```

- If system crashes before the completion of transactions:

   Case 1: Crash occurs just after the log record for write (B) operation.

   Log contents after the crash are:
```
            <T₀ start>
            <T₀, A, 950>
            <T₀, B, 2050>
```

<T_0 commit> is not written; hence no redo operation is possible.

The values of account remain unchanged i.e. account balance of A is ₹ 1000 and B is ₹ 2000.

Case 2: Crash occurs just after log record for write (C) operation.

The log contents after the crash are:

        <T_0 start>
        <T_0, A, 950>
        <T_0, B, 2050>
        <T_0 commit>
        <T_1, start>
        <T_1, C, 600>

When the system comes back it finds <T_0 start> and <T_0 commit>. But there is no <T_1 commit> for <T_0 start>. Hence, system can execute redo (T_0) but not redo <T_1>. Hence, the value of account C remains unchanged.

Case 3: Crash occurs just after the log record <T_1 commit>.

The log contents after the crash are:

        <T_0 start>
        <T_0, A, 950>
        <T_0, B, 2050>
        <T_0, commit>
        <T_1 start>
        <T, C, 600>
        <T_1 commit>

- When system comes back it can execute both redo (T_0) and redo (T_1) operations.
- For each commit record, the redo (T_i) operation is performed. redo (T_i) writes the values to the database independent of the values currently in the database. Hence, the redo (T_i) is idempotent.

5.4.3 Immediate Database Modification   (April 10, 12; Oct. 13)

- It allows the database modifications to be output to the database while transaction is still in active state.
- Database modifications written by active transactions are called **uncommitted modifications**.
- Execution of transaction proceeds as follows:
    1. Before T_i starts its execution, the record <T_i start> is written to the log.

2. Before executing any write (X) i.e. before modifying the database for write operation, it writes an update record <T_i, X, V_1, V_2> to the log.

3. When T_i partially commits, the record <T_i commit> is written to log.

- As an illustration consider the same example of bank accounts and transactions T_0 and T_1. Transactions T_0 and T_1 are executed serially.

- The log corresponding to this execution is given below:

   <T_0 start>
   <T_0, A, 1000, 950>
   <T_0, B, 2000, 2050>
   <T_0 commit>
   <T_1 start>
   <T_1, C, 700, 600>
   <T_1 commit>

- The order in which output took place to both database system and log as a result of execution of T_0 and T_1 is:

Data	Database
<T_0 start>	
<T_0, A, 1000, 950>	
<T_0, B, 2000, 2050>	
<T_0 commit> →	A = 950
	B = 2050
<T_1 start>	
<T_1, C, 700, 600> →	C = 600
<T_1 commit >	

- Using the log, the system can handle any failure. Two recovery procedures are there to recover:

  1. **Undo (T_i):** It restores the value of all data items updated by transaction T_i to the old values. **(Oct. 11, 13; April 13)**

  2. **Redo (T_i):** It sets the value of all data items updated by transaction T_i to the new values. **(Oct. 11, 13; April 13)**

- The undo (T_i) and redo (T_i) operations must be idempotent.

- Depending on the log, the recovery scheme determine which transaction need to be redone and which need to be undone.

- If the log record contains the record <T_i start> but does not contain the record <T_i commit> then T_i needs to be undone.

- If the log record contains both the records <T_i start> and <T_i commit> then T_i needs to be redone i.e. If a failure occurs before <T_i commit> the database modifications are rolled back by undo (T_i) operation. If a failure occurs after <T_i commit> then the transaction is reexecuted by redo (T_i) operation.

- Consider the following conditions of failure for transactions T_0 and T_1.

    Case 1: Failure occurs just after the log record for write (B) operation.
    Log contents and database are:

    ```
    Log                              Database
    <T0   start>
    <T0   A, 1000, 950>
    <T0,  B, 2000, 2050>
                                     A = 950
                                     B = 2050
    ```

- Log contains <T_0 start> but does not contain <T_0, commit>. Hence T_0 must be undone hence undo (T_0) is executed, the values of account A and B are restored to 1000 and 2000 respectively.

    Case 2: If some failure occurs just after log record for write (C) T_i has written to log.
    The log and database contents are:

    ```
    Log                              Database
    <T0   start>
    <T0   A, 1000, 950>
    <T0   B, 2000, 2050>
               database ─────────►   A = 950
                                     B = 2050
    <T0   commit>
    <T1   start>
    <T1   C, 700, 600>               C = 600
               database ─────────►   A = 950
    ```

- Log contains <T_0 start> and <T_0 commit>. Hence, the redo (T_0) is executed and values of accounts A and B are restored to the same (or new values) 950 and 2050 respectively. But the log doesn't contain <T_1 commit> for <T_1 start>. Hence, the value of account C to restored to old value by undo (T_1) operation. Hence value of C is ₹ 700.

    Case 3: If system crashes just after the log record <T_1 commit> has been written to log.

- The log and database contents are:

    ```
    Log                              Database
    <T0   start>
    <T0   A, 1000, 950>
    ```

```
        <T₀  B, 2000, 2050>
                    database ----> A = 950
                                   B = 2050
        <T₀  commit >
        <T₁  start >
        <T₁  C, 700, 600 >
                    database ----> C = 600
        <T₁  commit>
```

- Log contains <T₀ start>, <T₀ commit> and <T₁ start> <T₁ commit> operations. Hence recovery system executes redo (T₀) and redo (T₁) operations. The values of accounts A, B and C are ₹ 950, ₹ 2050 and ₹ 600 respectively.

5.4.4 Checkpoints   (Oct. 12, 13, April 14)

- When a system failure occurs, some transactions need to be redone and some need to be undone. Log record can find out this. But for that we need to search the entire log.
- There are two major difficulties with this approach.
   1. The search process is time consuming.
   2. Most of the transactions that will be redone have already written their updates into the database. Hence, it is better to avoid such redo operations.
- To reduce these types of overhead, checkpoints are introduced. During the execution the system keeps up log using immediate database modification technique or deferred database modification technique.
- In addition, the system periodically performs checkpoints, which require following sequence of operations:
   1. Output onto stable storage all log records currently stored in main memory.
   2. Output to the disk all modified buffer blocks.
   3. Output onto stable storage a log record <checkpoint>.
- Transactions are not allowed to perform any update actions, such as writing to a buffer block or writing a log record, while a checkpoint is in progress.
- The presence of <checkpoint> record in log allows the system to streamline its recovery procedure. After the failure has occurred, the recovery system examines the log to determine the most recent transaction T_i that started execution before the most recent checkpoint took place.
- It can find such a transaction by searching the log backward from the end of the log until it finds the first <checkpoint> record, then it continues the search backward until it finds the next <T_i start> record. This record identifies a transaction T_i.

- Once, the transaction is identified, redo or undo operation can be applied to transaction T_i and all the transactions T executing after T_i. The earlier part of transaction can be ignored.
- The recovery can be done by using immediate database modification or deferred database modification technique.

Shadow Paging

- Shadow paging is an alternative to log-based crash recovery technique. This is one possible form of indirect page allocation.
- **Paging:** Paging scheme is used in operating system for virtual memory management. The memory that is addressed by a process is called **virtual memory**.
- It is divided into pages, that are assumed to be of a certain size (1 KB or 4 KB). The virtual or logical pages are mapped onto physical memory blocks of same size. The mapping of pages is provided by means of table called as page table.

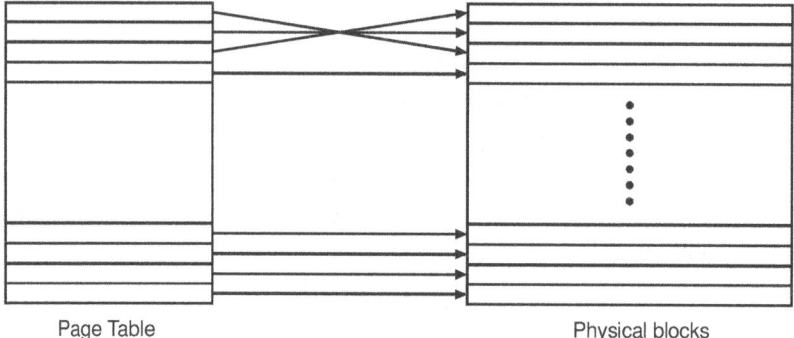

Page Table   Physical blocks

Fig. 5.2: Page Table

- Page table contains one entry for each logical page of the processes virtual address space. Page table is shown in the Fig. 5.2.
- In the shadow page scheme, the database is considered to be made up of logical units of storage called pages. The pages are mapped into physical blocks of storage by means of a page table with one entry for each logical page. This entry contains the block number of physical storage where this page is stored. The shadow page scheme uses two page tables.
    1. Current page table.
    2. Shadow page table.
- Transaction addresses the database using current page table. It may change the current page table entries. The changes are made whenever the transaction executes write operation.

- To modify a page, it copies that page to new blocks of physical storage. The page table entry corresponding to that page is made to point to new block of storage.
- The shadow page table is the original page table. It contains the entries that existed prior to the start of transaction. It remains unaltered by the transaction and it is used for undoing the transaction.
- Now, let us see how the transaction accesses data.
- The transaction uses the current page table to access the database blocks. The shadow paging scheme handles a write operation of transaction as follows:
    1. A free block of non-volatile storage is located from the pool of free blocks accessible by the database system.
    2. The block to be modified is copied onto this block.
    3. The original entry in the current page table is changed to point to this new block.
    4. The updates are propagated to the block pointed to by the current page table which in this case would be newly created block.

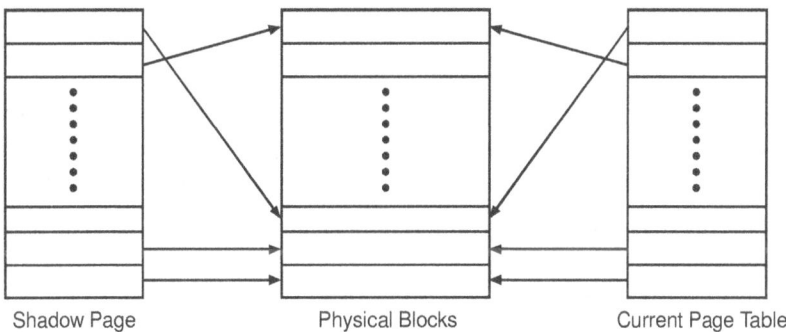

Before Starting the Transaction

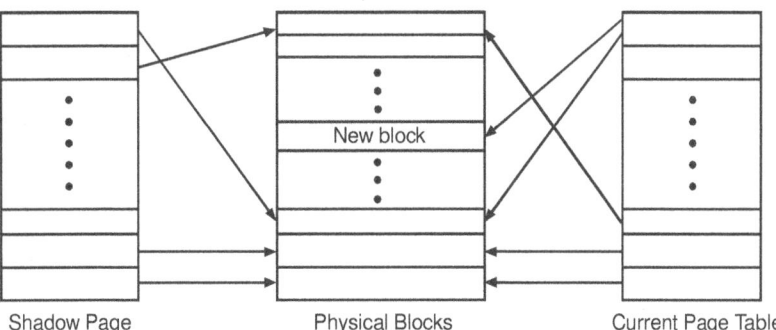

Fig. 5.3: After Executing Write Operation

- Any changes made to the database are propagated to the blocks pointed to by the current page table. Once, a transaction commits, all modifications made by the transaction and still in buffers are propagated to physical database. It causes the current page table to be written to non-volatile storage.
- In case of system crash before the transaction commits, the shadow page table and the corresponding blocks containing the old database will continue to be accessible.
- The old database is made accessible just by modifying a single pointer from shadow page table to current page table.
- Once, the transaction completes its execution successfully, the shadow block can be returned to the pool of available non-volatile storage blocks to be used for further transactions.
- Advantage of shadow paging scheme is: Recovery from system crash is relatively inexpensive and this is achieved without the overhead of logging.
- **Disadvantages of shadow paging scheme are:**

1. Over a period of time the database will be scattered over the physical memory and related records may require a very long access time.

2. When the transaction completed its execution, shadow blocks have to be returned to the pool of free blocks. If this is not done successfully, when a transaction commits, such blocks become inaccessible. This is called as **garbage collection operation**.

3. The commit of a single transaction using shadow paging requires multiple blocks to be output (the actual data blocks, the current page table, and disk address of the current page table log based schemes need to output only the log records.

5.5 RECOVERY WITH CONCURRENT TRANSACTIONS

(April 11; Oct. 11)

- Now we will discuss how user can modify and extend the log-based recovery scheme to deal with multiple concurrent transactions.
- The number of concurrent transactions, computer system has a single disk buffer and a single log. The buffer blocks are shared by all transactions.
- User allow immediate updates and the permit a buffer block to have data items updated by one or more transactions.

5.5.1 Transaction Rollback

(April 11; Oct. 11)

- User rollback a failed transaction, T_i, using the log.
- The log is scanned backward; for every log record of the form $<T_i, X_j, V_1, V_2>$ found in the log, the data item X_j is restored to its old value V_1.

- The scanning of the log terminates when the log record <T_i, start> is found.
- Scanning the log backward is more important, since a transaction may have updated a data item more than once. Consider the pair of log records as given below:

    <T_i A, 10, 20>

    <T_i A, 20, 30>

- They represent a modification of data item A by T_i, followed by another modification of A by T_i. Scanning the log backward set A correctly to 10.
- If the log were scanned in the forward direction, A would be set to 20, which value is incorrect.
- If strict two-phase locking is used for concurrency control, locks held by a transaction T may be released only after the transaction has been rolled back as described.
- Once, transaction T has updated a data item, no other transaction could have updated the same data item, due to the concurrency-control requirements.

Interaction with Concurrency Control

- The recovery scheme depends on the concurrency-control technique that is used. To roll back a failed transaction, user must undo the updates or modification performed by the transaction.
- Suppose that a transaction T_0 has to be rolled back and a data item Q that was updated by T_0 has to be restored to its old value. Using the log-based schemes for recovery, we restore the value using the undo information in a log record.
- Suppose a second transaction T_1 has performed yet another update on Q before T_0 is rolled back. Then, the updation performed by T_1 will be lost if T_0 is rolled back.
- If a transaction T has updated a data item Q, no other transaction may update the same data item until T has committed. We can ensure this requirement easily by using strict two-phase locking.

5.5.2 Restart Recovery   (Oct. 10)

1. **Undo List:** When the system recovers from a crash or failure, it constructs two lists: Which consists of transactions to be undone.
2. **Redo-list:** Which consists of transactions to be redone?
- These two lists are constructed on recovery, initially, they are both empty. User scan the log backward, examining each record, until the first <checkpoint> record is found:
   o For each record found of the form <T_i commit>, he/she adds T_i to redo-list.
   o For each record found of the form <T_i start>. If T_i is not in redo-list, then we add T_i to undo-list.

- When all the appropriate log records have been examined, user check the list L in the checkpoint record. For each transaction T_i in L, if T_i is not in *redo-list* then we add T_i to the *undo-list*.
- All transactions on the *undo-list* have been undone, those transactions on the *redo-list* are redone. It is important, to process the log forward. When the recovery process has completed, transaction-processing resumes.
- It is very important to undo the transaction in the *undo-list* before redoing transactions in the *redo-list*, using the preceding algorithm.
- Otherwise, the following problem may occur, suppose that data item X initially has the value 20. Suppose that a transaction T_i updated data item X to 30 and aborted; transaction rollback would bring back A to the value 20.
- Suppose that another transaction T_j then updated data item X to 40 and committed, after this the system crashed. The state of the log at the time of the crash or failure is,

    $<T_i, X, 20, 30>$

    $<T_j, X, 20, 40>$

    $<T_j \text{ commit}>$

- If the redo pass is performed first, X will be set to 40; then, in the undo pass, X will be set to 20 which is wrong. The final value of 'X' should be 40, which we can ensure by performing undo before performing redo.

Buffer Management

- Now, we consider several obvious details that are essential to the implementation of a crash-recovery scheme that ensures data consistency and causes a minimal amount of overhead on interactions with the database.

Log-Record Buffering

- We discussed earlier every log record is output to stable storage at the time it is created. This assumption causes a high overhead on system execution for the following reasons.
- Typically, output to stable storage is in units of blocks. In many cases, a log record is much smaller than a block. Thus, the output of each log record translates to a much larger output at the physical level.
- Due to the use of log buffering, a log record may be stored in only main memory for considerable time before it is output to stable storage.
- Since, such log records are lost if the system crashes or fails we must impose additional requirements on the recovery techniques to ensure transaction atomicity.
    1. T_i Transaction enters that commit state after the $<T_i \text{ commit}>$ log record has been output to stable storage.

2. Before the <T_i commit> log record can be output to stable storage, all log records belonging to transaction T_i must have been output to stable storage.
3. Before a block of data in main memory can be output to the database, all log records belonging to data in that block must have been output to stable storage.

Database Buffering

- The database is stored in non-volatile storage such as disks, tape etc. and blocks of data are brought into main memory as needed.
- Since, main memory is typically much smaller than the entire database, it may be necessary to overwrite B_1 block in main memory when another B_2 block needs to be brought into memory.
- If B_1 block has been changed, B_1 must be output before the input of B_2. This storage hierarchy is the standard operating system concept of virtual memory.
- The rules for the output of log records limit the freedom of the system to output blocks of data. If the input of B_2 block cause B_1 block to be chosen for output, all log records be bringing to data in B_1 block must be output to stable storage before B_1 block is output. Thus, the sequence of actions by the system would be as given below:
  - Output log records to stable storage until all log records belonging to B_1 block have been output.
  - Output B_1 block to disk.
  - Input B_2 block from disk to main memory.
- It is very important that no writes to the block B_1 be in progress while the preceding sequence of actions is carried out. User can ensure that there are no writes in progress by using a special means of locking.

5.6 REMOTE BACKUP SYSTEMS (Oct. 09)

- Backup is a database utility. It creates backup copy of database by storing entire database on storage devices.
- Normally magnetic tapes are used to store data. It is associated with restore utility.
- There are two basic approaches of database backup, are listed below:
  1. Hot Database Backup, and
  2. Cold Database Backup.
1. **Cold Backup (Offline Database Backup):** One of the simplest and easy methods of backup is called cold backup (also known as offline backup). In this technique the database is totally shut down and the physical files it is associated with are copied by means of normal operating system utilities, because the database is not in operation, the changes are not made to the physical files and hence the backup of the files is a consistent backup.

2. **Hot Backup (Online Database Backup):** Hot backup enables user to take backup of a database that has not been shutdown but is still active and used by the users. This is the most tedious backup but also the most flexible one.

- In general, backup and recovery refers to the various strategies and procedures involved in protecting your database against data loss and reconstructing the database after any kind of data loss.
- **A backup** is a copy of data from your database that can be used to reconstruct that data. Backups can be divided into physical backups and logical backups.
- **Physical backups** are backups of the physical files used in storing and recovering your database, such as datafiles, control files, and archived redo logs. Ultimately, every physical backup is a copy of files storing database information to some other location, whether on disk or some offline storage such as tape.
- **Logical backups** contain logical data (For example, tables or stored procedures) exported from a database with an Oracle export utility and stored in a binary file, for later re-importing into a database using the corresponding Oracle import utility.
- **A whole database backup** is a backup of every datafile in the database, plus the control file.
- **A tablespace backup** is a backup of the data files that constitute the tablespace. For example, if tablespace users contain datafiles 2, 3, and 4, then a backup of tablespace users backs up these three datafiles.
- A datafile backup is a backup of a single datafile.

5.6.1 Guidelines for Backup Strategy

1. Plan backup and recovery strategies before the database creation.
2. Decide whether to run in ARCHIVELOG mode or not is acceptable to loose any data ?
3. Maintain multiple Control Files and Redo Log Files to protect against the possible failure of the redo logs.
4. Test the backup and recovery strategies in the test environment before moving to the production environment.
5. Appropriately backup the database before and after modifying the database structures or making any structural changes to the data files or redo logs.
6. Backup extensively used tablespaces more often.
7. The more recent the backup the smaller is the number of redo logs to apply. Determine the amount of time to keep older backups.
8. Consider keeping two backups previous to the current backup.
9. Keep the backups in a place remote from the computer room.
10. Export database data for added protection and flexibility.

5.6.2 Remote Backup Systems (Oct. 09,12; April 11)

- Fig. 5.4 shows typical remote backup system. It provides high availability by allowing transaction processing to continue even if the primary site is destroyed.

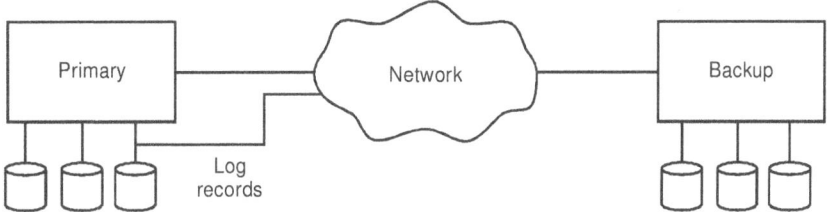

Fig. 5.4: Remote backup system

- Several key points for designing remote backup system are listed below:

    1. **Time to recover:** For reducing delay in takeover, backup site periodically processes the redo log records, performs a checkpoint. It can then delete earlier parts of the log.

    2. **Detection of failure:** The backup site must detect when primary site has failed. To distinguish primary site failure from link failure maintain several communication links or paths between the primary and the remote backup.

    3. **Alternative to remote backup:** In distributed database with replicated data remote backup is cheaper and faster, but less tolerant to failure.

    4. **Transfer of control:** To take over control backup site first perform recovery using its copy of the database. When the backup site takes over processing it becomes the new primary. To transfer control back to old primary when it recovers, old primary must receive redo logs from the old backup.

5.6.2.1 Advantages

- Remote backup has advantages over traditional backup methods:

    1. Remote backup maintains data offsite. Perhaps the most important aspect of backing up is that backups are stored in a different location from the original data. Traditional backup requires manually taking the backup media offsite.

    2. Remote backup does not require user intervention. The user does not have to change tapes, label CDs or perform other manual steps.

    3. Most remote backup services will use a 128 - 448 bit encryption to send data over unsecured links (i.e. internet).

    4. Unlimited data retentions.

5. A few remote backup services can reduce backup by only transmitting changed binary data bits.
6. Some remote backup services will work continuously, backing up files as they are changed.
7. Data storage abroad could be an advantage too.
8. Most remote backup services will maintain a list of versions of your files.

5.6.2.2 Disadvantages

- Remote backup has some disadvantages:
    1. Some backup service providers have no guarantee that stored data will be kept private - for example, from employees. As such, most recommend that files be encrypted before storing or automating this process.
    2. Depending on the available network bandwidth, the restoration of data can be slow. Because data is stored offsite, the data must be recovered either via the Internet or via tape or disk shipped from the online backup service provider.
    3. Bandwidth issues - backing up a whole hard drive can take a lot of bandwidth, and many broadband customers are limited to 5GB-50GB a month. This would make backing up large amount of data (e.g. 200GB) every day impossible.
    4. If encryption password is lost, no more data recovery will be possible. However with managed services this should not be a problem.
    5. It is possible that a remote backup service provider could go out of business or be purchased, which may affect the accessibility of one's data or the cost to continue using the service.

Practice Questions

1. What is mean by recovery?
2. What is Remote backup system?
3. Enlist various types of failures.
4. Explain the term Log-based recovery.
5. With neat diagram explain shadow paging.
6. What is recovery?
7. Explain the following terms:
    (a) Recovery and Atomicity
    (b) Failure with non-volatile storage.
8. Describe the term: Remote backup system.
9. Explain storage structure in detail.

10. Write short notes on:
    (a) Checkpoint
    (b) Buffer management.
11. Enlist various types of errors.
12. What do you meant by recovery system?
13. Enlist various storage types. Explain one of them in detail.

University Question & Answers

October 2009

1. Draw and explain architecture of remote back-up system. [4 M]
Ans. Please refer to Section 5.6.2.

2. Explain different types of failures. [2 M]
Ans. Please refer to Section 5.2.

3. Following are the log entries at the time of system crash:
   [Start – transaction, T1]
   [Write – item, T1, D, 20]
   [Commit, T1]
   [Checkpoint]
   [Start – transaction T4]
   [Write – item, T4, B, 15]
   [Commit, T4]
   [Start – transaction, T2]
   [Write – item, T2, B, 25]
   [Start – transaction, T3]
   [Write – item, T3, a, 30]
   [Write – item, T2, D, 25] ← System Crash

   If deferred update technique is used, what will be the recovery procedure?

April 2010

1. Explain log-based recovery. [4 M]
Ans. Please refer to Section 5.4.1.

2. Explain immediate data base modification with example. [4 M]
Ans. Please refer to Section 5.4.3.

3. Following are the log entries at the time of system crash?
   [start – transaction, T1]
   [read – item, T1, D]
   [Write – item, T1, D, 20]
   [commit, T1]

[checkpoint]
[start – transaction T2]
[read – item, T2, B]
[write – item, T2, B, 12]
[start – transaction, T3]
[Write – item, T3, A, 20] ← System Crash

If deferred update with checkpoint is used, what will be the recovery procedure?

October 2010

1. Define commit, Rollback. [2 M]
Ans. Please refer to Sections 5.5.1 and 5.5.2.

2. Explain different types of failure. [4 M]
Ans. Please refer to Section 5.2.

3. Explain recovery using deferred update method. [4 M]
Ans. Please refer to Section 5.4.2.

4. Following are log entries at the time of system crash:
   [Start - transaction T_1]
   [Read - item T_2, A]
   [Read - item T_1, D]
   [Write - item T_1, D, 20]
   [Commit T_1]
   [Check Point]
   [Start - transaction T_2]
   [Read - item T_2, B]
   [Write - item T_2, B, 12]
   [Start - transaction T_3]
   [Write - item T_3, C, 30]
   [Read - item T_3, D]
   [Write item T_3, D, 25] ← System Crash

   If deferred update with check point is used, what will be recovery procedure?

April 2011

1. Explain concurrent execution of transaction with example and advantages of concurrent execution. [4 M]
Ans. Please refer to Section 5.5.

2. Write a short note on storage type. [4 M]
Ans. Please refer to Section 5.3.1.

3. Following are the log entries at the time of system crash:

   [Start–transaction, T_1]

   [write_item T_1, D, 20]

   [commit T_1]

   [check point]

   [start_transaction T_4]

   [write_item T_4, B, 15]

   [commit T_4]

   [start_transaction T_2]

   [write_item T_2, B, 25]

   [start_transaction T_3]

   [write_item T_3, A, 30] ← System Crash

   If deferred update technique is used, what will be the recovery procedure?

October 2011

1. Explain deferred database modification with examples. [4 M]
Ans. Please refer to Section 5.4.2.

2. Define redo and undo operations. [2 M]
Ans. Please refer to Section 5.4.3.

3. Write note on storage type. [4 M]
Ans. Please refer to Section 5.3.1.

4. Explain different types of failures. [4 M]
Ans. Please refer to Section 5.2.

5. What are the various problems that occur in concurrent transaction. [4 M]
Ans. Please refer to Section 5.5.

6. Following are the log entries at the time of system crash ?

   [start_tansaction, T_1]

   [wtire_item T_1, D, 20]

   [commit T_1]

   [check point]

   [start_transaction T_4]

   [write_item T_4, B, 15]

   [commit T_4]

   [start_transaction T2]

[write_item T₂, b, 25]
[start_transaction T3]
[write_item T₃, A, 30]
[write_item, T₂, D, 25] ← System Crash

If deferred update technique is used, what will be the recovery procedure?

April 2012

1. Define the following terms: [2 M]
   (i) Commit, (ii) Rollback
Ans. Please refer to Section 5.5.1.

2. Explain different types of storage types. [4 M]
Ans. Please refer to Section 5.3.1.

3. Explain immediate database modification with example. [4 M]
Ans. Please refer to Section 5.4.3.

4. Following are the log entries at the time of system crash :
   [start_tansaction, T₁]
   [read_item T₁, D]
   [write_item T₁, D, B]
   [commit T₁]
   [check point]
   [start_transaction, T₂]
   [read_item T₂, B]
   [write_item T₂, B, 10]
   [start_transaction T₃]
   [write_item T₃, A, 20]
   [write_item T₂, D]
   [write_item, T₁, D, 20] ← System Crash

   If immediate update with checkpoint technique is used what will be the recovery procedure.

October 2012

1. List different type of storage. [2 M]
Ans. Please refer to Section 5.3.1.

2. What is checkpoint? [2 M]
Ans. Please refer to Section 5.4.4.

3. Explain log-based recovery. [4 M]
Ans. Please refer to Section 5.4.1.

4. Explain various type of failure that may occur in system. [4 M]
Ans. Please refer to Section 5.2.

5. Explain remote backup system with proper diagram. [4 M]
Ans. Please refer to Section 5.6.2.

6. Following are the log entries at the time of system crash

   [start transaction, T_1]

   [write_item, T_1, A, 30]

   [commit T_1]

   [checkpoint]

   [start_ transaction, T_3]

   [write_item T_3, C, 50]

   [commit T_3]

   [start_ transaction, T_2]

   [write—item T_2, C, 40]

   [start_ transaction, T_4]

   [write—item T_4, B, 30]

   [write — item T_2, D, 60] <--- System Crash

   If deferred update technique with checkpoint is used, what will be the recovery procedure?

April 2013

1. Define i) Comment ii) Rollback [2 M]
Ans. Please refer to Section 5.2.

2. List the type of failure. [2 M]
Ans. Please refer to Section 5.3.1.

3. Write a note on storage types. [4 M]
Ans. Please refer to Section 5.3.1.

4. Explain deferred database modification.
Ans. Please refer to Section 5.4.2.

5. Define:

   (i) Physical block, (ii) Buffer block, (iii) Redo, (iv) Undo.

Ans. Please refer to Section 5.4.3.

6. Following are the log entries at the time of system crash

   [start — transaction, T_1]

   [write_item, T_1, A, 10]

   [commit T_1]

   [start_transaction, T_3]

   [write_item T_3, B, 15]

   [checkpoint]

   [commit T_3]

   [start — transaction, T_2]

   [write_item T_2, B, 20]

   [start_transaction, T_4]

   [write_item, T_4, D, 25]

   [write_item T_2, C, 30] <— System Crash

   If deferred update technique with checkpoint is used, what will be the recovery procedure?

October 2013

1. Which are different types of storage? [2 M]

Ans. Please refer to Section 5.3.1.

2. Define : (i) Redo, (ii) Undo. [2 M]

Ans. Please refer to Section 5.4.3.

3. Explain immediate database modification technique with example. [4 M]

Ans. Please refer to Section 5.4.3.

4. Write note on checkpoint. [4 M]

Ans. Please refer to Section 5.4.4.

5. Following are the log entries at the time of system crash.

   [Start- Transaction, T_1)

   [Write - item, T_1, B, 100]

   [Commit, T_1]

   [Checkpoint]

   [Start- Transaction, T_2]

   [Write- item, T_2, D, 100]

   [Commit, T_2]

[Start- Transaction, T$_3$]

[Write - item, T$_3$, D, 200]

[Write - item, T$_3$, B, 200] <-- system crash.

If deferred update technique with checkpoint is used, What will be the recovery procedure?

April 2014

1. Define: i) Checkpoint, ii) Log [2 M]
Ans. Please refer to Section 5.4.4.

2. Write a note on storage types. [4 M]
Ans. Please refer to Section 5.3.1.

3. Explain log based recovery. [4 M]
Ans. Please refer to Section 5.4.1.

4. Following are the loj:efitri6s at.. the time .of system crash:

   [Start-Transaction, T$_1$]

   [Write-item, T$_1$, A, 10, 100]

   [Commit, T$_1$]

   [Checkpoint]

   [Start-Transaction, T$_2$]

   [Write-item, T$_2$, B, 20, 200]

   [Commit, T$_2$]

   [Start-Transaction, T$_3$]

   [Write-item, T$_3$, C, 30, 300] <---- System crash

   If immediate update technique with checkpoint is used, what will be the recovery procedure?

❖❖❖

UNIVERSITY QUESTION PAPER
April 2015

Time : 3 Hrs.   Maximum Marks : 80

Instructions : (1) All Questions are Compulsory.
(2) Figures to the right indicate full marks.

1. **Attempt all :**   16
   a) What is RDBMS? List any two features of RDBMS.
   Ans. : Please refer 1.1.3.
   b) What is difference between % type and %row type?
   Ans. : Please refer 2.3.1.
   c) What is serializability? List the types of serializability.
   Ans. : Please refer 3.6.
   d) Define: i) commit
   Ans. : Please refer 3.4.
       ii) rollback
   Ans. : Please refer 4.5.3.
   e) What is checkpoint?
   Ans. : Please refer 5.4.4.
   f) Define Recoverable schedule.
   Ans. : Please refer 5.4.
   g) Define i) upgrading ii) downgrading
   Ans. : Please refer 4.2.3.1 for both (i) and (ii).
   h) Write syntax of for loop in PL/SQL with example.
   Ans. : Please refer 2.3.3.2.

2. **Attempt any four :**   16
   a) Explain any two popular products of RDBMs.
   Ans. : Please refer 1.1.6.4.
   b) What is cursor? Explain different attributes used in it.
   Ans. : Please refer 2.7.
   c) What is transaction? Explain ACID properties of transaction.
   Ans. : Please refer 3.2, 3.3.1.
   d) What is PL/SQL? Explain block of PL/SQL.
   Ans. : Please refer 2.1.1, 2.3.
   e) What is deadlock? Explain how deadlock in recovered.
   Ans. : Please refer 4.5.

3. **Attempt any four :** 16
   a) Explain various types of failures that may occur in system.
   Ans. : Please refer 5.1.1
   b) What is trigger? Explain trigger with proper syntax and example.
   Ans. : Please refer 2.8.
   c) What are the various problems that occur in concurrent transaction?
   Ans. : Please refer 3.5.
   d) Explain Timestamp, ordering protocol.
   Ans. : Please refer 4.3.1.
   e) Explain deferred database modification technique with example.
   Ans. : Please refer 5.4.1.

4. **Attempt any four :** 16
   a) Consider the following relational database.
      Employee (empno, empname, city, deptname)
      Project (projno, proj name, status)
      Emp-proj (empno, proj no, number-of-days)
      Write a function which will return total number of employees working on any project for more than 60 days.
   Ans. :
   ```
   create or replace function f_cnt_emp return number as
     cnt number;
   begin
     select count(*) into cnt from employee_project where nod>60;
     return cnt;
   end f_cnt_emp;
   /

   Output :
   SQL> select f_cnt_emp() from dual;
   F_CNT_EMP()
   -----------
       5
   ```
   b) Consider the following relational database.
      Politician (pno, pname, description, partycode) Party (partycode, partyname)
      Write a clusor to display partywise details of politicians.
   Ans. :
   ```
   declare
     cursor pcur is select * from party;
     cursor polist(pn varchar) is select politician.* from
   ```

```
          party,politician where party.partycode=politician.partycode and
          party.partyname=pn;
          prec party%rowtype;
          polrec politician%rowtype;
begin
open pcur;
loop
    fetch pcur into prec;
    exit when pcur%notfound;
    dbms_output.put_line('Party Name : '||prec.partyname);
    open polist(prec.partyname);
    loop
      fetch polist into polrec;
      exit when polist%notfound;
      dbms_output.put_line('Name : '||polrec.pname||'   '||
                           'Description : '||'
'||polrec.desig);
    end loop;
    dbms_output.put_line('--------------------');
    close polist;
end loop;
close pcur;
end;
/

Output:
Party Name : AJP
Name : ANIL   Description :   MP
Name : RAJESH   Description :   MP
--------------------
Party Name : IP
Name : SMITA   Description :   MP
--------------------
Party Name : MJP
Name : MANDAR   Description :   MP
--------------------
Party Name : SDP
Name : MAHESH   Description :   MP
--------------------
PL/SQL procedure successfully completed.
```

c) Consider the following relational database.
   Department (deptno, deptname, location)
   Employee (empno, empname, salary, commission, designation, deptno)

Write a trigger for an employee table that restricts insertion or updation or deletion of data on 'sunday'.

Ans. :
```
create or replace trigger empl_time_trig before insert or update
or delete on empl for each row
begin
if(to_char(SYSDATE,'fmday')='sunday') then
   raise_application_error('-20010','Operation not allowed');
end if;
end empl_time_trig;
/


Output:
SQL> update empl set sal=10000 where empno=109;
update empl set sal=10000 where empno=109
          *
ERROR at line 1:
ORA-20010: Operation not allowed
ORA-06512: at "SCOTT.EMPL_TIME_TRIG", line 3
ORA-04088: error during execution of trigger
'SCOTT.EMPL_TIME_TRIG'

If the command is executed on a day other than Sunday:
SQL> update empl set sal=10000 where empno-109;
1 row updated.
```

d) Consider the following relational database
Book (bno, bname, pubname, price, dno)
Department (dno, dname)
Write a procedure which will display total expenditure on books by a given department.

Ans. :
```
create or replace procedure p_tot_exp(dpname in varchar) as
  tot number;
begin
  select sum(price) into tot from dept_info,book_info where
  dept_info.dno=book_info.dno and dname=dpname;
  dbms_output.put_line('Total Expenditure of '||dpname||
                   ' department is : '||tot);
end p_tot_exp;
/
```

```
Output:
SQL> execute p_tot_exp('COMPUTER');
Total Expenditure of COMPUTER department is : 450
PL/SQL procedure successfully completed.
```

e) Write a package which consist of one procedure and one function, consider relation student.

Student (Roll-no, stud-name, class, stud-addr, percentage) procedure of a package will display details of given student. Function of a package will count total number of students having percentage greater than 80 and class 'TYBCA!.

Ans. :

```
create or replace package stud_pack_1 as
procedure p_stud(num in number);
function f_stud_count return number;
PRAGMA RESTRICT_REFERENCES(f_stud_count, WNDS);
end stud_pack_1;
/

create or replace package body stud_pack_1 as
procedure p_stud(num in number) as
srec stud_info%rowtype;
begin
  select * into srec from stud_info where rollno=num;
  dbms_output.put_line('Name : '||srec.name||
  ' Address : '||srec.addr||' Class :'||srec.class||
  ' Percentage :'||srec.perc);
end p_stud;
function f_stud_count return number as
  cnt number;
begin
  select count(*) into cnt from stud_info where class='TYBCA'
  and perc>80;
  return cnt;
end f_stud_count;
end stud_pack_1;
/

Output:
SQL> set serveroutput on;
SQL> execute stud_pack_1.p_stud(1);
Name : ANIL Address : PUNE Class :TYBCA Percentage :77.71
PL/SQL procedure successfully completed.
```

```
SQL> select stud_pack_1.f_stud_count from dual;
F_STUD_COUNT
------------
           2
```

5. Attempt any four : 16

a) Consider the following transactions. Give two non-serial schedules that are serializable.

T_1	T_2
Read (A)	Read (A)
A=A+ 1000	A = A – 1000
Write (A)	Write (A)
Read (BC)	Read (B)
C=C-1000	B=B-1000
Write (C)	Write (B)
Read (B)	
B =B + 1000	
Write (B)	

Ans. : Following are two serializable schedules among the various concurrent (non-serial) schedules that are serializable.

(i)

T_1	T_2
Read(A)	
A=A+1000	
Write(A)	
Read(C)	
C=C-1000	
Write(C)	
	Read(A)
	A=A-1000
	Write(A)
Read(B)	
B=B+1000	
Write(B)	
	Read(B)
	B=B-1000
	Write(B)

(ii)

T_1	T_2
	Read(A)
	A=A-1000
	Write(A)
Read(A)	
A=A+1000	
Write(A)	
Read(C)	
C=C-1000	
Write(C)	
	Read(B)
	B=B-1000
	Write(B)
Read(B)	
B=B+1000	
Write(B)	

b) Consider the following transactions. Give two non-serial schedules that are serializable.

T₁	T₂	T₃
Read (A)	Read (C)	Read (B)
A=A+ 100	Read (B)	B = B + 200
Write (A)	B = B + C	Write (B)
Read (B)	Write (B)	Read (C)
B=B+ 100	Read (A)	C = C + 200
Write (B)	A = A – C	Write (C)
	Write (A)	

Ans. : Following are two serializable schedules among the various concurrent (non-serial) schedules that are serializable.

(i)

T₁	T₂	T₃
Read(A)		
A=A+100		
Write(A)		
Read(B)		
	Read(C)	
B=B+100		
Write(B)		
	Read(B)	
	B=B+C	
	Write(B)	
		Read(B)
		B=B+200
		Write(B)
	Read(A)	
	A=A-C	
	Write(A)	
		Read(C)
		C=C+200
		Write(C)

(ii)

T₁	T₂	T₃
Read(A)		
A=A+100		
Write(A)		
	Read(C)	
Read(B)		
B=B+100		
Write(B)		
	Read(B)	
	B=B+C	
	Write(B)	
		Read(B)
		B=B+200
		Write(B)
	Read(A)	
		Read(C)
	A=A-C	
	Write(A)	
		C=C+200
		Write(c)

c) Following is II list of events in an interleaved execution of set of transactions T_1, T_2, T_3 and T_4 with two phase locking protocol.

Time	Transaction	Code
t_1	T_1	Lock (B, S)
t_2	T_2	Lock (A, X)
t_3	T_3	Lock (C, S)
t_4	T_4	Lock (B, S)
t_5	T_1	Lock (A, S)
t_6	T_2	Lock (C, X)
t_7	T_3	Lock (A, X)
t_8	T_4	Lock (C, S)

Construct a wait for graph according to above request. Is there deadlock at any instance? Justify.

Ans. : As per the given list of events (from time t_1 to t_8) in the problem, the schedule can be written as follows :

T_1	T_2	T_3	T_4
S(B)			
	X(A)		
		S(C)	
			S(B)
S(A)			
	X(C)		
		X(A)	
			S(C)

Where X(A) indicates exclusive lock on object A.

The wait-for graph for the above schedule is as given below:

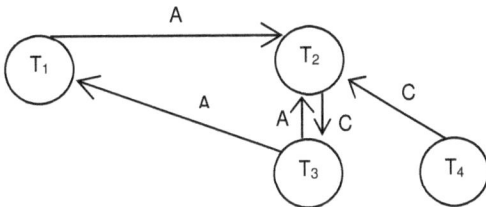

From the above wait-for graph, there is cycle. Hence there is a deadlock.

d) Following is a list of events in an interleaved execution of set of transactions T_1, T_2, T_3 and T_4 with two phase locking protocol.

Time	Transaction	Code
t_1	T_1	Lock (A, X)
t_2	T_2	Lock (B, S)
t_3	T_3	Lock (A, S)
t_4	T_4	Lock (C, S)
t_5	T_1	Lock (B, X)
t_6	T_2	Lock (C, X)
t_7	T_3	Lock (D, S)
t_8	T_4	Lock (D, X)

Construct a wait for graph according to above requests. Is there deadlock at any instance? Justify.

Ans. : As per the given list of events (from time t_1 to t_8) in the problem, the schedule can be written as follows :

T_1	T_2	T_3	T_4
X(A)			
	S(B)		
		S(A)	
			S(C)
X(B)			
	X(C)		
		S(D)	
			X(D)

Where X(A) indicates exclusive lock on object A.

The wait-for graph for the above schedule is as given below:

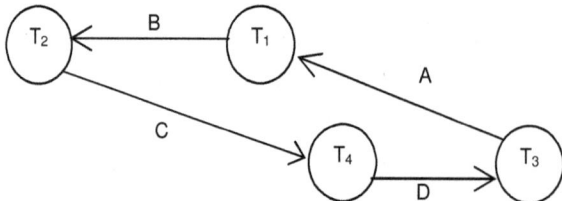

From the above wait-for graph, there is cycle. Hence there is a deadlock.

e) Following are the log entries at the time of system crash.

  [start - transaction, T_1]
  [write - item, T_1, A, 100]
  [commit . T_1]
  [start - transaction, T_3]
  [write - item, T_3, B, 200]
  [checkpoint]
  [commit, T_3]
  [start - transaction, T_2]
  [write - item, T_2, B, 300]
  [start - transaction, T_4]
  [write - item, T_4, D, 200]
  [write - item, T_2, C, 300] ← System crash

If deferred update technique with checkpoint is used, what will be the recovery procedure?

Ans. : Since transaction T_1 is committed before the checkpoint, it need not be considered. Transaction T_3 is committed after the checkpoint. Hence system can execute redo operation for T_3. Transactions T_2 and T_4 do not have commit instruction. Hence no redo for them and the values of B, C, D remain unchanged.

❖❖❖

October 2015

Time : 3 Hrs. **Maximum Marks : 80**

Instructions : (1) All Questions are Compulsory.
(2) Figures to the right indicate full marks.

1. **Attempt all of the following :** 16
    a) What is RDBMS? List any two features of RDBMS.
    Ans. : Please refer 1.1.3.
    b) What is PL/SQL ? Give advantages of PL/SQL.
    Ans. : Please refer 2.1.4.
    c) What is transaction ? State operations performed on transactions
    Ans. : Please refer 3.1 and 3.4.
    d) Define Deadlock.
    Ans. : Please refer 4.5.
    e) List the fields of update log record
    Ans. : Please refer 5.4.1.
    f) Give syntax of stored procedure in PL/SQL.
    Ans. : Please refer 2.6.
    g) Define cursor. Enlist attributes of cursor.
    Ans. : Please refer 2.6.1.
    h) Enlist the RDBMS products
    Ans. : Please refer 1.1.3.2.

2. **Attempt any four of the following :** 16
    a) Explain difference between DBMS and RDBMS.
    Ans. : Please refer 1.3.
    b) Write a note on exception handling in PL/SQL.
    Ans. : Please refer 2.4.
    c) What is Schedule ? Explain types of schedule with example.
    Ans. : Please refer 5.4.
    d) How is deadlock detected and how to recover deadlock ?
    Ans. : Please refer 4.4.2 and 4.4.3.
    e) Explain advantages and disadvantages of the remote backup system.
    Ans. : Please refer 5.6.2.

3. **Attempt any four of the following:** 16
    a) What is Trigger ? Explain types of trigger in detail.
    Ans. : Please refer 2.8.1.

b) Explain various states of transaction in detail.
Ans. : Please refer 3.4.
c) What is validation based protocol ? Explain in detail the conditions for the validation test.
Ans. : Please refer 4.4.
d) Write a note on Transaction Rollback.
Ans. : Please refer 5.5.1.
e) Explain immediate database modification with example.
Ans. : Please refer 5.4.3.

4. Attempt any four of the following : 16

a) Consider the following relational database.
Student (sno, sname, city, class)
Subject (subno, subname)
Stud-sub (sno, subno) '
Write a function which will take class as a parameter and will return total number of students.

Ans. :
```
create or replace function f_classtot(cname in varchar) return number as
   cnt number;
begin
   select count(*) into cnt from stud where class=cname;
   return cnt;
end f_classtot;
/
Output:
SQL> select f_classtot('SYBCA') from dual;
F_CLASSTOT('SYBCA')
-------------------
        3
```

b) Consider the following relational database
Publisher (pno, pname, pcity)
Book (bno, bname, price, pno)
Write a trigger which will restrict insertion or updation on price, price should not be less than zero.

Ans. :
```
create or replace trigger book_price_trig before insert or update
on book for each row
```

```
declare
  bn number;
begin
if inserting then
  if :new.price<0 then
    raise_application_error('-20010','Cannot insert ! Price should
    be above 0');
  end if;
end if;
if updating then
  if :new.price<0 then
    raise_application_error('-20010','Cannot update ! Price should
    be above 0');
  end if;
end if;
end book_price_trig;
/

Output:
SQL> insert into book values(5,'ALGORITHMS','ABC',-500);
insert into book values(5,'ALGORITHMS','ABC',-500)
            *
ERROR at line 1:
ORA-20010: Cannot insert ! Price should be above 0
ORA-06512: at "SCOTT.BOOK_PRICE_TRIG", line 6
ORA-04088: error during execution of trigger
'SCOTT.BOOK_PRICE_TRIG'

SQL> insert into book values(5,'ALGORITHMS','ABC',500);
1 row created.

SQL> update book set price=price-1000 where bno=1;
update book set price=price-1000 where bno=1
        *
ERROR at line 1:
ORA-20010: Cannot update ! Price should be above 0
ORA-06512: at "SCOTT.BOOK_PRICE_TRIG", line 11
ORA-04088: error during execution of trigger
'SCOTT.BOOK_PRICE_TRIG'
```

c) Consider the following relational database
Wholesaler (wno, wname, city)
Product (pno, pname, price)
Wp(wno, pno)
Write a cursor to display wholesalerwise product details.

Ans. :
```
declare
  cursor wcur is select * from wholesaler;
  cursor plist(wn varchar) is select wp.pno,pname,price from
  wholesaler,product,wp where wholesaler.wno=wp.wno and
  product.pno=wp.pno and wname=wn;
  wrec wholesaler%rowtype;
  pn wp.pno%type;
  pnm product.pname%type;
  prc product.price%type;
begin
open wcur;
loop
  fetch wcur into wrec;
  exit when wcur%notfound;
  dbms_output.put_line('Wholesaler Name : '||wrec.wname);
  open plist(wrec.wname);
  loop
    fetch plist into pn,pnm,prc;
    exit when plist%notfound;
    dbms_output.put_line('Product No. : '||pn||' '||
    'Product Name : '||pnm||' '||'Product Price : '||prc);
  end loop;
    dbms_output.put_line('-----------------------------------
-
                         -----');
    close plist;
end loop;
close wcur;
end;
/

Output:

Wholesaler Name : AMIT TRADERS
Product No. : 11   Product Name : STEEL BAR     Product Price : 340
Product No. : 12   Product Name : STEEL ANGLE   Product Price : 200
Product No. : 13   Product Name : STEEL ROOF    Product Price : 250
---------------------------------------------
```

```
Wholesaler Name : DIVYA AGENCY
Product No. : 12   Product Name : STEEL ANGLE   Product Price : 200
Product No. : 13   Product Name : STEEL ROOF    Product Price : 250
----------------------------------------------
Wholesaler Name : SWAPNIL TRADING CO
Product No. : 13   Product Name : STEEL ROOF    Product Price : 250
----------------------------------------------
PL/SQL procedure successfully completed.
```

d) Consider the following relational database

party (pcode, pname)

politician (pno, pname, pcity, pcode)

Write a procedure to display details of all politician of the given party.

Ans. :

```
create or replace procedure p_polit(pbname in varchar) as
  cursor bcur is select politician_info.* from
  party_info,politician_info where
  party_info.pcode=politician_info.pcode and
party_info.pname=pbname;
  prec politician_info%rowtype;
begin
  dbms_output.put_line('--------------------');
  dbms_output.put_line('PARTY : '||pbname);
  dbms_output.put_line('--------------------');
open bcur;
loop
  fetch bcur into prec;
  exit when bcur%notfound;
  dbms_output.put_line('PNO : '||prec.pno||' '||
              'NAME : '||prec.pname||' '||'CITY :
'||prec.pcity);
end loop;
close bcur;
end p_polit;
/
SQL> execute p_polit('AJP');
--------------------
PARTY : AJP
--------------------
PNO : 101   NAME : ANIL     CITY : AMRITSAR
PNO : 102   NAME : JEEVAN   CITY : ALLAHABAD
PNO : 104   NAME : SHIRISH  CITY : PUNE
PL/SQL procedure successfully completed.
```

e) Write a package which consist of one procedure and one function.
   Pass a number as a parameter to a procedure and print whether no. is +ve or —ve.
   Pass students rollno as a parameter to a function and print percentage of student.
   For this consider the following relation :
   student (rollno, name, addr, total, per).

Ans. :
```
create or replace package stud_pack
as
procedure p_pos_neg(num in number);
function f_perc(rn in number) return number;
PRAGMA RESTRICT_REFERENCES(f_perc, WNDS);
end stud_pack;
/
create or replace package body stud_pack as
procedure p_pos_neg(num in number) as
begin
  if num<0 then
    dbms_output.put_line(num||' is negative');
  else
    dbms_output.put_line(num||' is positive');
  end if;
end p_pos_neg;
function f_perc(rn in number) return number as
  per number;
begin
  select perc into per from stud_info where rollno=rn;
  return per;
end f_perc;
end stud_pack;
/

Output:
SQL> execute stud_pack.p_pos_neg(-1);
-1 is negative
PL/SQL procedure successfully completed.

SQL> select stud_pack.f_perc(1) from dual;
STUD_PACK.F_PERC(1)
-------------------
       77.71
```

5. Attempt any four : 16

a) Consider the following transactions. Give two non-serial schedules that are serializable.

T_1	T_2
Read (x)	Read (z)
x = x + 1000	Read (y)
Write (x)	y = y – z
Read (y)	Write (y)
y = y – 10	Read (x)
Write (y)	x = x + z
	Write (x)

Ans. :

T_1	T_2
Read(X)	
X = X + 10	
Write(X)	
	Read(Z)
Read(Y)	
Y = Y – 10	
Write(Y)	
	Read(Y)
	Y = Y – Z
	Write(Y)
	Read(X)
	X = X + Z
	Write(X)

T_1	T_2
Read(X)	
X = X + 10	
	Read(Z)
Write(X)	
Read(Y)	
Y = Y – 10	
Write(Y)	
	Read(Y)
	Y = Y – Z
	Write(Y)
	Read(X)
	X = X + Z
	Write(X)

b) Consider the following non-serial schedule. Is this schedule serializable ?

T_1	T_2	T_3
Read (A)		
	Read (A)	
Write (A)		
		Read (A)
		Write(A)

Ans. : The schedule given in the problem is serializable. The schedule is serializable and produces the result identical to $T_2 \rightarrow T_1 \rightarrow T_3$.

c) The following is the list of events in an interleaved execution if set T_1, T_2, T_3 and T_4 assuming 2 PL. Is there a deadlock ? If yes, which transactions are involved in deadlock ?

Time	Transaction	Code
t_1	T_1	Lock (A, X)
t_2	T_2	Lock (B, S)
t_3	T_3	Lock (A, S)
t_4	T_4	Lock (B, S)
t_5	T_1	Lock (C, S)
t_6	T_2	Lock (C, X)
t_7	T_3	Lock (D, S)
t_8	T_4	Lock (D, X)

Ans. : As per the given list of events (from time t_1 to t_8) in the problem, the schedule can be written as follows:

T_1	T_2	T_3	T_4
X(A)			
	S(B)		
		S(A)	
			S(B)
S(C)			
	X(C)		
		S(D)	
			X(D)

Where X(A) indicates exclusive lock on object A.

The waits-for graph for the above schedule is as given below:

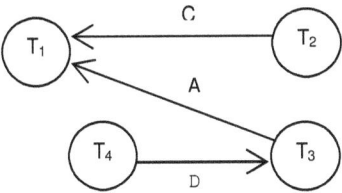

From the above waits-for graph, there is no cycle. Hence there is no deadlock.

d) The following is the list of events in an interleaved execution if set T_1, T_2, T_3 and T_4 assuming 2 PL. Is there a deadlock ? If yes, which transactions are involved in deadlock ?

Time	Transaction	Code
t_1	T_1	Lock (A, X)
t_2	T_2	Lock (B, S)
t_3	T_3	Lock (A, S)
t_4	T_4	Lock (C, S)
t_5	T_1	Lock (B, X)
t_6	T_2	Lock (C, X)
t_7	T_3	Lock (D, X)
t_8	T_4	Lock (D, S)

Ans. : As per the given list of events (from time t_1 to t_8) in the problem, the schedule can be written as follows:

T_1	T_2	T_3	T_4
X(A)			
	S(B)		
		S(A)	
			S(C)
X(C)			
	X(B)		
		X(D)	
			S(D)

Where X(A) indicates exclusive lock on object A.

The waits-for graph for the above schedule is as given below:

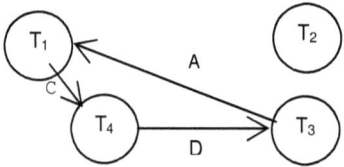

From the above waits-for graph, there is cycle among T_1, T_4 and T_3. Hence there is deadlock.

e) Following are the log entries at the time of system crash.

[start - transaction, T_1]

[write - item, T_1, A, 100]

[write - item, T_1, B, 100]

[commits, T_1]

[checkpoint]
[start - transaction, T_3]
[write - item, T_3, D, 500]
[commit, T_3]
[start - transaction, T_4]
[write - item, T_4, E, 400]
[start - transaction, T_2]
[write - item, T_2, C, 300] ← System crash

If deferred update technique with checkpoint is used, what will be the recovery procedure?

Ans. : T_1 is committed before the last system checkpoint, hence it need not be redone. T_3 is redone because its commit point is after the last system checkpoint.

T_2 and T_4 are not redone because there is no commit entry for these transactions. Hence, the values of C and E remain unchanged.

❖❖❖

www.ingramcontent.com/pod-product-compliance
Lightning Source LLC
Chambersburg PA
CBHW062133160426
43191CB00013B/2290